MALIGNED MASTER

Maligned Master

THE REAL STORY OF
ANTONIO SALIERI

by *Volkmar Braunbehrens*

TRANSLATED FROM THE GERMAN BY
Eveline L. Kanes

Fromm International Publishing Corporation
NEW YORK

Library of Congress Cataloging-in-Publication Data
Braunbehrens, Volkmar.
    [Salieri, ein Musiker im Schatten Mozarts. English]
    Maligned master : the real story of Antonio Salieri / by Volkmar
Braunbehrens; translated from the German by Eveline L. Kanes. —
1st U.S. ed.
     p. cm.
    Includes bibliographical references and index.
    ISBN 0-88064-140-1 $25.00
    1. Salieri, Antonio, 1750–1825. 2. Composers—Biography.
I. Title.
ML410.D16B713   1992
780'.92—dc20   92-28067
[B]   CIP
                                   MN

CONTENTS

FOREWORD

He was one of the most important composers of opera at the end of the eighteenth century. His works were performed all over Europe—from Naples to Copenhagen, from Lisbon to Moscow. In Paris he was esteemed as the legitimate heir to Christoph Willibald Gluck; the Paris Opera earned considerable profits for many years from one of his works. That particular opera dealt with an uncontrolled despot who is eventually replaced by a king chosen by the people, and its popularity spanned the period before, during, and even after the French Revolution. But the real center of his activities was Vienna. He had received his musical training there, having forgone the chance to study in Naples—an unusual choice for an Italian musician of his time. In Vienna he became the director of Italian Opera at the Nationaltheater, as well as the Hofkapell-meister; and later on he was one of the founders of the *Gesellschaft der Musikfreunde*. For decades he was the most influential musical personality in Vienna. In addition he was a sought-after teacher, whose students included Beethoven, Hummel, Moscheles, and Schubert; even Liszt studied with him as a young man.

But none of this prevented Antonio Salieri from being

quickly forgotten. He is known only by name, and even that not in connection with his seldom-performed work; he crops up in history uniquely as Mozart's competitor, the man who envied and supposedly poisoned him. In recent years the play and popular film *Amadeus* turned the legend into an event with great box-office appeal. Though musical historians early on denied the poison story, for a long time they did not lay the slanderous assertions of intrigue to rest, or reaffirm Salieri's musical significance. Salieri had a very different musical career from that of Mozart, and was considered by posterity to be a lesser talent. However, his importance can be properly understood only if that unjustified comparison is avoided.

For that reason, I devoted very little space to Salieri in my book *Mozart in Vienna*. In the following brief biography, I want to draw attention to the achievements of this important composer, who is so frequently discussed without any conception of his life and work independent of his relationship to Mozart. For it is only by considering the total picture that this relationship can be clarified, and the essentials of the often-cited "cabals" be fully grasped.

I am not concerned with sketching a hasty profile. In any case, information on Salieri's private life and ideas is very scant; few personal memoirs exist, and family letters appear not to have been preserved. Rather, what I want to do is present his musical career, and especially to give a critical analysis of his operas, which are virtually unknown today. Salieri's relationships with his most important librettists (Da Ponte, Beaumarchais, and Casti) interest me particularly, since they participated in his attempt to expand the confines of traditional operatic forms and develop new dramatic possibilities for music theater. In order to trace the progress of operatic reform from Gluck to Salieri, which is by no means direct, I have tried briefly to describe all of his operas, devoting greater detail to the more important ones. My chief concern is to provide a clear critical survey that might encourage the performance and study of Salieri's work.

Shortly after Salieri's death, Ignaz Franz von Mosel published a biography based on the composer's personal memoirs;

these have since disappeared. The well-known musicologist Alexander Wheelock Thayer later wrote a lengthy biographical article, to which *Dwight's Journal of Music* in Boston devoted nineteen issues. Thayer tried to give Salieri the recognition he deserved, but his attempt went unnoticed in Europe. The author's knowledge of Mozart scholarship could have prevented many erroneous conclusions about the supposed rivalry between Mozart and Salieri. Thayer's serialized piece was not mentioned in any of the relevant biographies I consulted, so that I was unaware of it when I wrote this book.*

Salieri was literally ignored for decades, aside from occasional references to him by musicologists, or mention in the volumes by Adolphe Jullien on the history of the Paris Opera. Several shorter scholarly works appeared later (such as those by Werner Bollert, Andrea Della Corte, Giuseppe Magnani, and Rudolf Nützlader), as well as a trivial novel, *Salieri und Mozart*, by Franz Farga. The subject of the latter was Salieri's supposedly boundless hatred for Mozart. Yet with all its distortions, even that book did not subscribe to the poison theory.

Musicologists did not become interested again in Salieri until about thirty years ago. Two parallel dissertations are especially noteworthy for attempting to summarize the facts of Salieri's life. Edward Elmgren Swenson put together a documentary biography in 1974; it is very reliable, but is available only in photocopy form. Rudolph Angermüller dealt with the longer operas in *Antonio Salieri. Sein Leben und seine weltlichen Werke unter besonderer Berücksichtigung seiner "grossen" Opern* (1971–1974); since then he has published numerous articles on aspects of Salieri's life and work. All future studies will have to be based on this research.†

The following libraries have been generous in helping me to obtain the necessary information and material, and permitting me to consult their valuable manuscript collections: the Theater Collection, and especially the Music Collection (where

---

* It is now available in book form: Alexander Wheelock Thayer, *Salieri— Rival of Mozart*, Theodore Albrecht (Kansas City: The Philharmonia of Greater Kansas City, 1989).
† All the works referred to above are cited in the bibliography.

the manuscripts and copies of Salieri's operas are housed), of the Österreichische Nationalbibliothek, Vienna; the Library of the *Gesellschaft der Musikfreunde,* which owns numerous Salieri manuscripts along with other items from his musical estate; further, the University Library and Musicological Institute of the University of Freiburg im Breisgau; the Staatsbibliothek in Berlin (West); and the City of Mannheim's Reiss Museum (which contains the remains of the Archives and Library of the Mannheimer Hof- und Nationaltheater). Special thanks are also due to Robert Pobitscha (in Vienna) for researching various items; to Bettina Kienlechner for her help with translation; to many friends for their valuable suggestions; but above all, to Gisela Beutler, who made this work possible.

INTRODUCTION

Whispers and Rumors

The most creative phase in the brief career of the Russian writer Aleksander Sergeevich Pushkin began when he went to spend a few weeks at Boldino, the family estate, in the autumn of 1830. There he completed *Eugene Onegin* and wrote about thirty poems, five stories, a verse epic, and five dramatic scenes and "little tragedies." The latter dealt with human passions in extreme situations, including self-destruction and death. The plans for these short plays dated back to the year 1825, but only in Boldino did Pushkin find the peace and inner equilibrium required for creative work. That happy time in the country lasted longer than expected, because Russia was already experiencing the cholera epidemic that was to devastate Central and Western Europe a year later. Of course, this was only a peaceful interlude before he was caught up in the social life he detested and which led to a deadly duel in 1837.

Among the long-planned work was a subject particularly congenial to Pushkin's constant reflections on creativity: Mozart and Salieri. He was not concerned with writing a historical play about the contrast between these two artists, or the nature of their supposed dissension; nor did he attempt to solve the mystery of Mozart's death through a psychological study.

Rather, Pushkin intended to compare two different artistic types, for whom Mozart and Salieri served as historic figurations. The dramatic action is almost incidental; and yet even in its sketchiness it is presented so indisputably that the two scenes entitled "Envy" in the manuscript substantiate the criminal case against Salieri beyond all doubt.

Salieri accuses God of being unjust for not rewarding his passionate love of art, his self-sacrifice, his struggles, his diligence and prayer with the gift of immortal genius—bestowing it instead on a madman and idler, in other words, on Mozart. For the first time, Salieri experiences something akin to envy. Mozart performs a new composition for Salieri and asks him for his opinion; this convinces Salieri that Mozart is unaware of his own genius. Salieri decides to poison this artist who he thinks has so transcended all earthly arts that he no longer serves them. In the second scene, Mozart tells Salieri of an anonymous commission for the *Requiem*. They happen to speak of Beaumarchais, and Mozart asks whether it can be true that he poisoned someone, since genius and crime are irreconcilable concepts. In that instant, Salieri secretly pours poison into his glass, Mozart drinks from it, and then sits down at the piano to play a passage from the *Requiem*. But he soon feels unwell and leaves. Alone again, Salieri continues to reflect on genius and crime—are they really irreconcilable?

Mozart and Salieri is the only one of the "little tragedies" that was published during Pushkin's lifetime; as of 1840 it was also available in its first German translation. The playlet has Salieri openly poison Mozart on the stage. How could such an outrageous accusation be made so readily and matter-of-factly? How did Pushkin come to believe so firmly in such a terrible crime that he could incorporate it almost incidentally into his short drama? And this dramatic development is not even essential to his play, since it merely shows Salieri poisoning Mozart's glass, and Mozart leaving the room shortly thereafter, feeling unwell. The little tragedy ends with Salieri's brief reflection on genius and crime. Obviously Pushkin was so thoroughly convinced of Salieri's crime that he could treat it as historical common knowledge. The scene is not intended as a portrayal of a criminal case; instead, it concentrates on comparing the divinely inspired genius to the composer who tries to achieve high art through ever-refined skills, by a deployment of talent, perseverance, and diligence. Yet despite all of Salieri's exertions, Pushkin asserts, he will never come even remotely close to producing the "snatches of song from heaven . . ." that the "son of harmony" creates so effortlessly, "to stir wingless desire in us, poor sons of dust. . . ."

Pushkin had adopted a fable that was no longer simply whispered in Europe, but had grown into a common, half-accepted rumor. The legend seemed to implicate Salieri, and to confirm the conjectures of murder by poisoning that had arisen soon after Mozart's death.

The first news of Mozart's death already referred to his having been poisoned. A report by a correspondent from Prague in the *Musikalische Wochenblatt* of Berlin stated:

> Mozart is—dead. He was sickly when he returned home from Prague, and remained ailing since then: he was thought to be retaining water, and he died in Vienna at the end of last week. Because his body swelled up after his death, it is even believed that he was poisoned.[1]

It is still not known today who was responsible for that assumption. And though it has been repeatedly claimed that Konstanze, Mozart's widow, herself contributed to the story, that is also rather unlikely, for no such suspicion on her part has come down to us. But from the very first, the legend continued to be embroidered upon. In his biography of 1798, Franz Niemetschek writes of a visit to the Prater by Mozart and his wife: ". . . as they sat together, Mozart began to speak of death and maintained that he was writing the *Requiem* for himself. Tears stood in the sensitive man's eyes. 'I feel it very acutely,' he went on, 'it won't be long now: I've surely been given poison! I can't let go of that thought.' "[2]

Niemetschek left the anecdote at that, without further comment. Though it found its way into all Mozart biographies, there is no mention anywhere of Salieri as the likely poisoner. Yet the rumor of a link with the "Italian faction" at the Vienna Opera must have soon developed, because a denial of such

accusations appeared in one of the earliest and least-noted
Mozart biographies:

> Mozart—like all great artists—certainly had a number of enemies,
> especially among the Italian opera composers who surely realized that
> with Mozart's rise their Italian singsong was finished. It is known how
> hard they tried to spoil *Figaro*; how after Mozart's plea the Emperor
> gave a special command to stop the performance between the first and
> second acts and ordered them to sing the arias properly or risk his
> displeasure. But if they wanted to get rid of Mozart, they could not
> afford to wait until he had given their mock serenades the coup de grâce;
> they had to go to work more quickly.
>   When he wrote *Figaro* in 1786, they were most angry, so would they
> have allowed him five more years—1786–1791—to increase his fame?
> That is unlikely, in view of the hot temper of the Italians and its not
> being in their interest to do so. And if someone did want to poison him,
> why the mysterious messenger? Why poison-pen letters, and a large
> reward for a composition that was destined to be destroyed for the same
> reason as its composer? There were easier ways of dealing with Mozart.
> His open, sincere character made him trust everyone, often even his
> worst enemies. Then why all the fuss? . . . The idea of being poisoned
> was surely just a figment of his imagination."[3]

But first of all, it is necessary to look into the question of
whether Salieri was actually the head of the Italian faction at
the Vienna Opera. In his position as Kapellmeister of the
Italian Opera, he did have occasional institutional differences with
Mozart, the famous "cabals" often mentioned by Mozart in his
letters. After all, Salieri was the established artist, whereas
Mozart had to make his way as a free-lance composer. While
a more collegial relationship between the two existed in the
year of Mozart's death, it made little overall difference. As
the above quotation from the Mozart biography suggests, the
notion that "the Italians" might have been capable of a murder
conspiracy existed as early as 1803. However, the author does
not implicate Salieri in this connection.

Rumors, hints, and insinuations whispered behind a shield-
ing hand cannot be pinned down; they are themselves a
creeping poison. It is impossible to determine at what point
the poison story was first mentioned, or when Salieri was
brought into it. It seems that Carl Maria von Weber learned
of these accusations when he visited Salieri in 1803, and on his
later visits to Vienna he deliberately avoided all contact with

him. Apparently Weber, who could claim family ties with Mozart, believed the rumors.[4]

Not until 1823 are there written records of conversations, though these provide an altogether new and tragic turn of events. Gioacchino Rossini, who was in Vienna in the early summer of 1822, was still able to discuss the rumors jokingly with Salieri; he had apparently learned of them as soon as he arrived.[5] But when Salieri suffered a physical and mental breakdown in the autumn of 1823 and was admitted to the Vienna general hospital in an enfeebled and mentally confused condition, it soon became known that in his deranged state of mind he accused himself of having killed Mozart. Naturally this caused a sensation, even if under the circumstances many people disbelieved it. Hints of such discussions can be found in Ludwig van Beethoven's *Conversation Books*.[6] In his more lucid moments Salieri was able to express himself more rationally. Ignaz Moscheles describes a deeply moving visit to the hospital:

> The reunion . . . was a sad one; even the sight of him shocked me and he spoke to me in broken sentences of his approaching death; finally he used these words: "Although this is my last illness, I can in all good faith swear that there is no truth to the absurd rumor; you know—I'm supposed to have poisoned Mozart. But no, it's spite, nothing but spite, tell that to the world, my dear Moscheles; old Salieri, who's going to die soon, told you that." I was greatly moved, and when the old man cried and thanked me again for my visit, after having overwhelmed me with thanks when I arrived, it was time for me to leave quickly so as not to be overcome. As to the rumor the dying man referred to, it had indeed circulated without ever influencing me. His intrigues certainly harmed him [Mozart] morally, and ruined many an hour for him.[7]

It was no longer possible to keep silent in public. Giuseppe Carpani published his *Letter in Defence of Salieri Regarding the Accusation of His Having Poisoned Mozart*.[8] The *Allgemeine musikalische Zeitung* of Leipzig carried reports from Paris on public repudiations of the accusation. One of the most serious and respected of musical publications, it even published an unequivocal "comment," as follows:

> Our worthy Salieri simply will not die, as the popular saying goes. His body suffers all the infirmities of old age and his mind is deranged.

In his unbalanced imagination he apparently at times claims to have been responsible for Mozart's early death, a delusion that no one except the poor bewildered old man really believes. Mozart's contemporaries know only too well that it was simply arduous work and fast living among ill-chosen company that shortened his precious life![9]

The virulence of the rumor was undeniable, and scarcely mitigated by these attempts to prove its unreliability. In view of Mozart's unparalleled fame throughout Europe, it is small wonder that such stories spread everywhere. And the denial in the *Allgemeine musikalische Zeitung*, well intentioned though it was, only encouraged the rumor.

How could Salieri's innocence be proved better than by pointing to the absurdity of the slander? After all, nothing but an assertion existed; there was not the least shred of evidence. Indeed, no one had ever wondered how Salieri was supposed to have carried out the poisoning. But could a defense make any difference? Carpani at least tried to deal with the essentials of the accusation by denying that Mozart had been poisoned at all. To substantiate this claim, he consulted competent specialists and obtained an opinion from one of the doctors who had actually seen Mozart's corpse. But this, too, made little difference. The poison theory continued to be advanced until recently, even by those who did not consider Salieri to be the murderer and looked for the culprit elsewhere.

It is generally accepted that Pushkin was familiar with the articles in the *Allgemeine musikalische Zeitung*, or at least with Salieri's obituary.[10] It was in the latter that Friedrich Rochlitz referred once again to the absurdity of the confused old man's self-accusations. But Pushkin was no longer receptive to such circumspection; perhaps he was too biased in favor of his idol Mozart. Still, there were thoughtful Russians, such as Pavel Alexandrovitch Katenin, who rightly took Pushkin to task for it:

Is there certain proof that Salieri murdered Mozart out of envy? If so, then it should be expressed in the preface in terms of criminal law; if not—is it permissible to defame the memory of an artist before posterity, even if he is only a mediocre one?[11]

In his argument, Katenin questions but does not refute Pushkin's theory of envy as a conceivable motive. But from a historical perspective, this must surely be viewed with some doubt. Salieri may have been very much aware of Mozart's artistic superiority; in his old age, after Mozart had died, he spoke of him with the greatest respect and admiration. But during Mozart's lifetime Salieri was just as successful with some, if not with all, of his own works. Several of his operas were published early as printed scores or pianoforte arrangements. And Salieri also brought back handsome honoraria from Paris. Moreover, he held one of the most influential positions in the musical life of Vienna. Did Salieri think so little of his own great success that his supposed resentment of Mozart's genius could lead him to commit a capital crime? Pushkin should have asked himself that; it is not a question that depends solely on historical distance and overview.

The success of Salieri's works gradually began to wane after 1800; but, of course, he did not write any new operas after 1802. Mozart, on the other hand—and this must not be overlooked—was the first composer whose works in all categories were performed with increasing frequency. Moreover, he was blessed with a posthumous reputation that has never declined, a previously unknown phenomenon.[12] So when it comes to envy and jealousy, Salieri may well have experienced these emotions as his bitterness increased—but only during the thirty-odd years by which he outlived Mozart. Besides, Salieri was not the grudging character that he has so often been portrayed as being.

Pushkin, and many others along with him, thus labored under a misconception that they could surely have corrected for themselves. Perhaps it was fostered by the increasing ignorance about Salieri, despite his high musical reputation in Vienna during his lifetime and for some time afterward. Indeed, until the end, when his powers suddenly failed him, he was actively connected with several of Vienna's musical organizations. Among these were the Tonkünstler Society, the *Gesellschaft der Musikfreunde* (which he helped found), and the Conservatory. He was also the leading authority on com-

position and voice, and taught such famous students as Beethoven, Hummel, Moscheles, Schubert, Liszt, and many others.
Pushkin would not have known much about that. And there is
proof that the Russian poet never saw a single one of Salieri's
operas performed. He lacked the opportunity to do so, never
having been in the West and having been banished from St.
Petersburg for many years on account of a political indiscretion.
This must have influenced his portrayal of Salieri as inferior
to Mozart, a typical representative of those *musici minores* who
possess talent, diligence, and perseverance, but no genius.

Salieri is one of those composers who were not performed
after their death. Very few composers escaped this fate before
the second half of the nineteenth century. The fact that
deceased composers (except for Mozart and Beethoven, to
whom this general rule does not apply) began to be heard
more frequently after 1850 is due to the institution of the
historical concert. Eighteenth-century operas, save for those by
Mozart, were repeated even more rarely; some of Gluck's
reform operas were put on, but even Handel had to wait for
a large-scale renaissance in the 1920s. Most works were produced only once. Not until the mass distribution of phonograph
records and the invention of radio, with its need to present
new material, was the range of the repertory quickly expanded.
Opera houses and established concert halls were less likely to
reflect this change. And it is only now, when one gets to hear
Salieri performed again, that one can examine what and how
he actually composed, what importance he gained among his
contemporaries, and how to represent him in a musicological
context.

The compulsion of today's culture industry to make redis-
coveries, influenced as it is by uneasiness with new musical
compositions, generally needs some external impetus—something that will spark a trend. And in this case it is Peter Shaffer's
brilliant and effective theatrical piece, *Amadeus*, that has allowed
us to take a fresh look at Salieri. Shaffer manages in a
remarkable way to disprove the thesis that Salieri was a murderer, while turning Salieri's alleged deadly hatred into the
subject of a drama. Shaffer's Salieri is scarcely involved in

Mozart's death, apart from the terrorizing psychodrama in which he appears nightly to Mozart as the embodiment of the latter's fearful fantasies of the "gray messenger." It is clear that in *Amadeus*, Salieri's taxing himself with Mozart's murder is simply a supreme effort to avoid being forgotten:

> By tonight they'll hear out there how I died—and they'll believe it's true! . . . Let them forget me then. For the rest of time whenever men say Mozart with love, they will say Salieri with loathing! . . . *I am going to be immortal after all!* And He is powerless to prevent it.
> [To God] So, *Signore*—see now if man is mocked![13]

Shaffer sticks to historical events and persons far more closely than did Pushkin, but essentially his concept differs little from Pushkin's. He contrasts a mediocrity about to be forgotten with a divine genius whose behavior in life is both childish and undignified, just as Salieri's rebellion against God was given a central focus in Pushkin's work. Shaffer merely reinterprets the confused rambling of an old man in decline as an ingenious ploy in the chess game of posthumous reputation. In that way, the motif of the poison legend is maintained, and Salieri remains a minor musician obsessed by jealousy, envy, and revenge, and never inspired to create anything remarkable.

Milos Forman's film *Amadeus* does away completely with Shaffer's cleverly managed theatricality in favor of an enthralling cinematic orgy. The suggestive power of the scenes, characters, and faces does the rest. More than thirty million people have seen this film. It fulfills the prediction made by Salieri at the end of Shaffer's play: that the catchword "Amadeus"—which since the beginning of the nineteenth century had referred only to Wolfgang Gottlieb Mozart—would henceforth include his own world-renowned theatrical-cinematic figure. And by a remarkable ironic twist, the composer Antonio Salieri (1750–1825), once almost forgotten and even ignored by musicologists, is now enjoying a revival and new performances of his works. It might be said that the first legend—that of Salieri the poisoner—banned the composer from the musical world. The second legend, on the other hand—that of Salieri as self-incriminator, and hence a partner in Mozart's fame—favored his rediscovery.

In his old age Salieri certainly thought about his posthumous fame. He intended to leave a well-ordered estate. He made specific and judicious arrangements for his compositions, whose manuscripts he had carefully preserved, ensuring their accessibility. After an interval of twenty to thirty years he wrote comments on the flyleaves of the original scores of twelve of his operas, including short critical reflections on the individual arias and their dramaturgical significance. He prepared a catalogue of his works, and began an unfinished outline of his life that was apparently only a rough account of the most important events. Certain manuscript pages contained jottings of his thoughts on music, its organization and the significance of its forms. This material was supplemented by a collection of anecdotes and brief descriptions of little incidents that Salieri probably jotted down throughout his life. It was not voluminous, like a journal, but rather occasional notes. He had evidently not thought of an autobiography but of a biographer, who after his death would be able to describe his life in relation to his works. Salieri wanted to prepare the necessary preliminary material for such a person. He enjoyed recollecting the various stages and experiences of his life, rereading and reviewing his works, and putting his estate in order. As he went over his compositions, he noted:

> It gives me pleasure . . . to find more good than bad in them, and if at times I manage to improve a section that I never liked and that I formerly tried to improve in vain, then no one is happier than me. It will be said that little satisfies me; this only proves the passion of an artist for his art, without which no one can ever accomplish anything good.[14]

Such statements give the impression of a modest artist, scarcely inclined to overvalue himself, who knows what he has accomplished and what he was competent to do, and who leaves a not insignificant body of work behind. Salieri certainly did not lack self-criticism, or the ability to appraise himself justly.

Salieri chose his own biographer. Ignaz Franz von Mosel

was a highly educated musical dilettante who served for many years as assistant director of the two Viennese court theaters, and later as librarian of the royal library. Aside from literary works, he had written three operas, with Salieri's encouragement; in addition, he had made a name for himself with arrangements of Handel oratorios and adaptations of Mozart operas for string quartet. Salieri showed Mosel the collection of sketches he intended to leave him.

But these jottings never reached a systematic conclusion, and when Mosel began his work, believing that he had merely to make a translation of a completed autobiography, he realized that the collection of anecdotes consisted of no more than "agreeable banter." Mosel described them as "little pleasantries, told in Salieri's lively fashion, whose presentation might well please a circle of good friends but which are not suitable for transmission to the public."[15] Mosel was therefore compelled to put together a biography based on his own thorough research. Among other sources, he used for this purpose Salieri's voluminous correspondence, a matter of great importance, as none of this material seems to have been preserved. Mosel must therefore be considered an authentic authority. Aware of the poisoning legend, as well as of the confused old man's self-incrimination (no one knows who had actually heard this, or who subsequently spread the rumor), Mosel did the best he could under the circumstances. He briefly described a thoroughly memorable life, and recalled the most important of Salieri's operas in some detail. This remained the only independent portrayal of Salieri for a century, aside from the work by Thayer, which was ignored. It appeared in a single edition and is available in only a few libraries.

CHAPTER ONE

Naples or Vienna 1750–1772

Antonio Salieri came from Legnago, a small border town between the Kingdom of Venice and the Duchy of Mantua. Situated on the Adige river, it was also a port of considerable importance for the grain trade. Such small towns were badly off because of the high taxes imposed by Venice. Moreover, a military base placed there to protect the frontier was not conducive to the development of its trade and commerce. Though there was an influential class of merchants who dominated the life of the city—they were able to support a theater for the 2500 inhabitants—the mood was depressed and the outlook for permanent economic improvement not very favorable. Venice clearly was living beyond its means and needed financial support, which meant that the *terra ferma*, the rural region belonging to Venice, suffered.

Salieri appears to have written and conveyed little concerning his childhood to Mosel, his biographer; aside from a few not very informative anecdotes, hardly anything is known about it. There is mention of a brother, a respected musician who performed frequently at village and church festivals in the area, and who took the young Antonio along on many such occasions. Once, when there was no room in the coach, the

ten-year-old boy followed it on foot and only returned home
in the evening. Another story tells of the boy's reluctance to
greet a familiar organist on the street, and how his father took
him to task for it. Antonio replied he had an aversion to the
man because he was a bad organist. When his father laughed
and said, "How can you judge that? You're still a beginner in
music," young Antonio responded cheekily, "That's true, but
even so I'd play with greater reverence." Such tales, however,
reveal little about any potential musical talent. Nor does Salieri
say much about his siblings, his lifestyle, or his education,
though some of it can be reconstructed.

His father, Antonio, who had lived in Legnago at least from
the beginning of the 1720s, seemed to have been a well-situated
merchant who traded in agricultural products. He had two
children from his first marriage, Giulia (born 1724) and Francesco Antonio (born 1737). His wife Elisabetta died in 1740,
whereupon, thinking no doubt of his three-year-old child, he
immediately remarried. In this second marriage, to Anna Maria
Scachi, he had a further nine (or ten) children, who were born
between 1741 and 1752 (the birth of the last one, Lucia, in
1756, cannot be positively confirmed). The family grew almost
yearly. Their names are somewhat confusing, for the first son
of the second marriage was also called Francesco Antonio,
though he was only four years younger than his step-brother.
The fourth child was a son, another Antonio, but he died in
his second year. The name Antonio was then used yet again,
for the eighth child of the second marriage. That was the
composer-to-be, Antonio Salieri, who was born in Legnago on
August 18, 1750.

We know nothing about the extent of the father's activities;
consequently, we cannot ascertain how his business fared in
the 1750s. But we do know that he submitted a petition to the
City Council in 1757, in which he asked that the taxes on his
bottega di grassina (fertilizer business) be lowered, referring to
the large family with which God had blessed him.

Education and music lessons held an important place in the
Salieri household. Francesco Antonio was sent to the conservatory in Padua, where he was a student of the celebrated

violinist Giuseppe Tartini, who taught there into his old age. Francesco Antonio also taught our Antonio to play the violin and the piano, and gave him his first singing lessons. Furthermore, young Antonio was sent to the Latin school, and was later allowed to continue his music lessons with Giuseppe Simoni, the organist at the cathedral in Legnago, who had studied with the famous Padre Giovanni Battista Martini in Bologna. Though the boy thus had access to various teachers, we know little about his musical ability or the results of these studies. The anecdotes reveal that he certainly had an inclination and desire for music, but it is uncertain at what point music was first considered to be a possible career for him.

One almost gets the impression that in later life Salieri was reluctant to recall his youth in Legnago. Subsequent contact with his siblings seems to have been minimal, and he maintained few other connections with his home town. Perhaps this was because Salieri became an orphan early on; his mother died in 1763 (he was then twelve), and his father soon thereafter. The date of his mother's death is verifiable in the parish register, but nothing is known about his father's, which must surely have been a trauma for the adolescent boy. Either the elder Salieri died away from Legnago—perhaps while on a trip—or else the often incomplete parish registers failed to record the event. Some of the siblings probably still lived at home, and these now had to be placed with relatives. We know that Antonio went to stay with one of his older brothers in Padua, who was a monk there at the church of San Francesco.[1] We do not know if Antonio, too, was destined for clerical robes, or if he was to receive further musical training at the Padua conservatory. We do not even know how long he stayed there.

More exact information does not become available until 1776, when an acquaintance of the Salieri family, Giovanni Mocenigo, showed an interest in the fifteen-year-old and took him to Venice. There he stayed in one of the Mocenigo family's palaces.

Mocenigo belonged to one of the wealthiest and most important aristocratic families of Venice. Except for the Contarinis, no other clan had produced as many doges; during the

eighteenth century alone, the Mocenigos ruled the republic for
thirty-five years. At the time of Salieri's arrival, Alvise IV was
the hundred and eighteenth of the hundred and twenty doges
in the history of this city. The family occupied at least seven
palaces, four of which were located along the "volta del canal,"
with a view of the Frari church spire. Aside from the dogate,
the family held many other significant public posts; they served
as ambassadors to the most important European courts and
played a leading role in the social life of this unique city. Of
course, the style of life of this particular nobility cannot be
compared with that of the Central European courts. Despite
the upper class's special position, because of the city's historical
and constitutional organization its members tended to live in
close proximity to the rest of the citizens and they led an
informal and quite similar way of life. Thus, nobles were listed
as the godparents of their employees, and members of lower
social classes were often chosen to be godparents to children
of the nobility. Venetians were prouder of their city than of
their social rank, and the subtle limitations placed on the
holding of public office were only to safeguard the power of
the oligarchy. But here, too, occasional concessions were made
when it was necessary to enlarge the circle of privileged families.
In such decisions, wealth was the key factor.

What must it have meant to Antonio, just turned fifteen,
suddenly to become the guest of this family in a Venetian
palace? To live in the midst of this European hotbed of pleasure
and luxury familiar from the accounts of Giacomo Casanova
or Lorenzo Da Ponte, from various travelers' tales and memoirs,
and from the paintings of Pietro Longhi? Except for Naples,
Venice was undoubtedly *the* city for music in a partitioned
Italy. Four opera houses and numerous theaters competed
there, and new operas were constantly being performed. As if
there were not enough theaters, operas were even presented
in the Mocenigo palace itself. In 1776, the year that Salieri
arrived in Venice, the popular composer Pietro Alessandro
Guglielmi had five new operas playing in four different Venetian theaters. Young Antonio must have been overwhelmed.
In later years he could still recall a moving scene: at one of

these productions he happened to be so close to the fur-clad Guglielmi—who was engaged in animated conversation with a lady—that, to his great delight, he was able to clasp one of the sleeves to his breast without Guglielmi's noticing.

Mocenigo did not permit the boy to be idle, but saw to it that he received proper instruction. Salieri began taking continuo lessons from Giovanni Battista Pescetti, the assistant Kapellmeister of the cathedral of San Marco. Pescetti had spent many years as conductor at the King's Theatre in London and enjoyed a successful career as an opera composer; however, he was already over sixty, and died a few weeks after the lessons began. Fernando Pacini, the tenor at San Marco who also lived with the Mocenigo family, was in charge of the youngster's singing lessons. But Pacini also performed in opera, and introduced Salieri to that world as well—not just as a spectator, but by giving him an insider's view of life at an opera house.

Mocenigo did not intend to keep young Salieri in Venice, but planned to send him to Naples for further study. This was not unusual. Scarcely any aspiring musicians had the resources to study composition or receive the instrumental training that would enable them to compete in the open market. The usual way of acquiring a musical education was through the patronage of either an aristocrat or the church. The only other possibility was to be accepted as a student by a musician who held a well-paid position; this involved a master-apprentice relationship, with board and lodging in the master's home in return for copying music, helping with various tasks connected with an orchestra, and similar duties. Salieri was fortunate, for with a patron like Mocenigo and a certain talent, he could expect to survive in Naples. It is not known what Mocenigo's motives were. Was it simply from friendship for the Salieri family that he took care of the young orphan? Or was it the boy's musical aptitude? And how did that aptitude reveal itself? No information exists about Salieri's qualities as an instrumentalist, nor about any of his early compositions—if indeed there were any.

Then something still more surprising happened. Pacini, his singing teacher and fellow resident in the Mocenigo palace, introduced him to a composer who was about to begin rehearsing a new opera. Florian Leopold Gassmann was not unknown in Venice, having lived there for some years, and producing an opera annually between 1757 and 1762. This composer was to prove of decisive importance in Salieri's life. Salieri probably did not record the initial encounter with him later on, otherwise his biographer Mosel would hardly have described it in so cursory a fashion:

> By chance he [Pacini] spoke with Kapellmeister *Gassmann* about his young fellow lodger, referring to him as a youth who had great talent and an even greater passion for music. The master asked to see him [Salieri]; the youth was introduced and made such a good impression with his fortepiano playing as well as with his singing, that he [Gassmann] asked his [Salieri's] patron's permission to take him to Vienna and to teach him musical composition.[2]

What could have induced Gassmann without a thought to accept responsibility for a young orphan, and take him to Vienna? While Gassmann had a lucrative position at the Viennese court, he was, after all, a bachelor and lived alone. Hence he not only had to have an apartment large enough to accommodate Salieri, but a staff of servants to take care of such things as clothing, laundry, food, barbering, and other basic necessities that were difficult to manage by oneself in the eighteenth century. Salieri had no money of his own, unless Mocenigo was prepared to contribute something. So Gassmann must have assessed, and been convinced by, the boy's overall musical talents; a teenager's ability to sing well shortly before his voice broke would not in itself have been enough. As for the expensive journey to Vienna, that was not a problem, as Emperor Joseph II had already taken care of Gassmann's travel expenses.

This was not a case of Gassmann's charitably helping a destitute person, or taking pity on an orphan whose plight might appeal to his sensitive nature. Gassmann himself had run away from home as a boy, and ended up in Italy some time afterward—apparently on the assumption that a career in music could begin only there. A priest found him in the street; completely penniless, and took him in charge; he not only had him educated, but eventually even sent him to Padre Martini, in Bologna, where he received the best basic musical training available. There Gassmann himself had an unusual experience: he was discovered by a Venetian nobleman, who took him into his house and treated him as an equal. He was given an entire floor to himself, and was showered with honors—it was the beginning of Gassmann's musical career. In taking on Salieri, was Gassmann trying in some way to reciprocate for his own good fortune?

But Salieri had already found a patron in Mocenigo, who was about to send him to Naples. (What must Mocenigo have thought about his self-imposed responsibility for the orphan suddenly being taken from him?) It was every musician's highest goal to spend some time in Italy, to perfect his training there. But why should Salieri choose Vienna? Except in Paris, the general trend in composition was the Italian style with its emphasis on vocal melody. Vienna had adapted this model, blending it with its own tradition of counterpoint and dramatic orchestration. Moreover, Gluck had just introduced a completely new style there, in which he tried to transform the traditional French and Italian opera into something quite new. He did this by replacing the *secco* recit with *recitativo accompagnato*, and by increasing the role of drama over that of the voice.

What must the young Italian have felt—assured of a stipend for Naples, yet about to face instead the uncertainties of life in Vienna, a life that offered far fewer opportunities for advancement? Or did he think that he could learn more there? Perhaps he believed that he carried sufficient "italianità" with him to make his way north of the Alps. However it was arrived at, the decision to go to Vienna carried completely different portents for his career. Salieri turned his back on Italy forever—he made only three short trips there afterward—and was instead adopted by Vienna. Indeed, he did not become a composer in the "Italian" style at all, but developed into a Viennese composer in the tradition of Gluck.

Gassmann and Salieri arrived in Vienna on Sunday, June 15, 1766. For the rest of his life, Salieri remembered it as the day of his "hegira." His boundless gratitude to Gassmann was forever entwined with this memory, and the aging Salieri referred to it yet again:

> The day after my arrival in this residency my master took me to the Italian Church for services. As we were going home he said to me: "I thought I ought to begin your musical education with God. Now it is up to you whether it will have a good or a bad effect; I shall have done my duty whatever happens." Such men are rare! I expressed my eternal gratitude for all the good he would teach me and, blessed be the Lord!, I am proud to say that I demonstrated it to him in all sincerity as long as he lived, and thereafter to his family.[3]

Gassmann took his role as mentor very seriously, and organized an exemplary curriculum for his protégé. He worked out a whole program of subjects to cover a two-year period, for which teachers were expressly engaged. Thus Salieri had both a German and a French language teacher, and another for Latin, who also gave him Italian lessons. The latter subjects were to be of great importance subsequently, when he had to work with Italian opera libretti. (One wonders whether the Abbot Pietro Tommasi, who taught this subject, was really the right man to help Salieri develop the discrimination he would need in his career. Salieri did not always exhibit reliable judgment in his later choices of texts.) A Bohemian musician came to the house to teach such musical subjects as violin, *continuo*, and score reading. But Salieri's training was focused on counterpoint as the core of compositional theory, and that was taught by Gassmann himself. The text used was the Latin edition of *Gradus ad Parnassum* by Johann Joseph Fux, which Salieri had to translate during his Latin lessons. Obviously the entire curriculum was efficiently interconnected. That instruction in singing was not continued is easily explained by the young student's change of voice.

It was evident that Gassmann's commitment to Salieri was extraordinary, for he must have paid for all this instruction out of his own pocket. At this point in his life Gassmann was a very successful composer, but he had by no means reached the peak of his career; after all, he was only thirty-seven. He had come to Vienna three years earlier, and held the positions of composer at the ballet and Kapellmeister at the theater. In addition, Emperor Joseph II had made him a member of the chamber music group with which the ruler played for an hour daily. All in all, Gassmann had a not inconsiderable annual income of 2,200 florins, which enabled him to maintain his own household with the necessary staff. At first he lived near the Wasserkunst-Bastei, with a beautiful view over the southern and southeastern suburbs of Wieden and Landstrasse; beyond the five-hundred-meter-wide glacis, one could see the St. Charles Church and the Schwarzenberg palace in the foreground, with the Belvedere behind it. This was Salieri's first home in Vienna.

Gassmann considered it his task to provide not only good instruction for his pupil, but also that necessity for a successful career, introductions to the right people. Salieri owed three decisive meetings to his teacher and knew how to make use of them, modest, self-confident, and eager to learn as he was.

His contact with Joseph II came about by chance, during one of the chamber music sessions, when the emperor found out that Gassmann had brought a student from Venice whom he wished to introduce. There was no set program for these musical gatherings; the musicians alternated chairs in the quartets they performed, and opera roles were distributed according to the voices available. The emperor wanted to become familiar with new operas by participating in these sessions, playing the harpsichord or the cello, or singing. Musical education had been given high priority in the Habsburg family for generations. When young Salieri was brought along for the first time by Gassmann, he naturally had to take part immediately; no doubt this was also partly to test the young man's ability. Salieri later recalled quite clearly that Johann Adolf Hasse's opera *Alcide al bivio* was being studied, and that at first he had to sing alto in the choruses. As he did quite well at this, he was then allowed to sight-read a few solo sections, and the emperor was so well pleased that he urged Gassmann to bring his student along on a regular basis. In this way Salieri imperceptibly became firmly attached to the court of Joseph II, even if at his level of competence he was far from receiving a formal appointment.

Emperor Joseph II's musical interests were very versatile;

he by no means sought merely fashionable entertainment. Mozart's letters speak of the emperor's preference for fugues, which at that time were used mostly in sacred music. Gassmann especially enjoyed and practiced the art of counterpoint. His string quartets, containing up to two fugue sections, could hardly have been published without the emperor's interest. As for opera, it is always claimed that Joseph II was biased in favor of Italian opera, but there is no proof of this. We know nothing of his attitude toward Gluck's new style of opera. Moreover, the emperor was one of the initiators of the German *Singspiel*. Not only did he adopt the North German version, he lent his personal support to its development as a national music theater based in Vienna. It was generally conceded that except for Mozart's *Entführung aus dem Serail*, the results were unsatisfactory (and a separate theater could not be maintained merely for that). But in his admiration for and sponsorship of Mozart, one can see that Joseph II had an unfailing sense of quality, and was by no means ruled by convention.

Although stingy, Joseph nevertheless did not let achievement go unrewarded. Young Salieri received a New Year's gift of 50 ducats (225 florins) for his weekly participation as a guest at the musical gatherings. The following year it was increased to 80 ducats (360 florins). That money was the first he had ever earned, and he immediately gave it to Gassmann.

The second important person Salieri met was Pietro Metastasio, probably the most renowned librettist who ever lived. He was the unchallenged authority on *opera seria*; several of his thirty librettos were set to music more than fifty times. His dramas, often with complicated plots, were all set in Greece or Rome and celebrated morality, exalted love, and incomparable bravery. All gross and excessive characteristics were omitted; catastrophes were avoided. Decency, dignity, and a frequently improbable virtue inform these plays, which ideally reflected the court's taste. But in depicting the victory of ethics and morality over baseness and evil, they also embodied bourgeois values. Naturally, Metastasio could hardly have become so important had his refined linguistic skills not enabled him to write light and melodious verse that blended pleasingly with music.

This leading figure of Italian literature lived in Vienna as poet of the imperial court for over fifty years, without once visiting his homeland. He lived in modest seclusion with his friends, the Martinez family—he did not even have his own home—secretly amassing wealth, and dressed as discreetly as an abbot. He was a poet to whom all of Europe paid homage, and he maintained an extensive correspondence. Moreover, he was most helpful (provided money was not involved) and friendly, a man accessible to everyone. He held an open house each Sunday morning from nine to twelve o'clock, at which the most cultivated Viennese residents and foreign visitors gathered.

It was easy for Gassmann to introduce Salieri to these gatherings, where one could always meet influential people. But for the time being, Salieri's main interest was not so much to make useful acquaintances as it was to study musical texts. Metastasio was generous enough to receive the eager young man in private, when no admirers would disturb the poetic-musical instruction—perhaps Metastasio was as receptive to flattery as he was skilful in practicing it. Salieri thus received private instruction in declamation from Metastasio, which was useful not only to the future composer of opera, but also to the later voice teacher. This made for such a friendly relationship that Salieri now became a regular guest at the evening gatherings of Metastasio's hosts, the Martinez family.

Gluck, who later would advance Salieri's fortunes, lived right next door. When Count Giacomo Durazzo ceased being director of the opera in 1764, Gluck had had to relinquish his position as ballet composer to Gassmann, who soon turned out to be receptive to Gluck's operatic reforms. As for Gluck himself, he now had the leisure to develop farther the kind of composition he had begun with *Don Juan* (1761) and *Orfeo ed Euridice* (1762). It is not known when Salieri met Gluck for the first time, but he must have early become familiar with Gluck's ideas through Gassmann, who was working on *Amor e Psiche*, scheduled for production in the fall of 1767. This opera could not have been written without *Orfeo* as its model. No doubt Salieri was present during rehearsals, as it was part of Gassmann's teaching method to accustom his student to opera

praxis from the very beginning. This soon included accompanying on the harpsichord; in fact, Salieri apparently played
the harpsichord at the premiere of Gluck's *Alceste* in December
1767.

It must have been among the more memorable of Salieri's
experiences to arrive in Vienna at the very moment when
Metastasio's dominating influence on operatic style came to an
end. The first new works to break away from the Metastasian
model were given very mixed receptions. Of course, it was
impossible to foresee the far-reaching consequences of these
initial attempts to formulate a new esthetic. The idea of
replacing unnatural, ornate language, complicated intrigues,
and schematic, undramatic plots with simplicity, truth, and
artlessness was surely much debated. Something so fundamen-
tally new was happening here that it was later referred to as a
revolution in opera—and Salieri could say to himself that he
had witnessed it almost from the beginning. That he preferred
to risk the unknown in Vienna, rather than study in Naples
with an assured stipend and the protection of an influential
nobleman, may have seemed strange to the Venetians. Yet
whatever may have influenced young Salieri's decision at the
time, its uncertainties were soon followed by more positive
developments.

Metastasio's texts continued to be set to music (even Gassmann did so with *Ezio* in 1770, though that was for a Roman
rather than for the Viennese theater); but this became increasingly rare, with only an occasional work appearing after the
turn of the century. It is significant that when Mozart received
his commission for an opera in honor of the coronation in
Prague in 1791 (based on the text of Metastasio's *La clemenza
di Tito*), he undertook an arrangement that he described as a
"transformation into true opera." No one would have dared
to tamper with Metastasio's libretti twenty-five years earlier,
when they were still considered sacrosanct.

The child Mozart arrived in Vienna (with his family and a
servant) just in time to hear the new operas by Gluck, and he
stayed there for almost a year and a half. Naturally Leopold
Mozart took his eleven-year-old son to the opera; in letters to

Salzburg, Leopold specifically mentioned *Amor e Psiche* as well as *Alceste*. After all, the "prodigy" was supposed to write an opera himself in Vienna, even though it was to be an *opera buffa*—"but not a short *opera buffa*, rather one that is two-and-a-half to three hours long," as Leopold Mozart writes. Mozart must have seen Salieri, who was about seventeen then, at the Gluck operas for the first time. He probably paid little attention to the lanky, inconspicuous youth at the harpsichord, who had not yet made his mark.

Salieri, on the other hand, had in all likelihood heard of this phenomenal prodigy, and would have had the opportunity to admire the genius at the pianoforte during one of his numerous performances. For Leopold Mozart did not miss any chance to attract attention to his son. And of course Salieri must have heard that this eleven-year-old child wanted to write an opera for the opera house where he, Salieri, played the harpsichord often enough of an evening. This, however, was a project that no one deemed possible. Many saw it as a fraud perpetrated by an impresario father who was not content with the unquestionable talents of his "young genius" at the piano-forte.

Most of the composers in Vienna thought that it would prove a dubious and silly spectacle that ought to be prevented—and only with hindsight was this a mistaken view. No one could have known that Mozart was so exceptional; no one like him had ever existed before. In the end, this opera, *La finta semplice*, was not performed in Vienna, though Emperor Joseph himself had been in favor of it. Gluck seems to have been quite set against the experiment, for which the vindictive Leopold Mozart held a longstanding grudge against him. But did Gluck really have so much influence at the opera at that time? For he was now on the point of assuming a lesser role in public life. And what about Gassmann, who did hold an influential position at the opera house? Leopold Mozart makes no mention of him at all in connection with the intrigues.

In the same period young Salieri earned his compositional spurs with short adaptations or insertions for the opera, written with Gassmann's guidance and approval during his daily theater praxis. He also composed a few smaller works for the church, and some instrumental music that he later destroyed, for the most part. He still considered himself a student; it was in that spirit that he secretly set to music the same pieces his teacher was currently working on, in order to compare them. There is some mention of an early opera from this period, *La vestale*, that has not been preserved. Presumably this, too, was designed as a comparative piece, for in 1768 Gluck actually published a new version of an older opera with the same title. The important entrance of the chorus in that piece was a suitable challenge to a student taking his first steps in a new form.

There is a little anecdote from this time that reveals the unpleasant side of the daily life of the theater as much as it does Salieri's temperament, and was probably told to Mosel by Salieri himself. The theater had a spinet that was in pitiful shape and did not stay in tune even for the duration of a rehearsal. Although it had broken plectra and failing springs, it was not replaced. Presumably this was during the era of the impresario Giuseppe Affligio (1767–1770), soon to end in economic disaster.

One day Salieri

> . . . finally had the urge to put an end to the impresario's stinginess or carelessness; he opened up the spinet, moved a chair next to it, stood on it and jumped into the spinet. Anyone familiar with the mechanism of such an instrument can picture what he managed to do to it! . . . An opera was to be performed that evening, and the spinet was taken into the orchestra pit; the tuner arrived an hour before the performance and opened it to tune it. "Mercy!" he called out and sank back into his chair. Almost all the strings were broken and the sound-board was smashed. . . . "Some devil must have jumped into it." "This good man just about guessed it," thought *Salieri*, who was standing there quietly and whom no one suspected, or at least of whom no one voiced a suspicion, but who did not feel entirely at ease until he heard the maestro say: "Let it stay the way it is! Heaven be praised that the impresario is finally forced to have a new instrument made." And that's what happened.[4]

Gassmann's teaching was supposed to last two years, but there seems to be no official point at which it was terminated. Early on Salieri slipped informally into the role of *répétiteur* at the opera, as Gassmann's assistant, so to speak. However, he continued to live with Gassmann, who moved to Josephstadt (taking up residence at the "Zur goldenen Säule" inn no later than the fall of 1768) and married. Salieri was still completely dependent on Gassmann, having no steady income of his own.

A year later an opportunity arose for him to work on his first piece as an apprentice composer. This came about through one of the dancers at the opera, Giovanni Gastone Boccherini, who was a friend of Ranieri de' Calzabigi (the librettist for Gluck's reform operas and the power behind the reform movement). Boccherini wanted to try his hand at writing a libretto. He had actually written the commedia per musica *Le donne letterate* for Gassmann, but the latter was busy with a commission for Rome, so Calzabigi advised him to entrust this opera to Salieri, who was a beginner as well. Salieri describes what took place:

Aha! I thought, so they consider you ready to compose operas! Courage! We won't waste an opportunity! —I asked the poet, with great impatience, to inform me of the subject of his opera and to bring his libretto himself. That is what happened; and after we had distributed the roles according to the competence of the singers at that time, *Boccherini* said: "I'm going to leave you now; meantime you can make your comments and if you need some changes made here and there in regard to the musical effect, we can make them together when I return." When I was alone again I locked myself in and with my face aflame— as happened to me later on as well, whenever I worked on a piece with pleasure and love—I reread the text, and found it quite suitable for the music; after I had read the segments for voice for the third time, I began by determining the key that would match the nature of each aria, as I had learnt to do from my master. . . .

As soon as I found myself alone I had an irresistible urge to set the introduction to the opera to music. Hence I tried to visualize the characters and circumstances of the protagonists as clearly as possible, and suddenly I thought of a phrase for the orchestra that seemed appropriate to carry and link the interspersed vocal sections of the composition. I imagined myself in the theater's orchestra seats and heard my concepts being performed; they seemed full of character to me; I wrote them down, checked them again and as I felt satisfied I continued my work. Thus the introduction was sketched out on the music sheet in half an hour. . . .

In short, after continuing the work with the same eagerness, I had a good two-thirds of the opera score and the instrumentation completed within four weeks. It was my intention to finish it without delay, but not to let it be performed until my master had returned from Rome and was able to correct it. But existing circumstances decreed otherwise. The impresario had just produced an opera that the public disliked, and hence found it necessary to follow it up with another new work.

Given this predicament, Boccherini adroitly called attention to the almost completed work by Salieri, and he was asked to present whatever was finished.

> I was somewhat surprised to find the impresario and the *Kapellmeisters Gluck* and *Scarlatti* there, but thought they had just come out of curiosity and was tremendously pleased by their presence. I sang and played whatever was finished; *Gluck* and *Scarlatti* joined in the arias for multiple voices. *Gluck*, who had always loved and encouraged me, showed he was satisfied with my work right from the start; *Scarlatti*, who now and then criticized small grammatical errors, nevertheless praised each aria in its entirety, and at the end both masters told the impresario that if I were willing to complete the unfinished sections, the opera could be rehearsed and performed promptly, since (*Gluck's* words) "the work contains enough to entertain the public."[5]

Though not lavish praise, this was, after all, a commendation by Gluck. The work shows that Salieri had already mastered something of the new trend. Thus, there are accompanied *recitativos* instead of *secco recitativos*, ensembles, and a finale at the end of each act; the arias are not *da capo*, and are effectively designed to bring out the character of the protagonists. However, there are some redundancies (already present in the text), as is frequent among beginners. Though the plot is simple, the work requires eight singers and has three different choruses scattered throughout. It deals with a family that seems to be rather intellectual (two sisters study philosophy and astronomy; the husband of one of them is writing a tragedy on Caracalla, and wants to earn his doctorate). An orphan named Corilla lives with the family and is supposed to marry a poet or an academic. After numerous complications, she manages to get the man she loves, and the one who best suits her unaffected innocence.

One can imagine that Salieri rehearsed this opera carefully; he was so excited that he could hardly wait to see his name printed on the posters for the first time. At the end of the successful premiere he mingled with the public to catch whatever scraps of praise (or criticism) he could overhear. How successful it was, we do not know; at any rate, it was performed once more in Prague (1773). Gassmann only got to know this initial work on his return from Rome, when Emperor Joseph had it played during his musicale. He was, as Mosel writes, "uncommonly satisfied with the treatment of each individual passage, with the musical concepts, the overall character of the music, and especially with its relationship to the subject of the opera."[6]

That apparently concluded Salieri's apprenticeship; it was his first chance to receive a regular fee, and he now became one of the composers whose works were performed at the imperial Burgtheater. He did not let much time elapse before writing his second piece, *L'amore innocente*, a pastorale that appeared in the same year, again with Boccherini as its author.

The unique quality of this little work is that it is specifically set in the mountain village of Klausen in the magnificent Tyrolean Alps (the village lies between Bressanone and Bolzano, along the Isarco river), instead of the usual bucolic southern landscape. It deals with a shepherd who has a rather city-oriented daughter, as well as a ward who prefers the countryside and has promised to marry a shepherd. The daughter also likes the shepherd, and institutes a rash of intrigues in order to get him. Up to the last minute, she seems to have succeeded, but then an unexpected solution brings about the required rustic bliss.

Salieri chose to have the role of the simple country girl sung by a coloratura, which, of course, required bravura arias. Perhaps this was why the piece was set in the Alps—coloratura as yodeling. At any rate, Salieri managed the characterization skillfully: he juxtaposed the coloratura soprano of the country ward against the shepherd's capricious daughter, whose assumed worldliness contrasts effectively with the alpine setting. On the other hand, the wooed swain is portrayed as utterly confused. All this was cleverly achieved with the simplest of means, and the work was later produced at least three more times.

These first two operas, though not wild successes, were encouraging. Salieri seemed to think he had to display all his talents at once, and that same year (1770) he produced another opera, again in a quite different category. *Don Chisciotte alle nozze di Gamace* is a ballet-opera in one act with very little plot.

Its most amusing feature is the rhythmic jingle of its title. While Gamace is celebrating a country wedding, Don Chisciotte and a knight pass by with their servants, and are invited to join in. Salieri himself says that this work "received the most scanty applause," from which perfunctory reception even the dances by the famous choreographer Jean-Georges Noverre could not rescue it. There are times when even the biggest names are of no help.

Before Salieri embarked on his first great triumph, he contributed certain segments to a pasticcio, *La moda ossia I scompigli domestici*, a casual and quickly written piece intended as a program filler.

Only then did Salieri attempt a piece on a grander scale, the *dramma per musica Armida*, based on a text by Marco Coltellini. In this "opera containing magic, heroes, and love, which also touches on the tragic," as Salieri characterizes it, he set to music a work that has dances, choruses, arias, and ensembles. Even the overture is worthy of attention. It is not a symphony whose musical motifs are scarcely related to its dramatic themes, as was customary; rather, it tries to express the events that precede the action of the opera by musical means:

> . . . Ubaldo's arrival on Armida's island in the dense, dark fog surrounding it; the monsters, standing guard, that attack him at the foot of the cliff to frighten him; the terrible howls and confusion with which they are put to flight on being confronted by his magic shield; the effort and utmost exertion with which he climbs to the top of the overhanging cliff; finally, his quick progress bringing him to the crest of the mountain into a more pleasant and enchanting region.

Carl Friedrich Cramer, who printed Salieri's description in his *Magazin der Musik* (1783), added: "Merely to have conceived of this is proof of Salieri's great descriptive genius; but now it has to be executed!"[7]

In general, the music of the overture was supposed to convey a sense of drama without the simultaneous presentation of pantomime or dance on stage. This could be achieved only if the public was already familiar with the outlines of the plot and merely had to recall it, but it required the composer to have a capacity for tone painting. *Armida* was a subject made familiar in numerous editions and translations of Torquato Tasso's verse epic on Gottfried of Bouillon and "the liberation of Jerusalem." Coltellini and Salieri did not bother with the complete highly complex story of Armida, but reduced the action to three main characters and a minor one, Armida's confidante.

The plot concerns Armida, daughter of the king of Damascus, who is used as a decoy for the Christian knights camped outside Jerusalem. She has not only mastered all the arts of love, but also possesses the magic power to entrap Rinaldo—a knight seeking adventure—on an island of love in the Dead Sea(!); now she herself has become enthralled by him. Salieri's opera begins with the daring attempt by Ubaldo to free Rinaldo from his involvement with Armida and bring him back to perform his Christian duty of laying siege to Jerusalem. The overture depicts Ubaldo's landing on the magic island. The first act gives an attractive picture of the magic island, where nymphs immediately invite Ubaldo to take part in wanton games; he withstands this temptation, and then holds off the threatening demons with a magic wand. The second act shows Rinaldo's entanglement with Armida; Ubaldo eventually comes upon the two of them, but finds it almost impossible to talk to Rinaldo, who is under the spell of love, while Armida suspects danger and becomes very worried. The freeing of Rinaldo finally takes place in the third act. At first he still vacillates between love and Christian duty, but Ubaldo increasingly learns how to loosen the bonds of love. When Armida joins them, she can no longer change Rinaldo's mind, and he boards the ship to Jerusalem. Armida slowly emerges from her numbing disappointment, and in an aria of revenge she once again summons all her magic powers to make the island collapse and the sea rage angrily.

Coltellini knew how to write an opera text in which—just as in Calzabigi's and Gluck's conceptions—dances and choruses effectively form part of a simple action based on entertaining images. He had found a language for it that was completely free of Metastasio's metaphors and "concetti," and that, moreover, managed to express the emotions of the three main characters in a straightforward and pleasing fashion. It is probably his best libretto.

Salieri had similarly distanced himself from the traditions of *opera seria*, and composed a work that already showed close affinities with Gluck's reform operas. (Gluck had not yet written his *Iphigénie* operas.) The rudimentary interchange between recitative and aria was largely dispensed with, in favor of more complex dramatic scenes in the first and third acts, in which the chorus is given an important role; these sections are often interspersed with solos, and are thus closely connected to the action. The recitatives are rarely mere *secco* recitatives; they generally make a smooth transition into segments accompanied by the orchestra. But above all, the opera concentrates on a linear plot that saves the subject from being overwhelmed by subplots, as it was in other versions. Even Gluck's *Armide*, not written until six years later, still included a great deal of secondary material.

In terms of musicological history, Salieri's *Armida* was the first work written after Gluck's *Alceste* and *Paride ed Elena* to use the central concepts of Gluck's reform operas. Of course, the twenty-year-old Salieri still lacked experience in the psychological development of characters. The arias are still encumbered with the conventional and schematic devices of *opera seria*, especially the use of bravura coloraturas—a concession to solo performers unsuitable in this case. On the other hand, it is also evident how hard Salieri tried to adapt such devices to his own dramatic effects. Even if he lacks Gluck's firm consistency, which a beginner could not be expected to achieve, *Armida* is by no means an imitative work. It tends rather to replace Gluck's pathetic tone with the conscious blending of the most diverse elements of style that was to be characteristic of Salieri's later operas. And no other subject was better suited for that type of music than this tragic, magic, heroic, and romantic story.

Later, Salieri kept trying to improve the work; in 1789 he even undertook a thorough revision that included the instrumental parts—a revision prompted by the great success of this opera, the first of his works to be printed in its entirety. Salieri was not very pleased when he heard that Cramer was adapting an excerpt from it for pianoforte, with a German text, in 1782. However, the transposition turned out to have been done with so much care that his reservations quickly disappeared.

Salieri elaborated his ideas on the opera in some detail in his letters to Cramer, revealing a rather self-critical and modest side of himself. He writes of "unforgivable immaturity, which makes me blush" (September 7, 1783),[8] and of "mistakes in the theatrical organization, of misleading passages, etc." that

> make me look at my first Armida with dissatisfied eyes. . . . So, just to repeat it again: nothing is more important to me in vocal music than the truth—the truth that I hear in entire works, as well as in the details of the tragedies by the inimitable master, Gluck, and that I could find only in very few masters in other categories of music; it is this that I try to put into all my operas, that requires the effort of thorough study, and only this has determined any changes I have made, and am still making in Armida (July 20, 1784).[9]

Another letter to Cramer indicates that Salieri considered that the lapse of time within the play, as well as the instrumentation, needed improvement; he writes that the "greater part of the changes consists of an expansion of the instrumental sections, involving both the type of instrumentation and what is known in music as *colpo di teatro* (surprise effect)." His only request is that in the foreword to the keyboard adaptation "the public be informed that this is my first *opera seria* and the fourth product of my modest talent. In this way, anyone who knows about the art of composition and the difficulties connected with it will understand the mistakes and, I continue to hope, will forgive them. I implore you to do this" (February 25, 1783).[10]

It is understandable that Salieri was not very happy that this work was to be published without corrections, especially as he himself was preparing a new version for a performance (Copenhagen, 1784?). On the other hand, a keyboard excerpt seemed to him most suitable for study and performance by amateurs at home, especially as it was impossible to reproduce the theatrical effect in an adaptation for the harpsichord. Only

the complete score could form the basis for performances. Yet
Cramer's keyboard adaptation was done so carefully that it was
long considered a model of its kind, along with that of Johann
Gottlieb Naumann's *Cora och Alonzo*. The work was published
with much attendant publicity. Cramer used the occasion to
reprint his chauvinistic foreword—in which he barely acknowledged Salieri as an Italian musician—along with the entire text
in German translation in his *Magazin der Musik*.

The speed with which works were composed in the eighteenth century is amazing; an opera composer could write up
to four works a year, always chasing restlessly after fresh
commissions. Indeed, composers had little opportunity to distance themselves from their work in order to revise. Each piece
was written for immediate production; it was worked on up to
the very last minute, and along the way there were many who
wanted to have their say. Evidence exists of numerous special
requests by male and female performers who were unwilling
to sing a single note that did not fall within their range and
style of singing. It was advisable to pay attention to such
requests, as they could have a great influence on the success
of the performance. Of course, this necessitated constant
changes, which affected a particular performance rather than
the work itself. We know that a composer like Gluck plagiarized
himself shamelessly in the period before his reform operas,
constantly reworking his own older material and inserting it
into new pieces. Sometimes the greater part of an opera was
no more than a collage of self-quotations; but in later years all
that changed radically.

Salieri began to work on other operas as soon as he finished
Armida. He wrote three new ones in 1772, though they cannot
be said to be among his best. Eighteenth-century opera sacrificed much intellectual power to the daily requirements of the
theater. Understandably, people always wanted to see something new, and considered the artistic creations of the past as
foreign to their taste. At best, these were thought of as subjects
for academic study, and only the most current works of art
received wide attention. Moreover, it was not only the general
quality of libretto and music that determined the success of a
performance—that is, its frequent repetition—but also such

elements as arias that became especially popular, virtuoso contributions by great artists, stage effects, and the like. And from today's vantage point, it is not always easy to judge why one piece was more successful than another.

Salieri's next opera, *La fiera di Venezia*, belongs among his most acclaimed compositions, and was produced all over Europe on more than thirty occasions during his lifetime; yet it contains scarcely anything worthy of the composer of *Armida*. Even in that earlier work Salieri had tried harder to avoid the all-too-insipid conventions of the current *opera buffa*. Here not only was the musical treatment unimaginative, but the libretto's complex plot failed to create suspense. Boccherini proved to be a librettist who did not develop any particular individuality; yet Salieri was faithful to the man with whom he had begun. It is precisely in this work that Salieri freely utilizes the uninspired intricacies of the Italian *opera buffa* (which he had tried to avoid in his first piece). It is as though in recalling Venice—for that is where the opera takes place—he had a lump in his throat.

Leopold Mozart, who saw this opera in Salzburg in 1785, wrote of it harshly and succinctly: ". . . there is another *opera buffa* being performed, *La fiera di Venezia* by Salieri, that pains me; because as far as the music is concerned, it is full of the most banal, commonplace concepts, it is antiquated, forced and rather lacking in harmony: the individual finales are just about bearable: the subject of the piece is as always a *silly piece of Italian foolishness*, contrary to all common sense."[11]

It must have been the fair in the first act and the masquerade in the second act, the inevitable Venetian local color, that appealed to contemporary tastes. The plot involves a rich and extravagant Venetian nobleman, who returns to his bride after leaving her temporarily. The work is more like a portrait of society in which three couples come together, each pair from a different social level—the nobility, the bourgeoisie, and the common people—in which everything is organized as it should be, and thus offers little drama. Perhaps it was this very confirmation of the obvious that pleased contemporary operagoers.

Giuseppe Petrosellini's libretto for the second opera of that year, *Il barone di Rocca antica*, is much more effective. It is a typical small-scale *opera buffa* without tasteless exaggerations or crude stylizations of the four characters who make up the cast. The story concerns a baron who had once carelessly made a written promise of marriage while a student in Cremona. He is now expecting a visit from a lady whom he wants to marry, if she pleases him. A female pilgrim enters, and tells his future; then his expected visitor arrives, and she behaves so badly that he prefers to remember the promise of marriage he made as a student. Thereupon his visitor reveals herself to be both his first love and the pilgrim. There is a parallel subplot dealing with the manager of the baron's estate, who had also once promised to marry someone, but who is now more interested in military service. Considerable pressure has to be exerted to make him keep his promise.

The music Salieri wrote for this work was not especially inspiring; at a later performance, Charles Burney found it "boring." Not until the prima donna appeared, the famous coloratura singer Costanza Baglioni, who had the role of the lady in various disguises, did Burney, and apparently others, become fascinated: "Her notes were all so rounded and pure that everything she did was pleasing; a few simple, slow notes by her were worth more to the listeners than an entire elaborate aria by any of the others."[12]

The third opera again had Boccherini as its librettist; this time he used a famous Italian play, Alessandro Tassoni's *La secchia rapita*, though he oversimplified it to such an extent that nothing remained of Tassoni's blend of the heroic and the comic. In the original version, a verse epic in twelve cantos, Tassoni turned the ancient gods into pathetic down-and-out characters who intervene in a historic war between Modena and Bologna. Boccherini had no use for the gods; he reduced the plot to the theft of a bucket that causes a war. The foreword to Salieri's opera states:

As Tassoni's verse is mainly nothing but a parody of the divine writing of Homer, Petrarch, and Ariosto, it was decided to imitate the most famous heroic epics in the scenic arrangement and the expression of the arias, with a view to choosing ideas that would once again please the public, though cast in a cheerful style.[13]

Thus the opera was turned into a harmless burlesque to which even Salieri contributed little that was original. Nevertheless, it later received four different productions. However, Salieri must have realized that working with Boccherini could scarcely continue to be fruitful for him; *La secchia rapita* turned out to be their final collaboration.

Salieri had his first real breakthrough in the "Italian specialty" of the *opera buffa* with *La locandiera*. This piece by Goldoni, about the self-confident Mirandolina, was adapted for Salieri by Domenico Poggi. Poggi and his wife Clementina Baglioni both came from famous Italian families of singers and lived in Vienna from the 1760s to 1774. Poggi had sung the role of the oracle in the memorable premiere of Gluck's *Alceste*. He not only had a very beautiful bass voice but was above all an excellent actor. Theater professional that he was, he had immediately given himself the important role of the waiter Fabrizio; his sister-in-law, Costanza Baglioni, sang the leading role of Mirandolina; and her sister Rosa had the part of the chambermaid Lena. So it was a real family venture, for which Salieri wrote some very lively and fast-paced music.

The work has very few grand arias, and the texts are repeated only twice; two-part arias, *cavatinas*, or *ariosos* predominate, and permit a musically fluid transition to accompanied recitatives. In this way an overall rapid *parlando* style is achieved that also prevails in the final scenes, with connecting motifs providing uniformity among all the sections. To conform with this, only two real duets occur in the opera itself; however, the three participants in the sole terzetto never sing simultaneously, but always alternate. Salieri had managed to create a musical comedy that does not rely on pretty melodies and accessible music, but rather demands singers who are also outstanding actors. For Goldoni's protagonists are not comic types, not the crude masks of the commedia dell'arte, but cleverly observed individuals whose differentiated characters are revealed only by the intrigue-laden plot. The beautiful and lively innkeeper, Mirandolina, who makes fools of three of her guests in a rather audacious manner, ends up with the waiter, whom she really wants and who had been chosen for her by her father. She is a self-determined woman who never lets go of the reins.

The work became very successful in Vienna, no doubt thanks to its ideal casting, but was performed all over Europe as well. It advanced the twenty-three-year-old Salieri to the status of a full-fledged composer. Yet a German version that was put on at the national *Singspiel* in Vienna in 1782 had only limited success. Apart from the fact that the cast there probably were not good actors, translation of the rapid *parlando* into unaffected German must have caused numerous problems—a difficulty familiar from Mozart operas as well.

Mozart came to Vienna again in the summer of 1773, this time accompanied only by his father. The two naturally wanted to investigate future prospects; after all, they did not intend to go to seed in Salzburg. Mozart was now seventeen; over the previous two years he had made three trips to Italy, and had been highly successful there as a composer of opera. But what were the real purposes of this visit to Vienna? Did Leopold Mozart nurse the hope that his youthful son would find an official position at the imperial court? Leopold's letters contain hints that are still puzzling today. There is constant talk of "circumstances that I do not wish to mention"; he did not seem to trust the mail, or was he afraid his letters would be passed around in Salzburg and lead to dangerous gossip? Among the many visits the Mozarts paid there was one to the Martinez family, where Metastasio lived. They might also have met Salieri there. At any rate, that autumn Mozart wrote *Sechs Variationen über ein Thema aus der Oper "La fiera di Venezia,"* a pleasant if not very significant occasional piece. It was published some years later (1778), and was certainly a friendly compliment to his elder.

CHAPTER TWO

The Emperor's Protégé 1773–1777

The young composer soon became known outside Vienna as well. In 1772 Salieri's operas were seen for the first time in Dresden (*L'amore innocente*), Mannheim (*La fiera di Venezia*), and Florence (*Il barone di Rocca antica*); then, in 1773, performances were given in Prague (*Le donne letterate*) and Copenhagen (*Armida*). People everywhere were eager to put on the latest works that had been publicized through the active network of musicians and singers rather than in the daily press. Apparently Salieri was considered a rising star in the operatic firmament. It is only in such a context that a comment by Mosel can be understood:

> At this time he received a three-year appointment to the court theater in Stockholm. But as this visit did not get much encouragement from the emperor, *Salieri* remained in Vienna and subsequently had no cause to regret the decision.[1]

Salieri was not offered a firm position in Stockholm; he was simply invited for an extended stay, possibly to write a few operas. King Gustav III, who had just ascended the throne, was in fact engaged in giving a fresh impetus to Swedish musical life. As he himself attempted to write librettos, he was especially interested in establishing a national music theater where material drawn from Swedish history—and, above all, written in Swedish—could be performed. Since there was as yet no indigenous talent, the king had to depend on foreigners. Francesco Antonio Uttini had been at the Swedish court since 1755; his *Thetis och Pelée* became the first Swedish opera. Later there were compositions by other foreign composers, such as Joseph Martin Kraus, Johann Gottlieb Naumann, and Georg Joseph Vogler.

Salieri's life would probably have turned out very differently had he accepted the offer from Stockholm. His musical development would most likely have led to an even more thorough study of Gluck, whose works were immediately translated into Swedish during the Gustavian period, and served as the model for the new national opera. Historical and mythological subjects were preeminent, "grand" opera in which the chorus filled important functions. At the same time, a willingness to embark on new and experimental styles placed operatic composition at a far remove from the conventions of Metastasio's *opera seria*. Apparently those who had transmitted the new ideas to Sweden had listened closely to *Armida*. What Salieri had attempted there fitted in well with the esthetic discussions held in Johan Henrik Kellgren's circle.[2] Veracity, naturalness, and simplicity did more than merely shake up a traditional *opera seria* that had become set in its formal modes. A pompous and affected court ceremonial was replaced by a universal form expressing natural dignity and equality. It was the birth of classicism in the realm of music—not simply a style, but an esthetic program that accompanied the end of reactionary systems such as the *ancien régime*. This had nothing to do with the dispute between the followers of Gluck and those of Niccolò Piccinni; that was merely a feud between blind partisans, since Gluck and Piccinni themselves had already accepted each other in a respectful and fraternal way. The new trend really had to do with a new understanding of music theater, a dramatic form expressed in music, in which music itself is the language of action. This innovative approach to opera quickly gained acceptance, transmitted not only from the operatic center of Paris, but also from the peripheries. Seen from this perspective, Stockholm was not a backward province.

The fact that Salieri did not go to Stockholm, though he had no firm position in Vienna and nothing to lose by accepting the invitation, was indeed due solely to Emperor Joseph II; there is not the slightest reason to doubt Mosel's explanation. After all, since his early days in Vienna, Salieri had been part of the emperor's private musical ensemble, which had inevitably led to a natural and friendly relationship. An honorable offer such as the one from Stockholm had of course to be made known and discussed in that setting. And if Joseph II advised that the offer be turned down, he was taking personal responsibility for ensuring that the decision would not be to Salieri's disadvantage.

It is always said that Emperor Joseph II had a great preference for "Italian" musicians because he himself was partial to the prevailing Italian style, with its accessible melodic patterns. One incident that is given as evidence of this concerns a visit Joseph II made to his royal sister, Marie Antoinette, in Paris. He advised her to support Antonio Sacchini, as demanded by the followers of Piccinni; but in fact Sacchini's latest works had clearly shown him to be moving in Gluck's direction. And Salieri, given his entire training and the range of his models, was anything but a composer of the Italian school. Of course, the Italian school had dominated Europe for decades, and even Gluck had composed in that style until the early 1760s. The reform movement exploring new artistic ground got under way rather slowly. But from the beginning of his compositional career Salieri had assimilated and developed these new concepts. Finally, there was not *one* typical representative of the Italian school in the emperor's chamber music circle. Its members tended to be conservatives who still had ties to the older Viennese tradition. And the emperor's well-known love of the fugue hardly indicated a preference for Italian opera. There was also his attempt to start a national German *Singspiel* and found a German-language tradition of music theater. That was surely not a momentary whim, but an idea developed over years. Indeed, it reflected an unusual optimism about a feasible counterbalance to Italian opera, and confidence that innovation and creativity would prove strong once there was a theater for them.

Though Joseph II did not make a formal counter-offer to Salieri, he left him in no doubt as to his patronage and esteem, so the effect was that of a better offer. Salieri was given to understand that he would receive special consideration the next time a position became available, and there was probably some guarantee that he would not go penniless until then. He already received a personal "gratuity" for his participation in the chamber music group, and an honorarium, though not a lavish one, was paid for operas that were performed in Vienna.

The emperor was also well aware that Gassmann, who still belonged to the chamber music group, had been seriously ill for some time. This probably dated back to an accident Gassmann had on his trip to Italy in 1769–1770. The *Wiener Theater Almanach für das Jahr 1795* notes:

> On one of his journeys to Italy his horses bolted; he wanted to jump out of the carriage but got caught in the chains. The horses dragged him along for three quarters of an hour and two of his ribs were bent inward in his chest. Since that time he was noticed to have an extraordinarily strong pulse, even in areas where one does not usually notice a pulse beat, i.e., in his fingertips. . . . As of that time he also managed to get very little sleep; he generally slept for only one or two hours. Baron von Quarin, who is widely known for his keen eye in judging sicknesses, predicted the overall condition of his body to the emperor, and when the postmortem was performed everything was just as Quarin had foretold.[3]

Presumably Salieri still lived with his esteemed teacher,[4] and had to watch him gradually decline. Gassmann finally died in his mid-forties, in January 1774.

The administrative merry-go-round immediately went into action. Giuseppe Bonno, who had been court composer, was appointed successor to Gassmann as the Hofkapellmeister. Eventually the post of composer of the imperial chamber became vacant. It was not an important position in the court and state system, more of a makeshift office to be bestowed as the emperor pleased. Since Gassmann had held this title, no elaborate decision-making process was required to fill the position again—with Antonio Salieri. It came with the low salary of 100 ducats, but also with a rent-free court residence (one of the second-floor apartments that had to be left vacant by the owner of every house for the accommodation of court officials). Salieri went to live at Heidenschuss No. 361, in what had formerly been a deep fortification. Given the high rents in Vienna, a court residence was equivalent to a substantial allowance. (Joseph II, however, abolished the entire arrangement once Maria Theresa died.) More important, Salieri was given a concurrent appointment as Kapellmeister at the opera, and for this he received another 300 ducats. Thus he had a secure and influential position at the Burgtheater and the expectation of being appointed Hofkapellmeister, for Bonno was already over sixty years old. The emperor had indeed provided an appointment for his protégé Salieri that far exceeded the Stockholm offer.

At this point Salieri met his future wife, an event that he himself preserved for his biographer in a long-winded account. Not many documents exist in which Salieri recounts personal events, describes his private life, or provides insight into his modest, rather shy way of thinking. Theresa von Helferstorfer was the daughter of a retired official, and was raised in a convent where Salieri gave music lessons to a young countess:

From the very first day I gave my lessons there, one of the girls—of slender build, somewhat taller than the rest, about eighteen years old and dressed in pink taffeta—made a strong impression on me. I saw her pass twice; the third and fourth times I did not notice her among her friends and did not know why she had stayed away; that made me very anxious. The fifth time the others again came without her; just as I began to feel my anxiety increase she entered the room alone, having followed her friends. I was so overwhelmed by the unexpected pleasure I experienced that I greeted her—though with the same respect as usual—in a way that clearly showed that it had pained me not to have seen her on the previous days; and I thought I could tell just as plainly from her little face that this was not unwelcome news to her.

As of that moment her image was embedded in my mind and heart; but the pleasant feeling inside me that had accompanied it was marred by many bitter thoughts. "What folly," I told myself, "to develop such a sudden passion for a girl you have only seen three times, who most likely only came to know you in the convent, to whom you have never spoken and probably will never be able to speak!" . . . Such was my agitated state when, on the second Sunday after my first encounter with the charming stranger, chance (or rather divine providence) created the opportunity for me to address her for the first time. It was my habit on Sundays to attend the afternoon services in the cathedral as often as I could; . . . What a wonderful surprise awaited me! I greeted her respectfully but without speaking to her; she did the same with much grace. I did not hesitate a moment in following her. I left the church, saw that she was going in the direction of the convent with her companion, and hurried along the back streets in order to meet up with her. I wanted to approach her and did not dare to do so. Finally the fear of losing a favorable opportunity so aroused my courage that, under the assumption that she understood French, I asked her in that language to forgive my daring and to permit me to accompany her to the convent. She answered, also in French, but in the voice and manner of an angel, that it would give her pleasure.

It would be impossible to try to express the inner joy these words gave me, and the realization that she was not offended by my address. In a voice that trembled with delight I now continued talking to her; . . . The following Sunday it had barely struck four o'clock when I hurried to the church and took up my position at the gate through which she had to pass coming from her father's apartment. . . . After the service was over I followed her, like the first time, and found sweet solace for all my suffering in her assurance that she was pleased to see me again. . . . I did not know where to begin, and the short time at my disposal was almost over, when I gathered the courage to say I had a secret to divulge that concerned my peace of mind, but begged her to promise me that she would give me a definite answer. She promised and encouraged me to speak, with such grace and delicate curiosity, that I finally dared to tell her that I loved her passionately and wanted to know whether I could hope for any love from her. "The same affection," she answered in a low voice. "The same affection!" I called out in delight, reaching for her hand and covering it with kisses. "The very same," she confirmed and shyly pressed my hand lightly. Feeling beside myself with happiness, I assured her that these words overjoyed me, and asked her when I might introduce myself to her father in the event that she approved of this decision. "In a week from today," she answered; "I shall prepare him for your visit and you will be welcome for my father already knows you from your reputation." I had indeed made a name for myself by then with a few successful operas like *Armida, La fiera di Venezia*, and *La secchia rapita*, and the emperor's gracious opinion of me was equally known. Meanwhile, I was not destined to ask my beloved's father for her hand in marriage; this noble old man, whom everyone esteemed and who had been ill for some time, was quite unexpectedly summoned by God in the course of the following week; . . .

Herr *v. Helferstorfer* had arranged for an upright and wealthy man to be the guardian of his daughter and two sons. He was a widower, still in his prime, and, being unaware of his ward's romantic attachment, intended to marry her, and informed her of this soon after her father's death. There was nothing Theresa could do but confess that her heart was no longer free and to reveal the object of her affection. As soon as I learned of this I hastened to see the guardian, accompanied by a respected man, and formally requested the hand of my beloved. He received me politely and declared with apparent calm that as his ward was satisfied, he also agreed to my request; but he had to make sure first that I had sufficient means to support a woman from a noble family who possessed a considerable fortune. I replied that I received three hundred ducats as conductor of the Italian Opera, and a hundred ducats as composer of the imperial chamber, and that I had hopes of becoming the Hofkapellmeister some day; moreover, my compositions and my lessons brought in another three hundred ducats annually, so that my total income could be said to amount to seven hundred ducats. The guardian answered, "That would be more than enough if it were assured; but of all of these sources you can really only depend on the hundred ducats that you receive from the court, and as guardian I must therefore ask you to wait until your position becomes more secure before I can consent to this marriage."

I had to concede that the honest man was basically doing his duty. So I asked him merely to keep the matter secret, which (fortunately) he did *not* do.

Two days later I went to play chamber music at the emperor's at three o'clock in the afternoon, as was my duty. When I entered the antechamber I saw the monarch there alone by the fireplace, his back toward me, deep in thought. He turned slightly to see who had come and thanked me for my reverential bow with his usual grace. On the other side of the room were the emperor's personal valet and two others, one of whom was a very good friend of mine, employed at the court library and well liked by the sovereign. I joined them, quietly, and my friend smiled and teased me by thumbing his nose at me. The emperor turned around again just at that moment, noticed the joke, and came toward us asking what this was all about? I pretended not to understand the joke that I understood only too well; the dismayed librarian stuttered that I wanted to marry a beautiful orphan but had found a rival in her guardian. The monarch, somewhat surprised at first, also smiled and asked me whether this was true? I was forced to recount the whole story of my love; it seemed to entertain the emperor greatly and ended with the request that His Majesty should forgive my having kept this matter secret up to now, but that I had done so because I was uncertain of my success. When I mentioned the reason for which the guardian refused his consent, I noticed a sudden serious expression on the monarch's face; but when I had finished speaking he walked away and said, as though reflecting, "Well now, you're going to have to have patience." Meanwhile the other musicians had arrived and the concert began as usual, without any further discussion of the matter dear to my heart.

The next morning the director of the court orchestra requested my presence. I hastened there and he greeted me with these words: "Please accept my congratulations, Herr Kapellmeister; the emperor has raised your salary from one hundred to *three hundred* ducats, with the only stipulation that you help to ease the duties of the meritorious, but already very aged and often sick Hofkapellmeister *Bonno*, and that you conduct the Italian Opera even when His Majesty begins to take charge of it himself. . . ."

Anyone can easily guess that I then rushed off to see the guardian who could no longer refuse to give his consent, that His Gracious Majesty heard of it with pleasure, and what the outcome was; . . .[5]

The account of the less pleasant aspects of this courtship is almost twice as long as what is cited here. But even in this shortened version, one senses the resoluteness and certainty of a man in love who patiently overcomes all obstacles, and in the end even finds considerate words for his rival. Joseph II, who was generally known for his stringent thriftiness, revealed himself here to be an unexpected friendly savior. The wedding took place on October 10, 1774.[6] It would not be inappropriate to assume that an *Alleluja* for choir and orchestra composed that year was a personal hymn of gratitude by the deeply religious musician.

In raising the issue of the uncertain income Salieri could expect from the Italian Opera, the bride's guardian, Leopold Hofmann, was very likely prompted by his own interests. Indeed Hofmann, Kapellmeister at the Cathedral of St. Stefan, had touched on a sore point. For conditions at the Viennese "Theater next to the Burg" and at the Kärntnertortheater had for years been anything but secure, and no one knew what would happen. Both venues, formerly court theaters, had been rented since the period of mourning for Emperor Franz I, Maria Theresa's husband, and were subject to the rather fluctuating fortunes that affected music theater in particular. The first impresario, Giuseppe Affligio, managed to stay in business for only a short period, despite help from a banker, and had to flee an enormous debt. Gluck, who became involved there in the interim, also lost his fortune. Next in line was a completely inexperienced but art-loving nobleman, Count Johann Koháry, who had to file for bankruptcy after a short time. He was followed as a trustee by Count Joseph Keglevich, who could do no more under these circumstances than take care of the most necessary administrative work and continue running the theaters.

These difficulties arose because the theaters catered to people from all levels of society and with varied interests in drama and opera. The "noblesse" had a pronounced taste for French drama—a penchant surely connected with the language itself, French being the idiom of the aristocracy and of diplomacy, but not of the bourgeoisie, who now crowded the theater and the opera in greater numbers. It can hardly be assumed that the nobility considered French theater to be the best, with the best plays and the best actors. Rather, it was an expression of pride in their rank, the wish to maintain an exclusive court theater, and a dislike of having to rub shoulders with the ordinary public. Others, especially among the bourgeois public, were more interested in German theater. Then there was the large circle of lovers of opera (which meant primarily Italian opera) and ballet. But this was also the most expensive entertainment, which only the wealthiest bourgeois could afford to attend frequently. Finally, there was the popular theater, which had always been particularly encouraged in Vienna, and was so well attended that certain companies were even in a position to rent the Kärntnertortheater. The administration of the overall theater program had the task—impossible even theoretically—of trying to satisfy all these various interests, while achieving an artistic and economically viable result.

As director of the court theater, Count Giacomo Durazzo produced French plays, Italian opera, and French opéra-comique at the Burgtheater until 1764; but he also actively supported the first attempts of Gluck's reform. The Kärntner-tortheater, on the other hand, was reserved for popular drama. However, when the theater was leased out, there was neither the professional management nor any plan that would have been in keeping with the economic possibilities. Affligio, who was in charge between 1767 and 1770, wanted to satisfy everyone. He kept the French ensemble and the Italian Opera company, permitted German actors to appear, and as a way of attracting the public, brought Jean Georges Noverre, the most famous choreographer and ballet master to Vienna. Not surprisingly, all this was impossible to finance. In the time of Count Koháry (1770–1772), and during the curatorship of his successor, Count Keglevich (1772–1776), *opera buffa* and *opera seria* experienced a great boom, whereas the French ensemble was let go in 1772. This was when Salieri was having his first experience of theater and opera.

It was clear to everyone that the administration of the bankrupt enterprise under Count Keglevich could only be an interim, not a satisfactory permanent solution. Joseph II now began to involve himself in the affairs of the theater to an ever greater extent, though he tried not to give the impression that he intended to restore a court theater. Salieri's appointment as Kapellmeister of the Italian Opera therefore depended entirely on its future development, including the possibility that Joseph II would himself take over its administrative affairs. "Italian Opera" in this instance did not represent a preference for one or the other trend, or for a particular traditional school; it merely signified the existence of an ensemble for *opera buffa* and *seria* that sang in Italian. Singers were employed whose vocal characteristics and range of roles enabled them to perform in either type of opera. Eventually it became clear that the continuance of the Italian Opera was uncertain, but that the protection Salieri received from Joseph II was nevertheless firmly established.

In this same period Salieri also revealed himself as a composer of instrumental works; he produced an organ concerto, two piano concertos, and a triple concerto for violin, oboe, and cello, as well as a concerto for flute and oboe with orchestral accompaniment. These concerti were surely written for specific occasions about which nothing is known. They do not deserve to be dismissed as mere occasional pieces, for they certainly compare favorably with the concerti of Haydn and Mozart. Perhaps their organization lacks the same strict clarity, and the themes tend at times to be somewhat dull or superficial; but there are sections (as in the first movement of the Concerto for Flute, Oboe, and Orchestra) in which Salieri's music is very elegant and rich in ideas. There are also some thoroughly dramatic passages in the first movement of the Piano Concerto in B Major, while the *adagio* is a delicate elegiac movement interspersed with some powerful passages. The conclusion consists of variations in minuet form. The Piano Concerto in C Major has a first movement that is arranged somewhat theatrically, though with virtuoso brilliance; the *larghetto* is a *siciliano* rich in nuances; and the finale consists of a lively *minuet-rondo*. In these concerti Salieri demonstrates a very colorful and varied instrumentation with distinctive tonal effects. It is regrettable that only these few concerti exist, and that Salieri did not write a single symphony in the classic sense (the works called "sinfonia" are overtures to his operas). No doubt this is due not only to the fact that his primary interest was opera, but also to his practical experience in that field right from the beginning of his career. His instrumental competence was probably not sufficient for solo performance (unlike Mozart's, whose virtuosity on the pianoforte inspired a large body of his work).

While the administration of the Italian Opera was still in a state of confusion, Salieri became a sort of resident composer there, hardly surprising after the box-office success of *La fiera di Venezia* and *La locandiera*. He lived in Vienna, and so was available for the often urgent demands of the theater; he enjoyed the emperor's protection—highly important in those times of upheaval—and he wrote the kind of music that appealed to the public. But so much success had its pitfalls. Perhaps Salieri was too closely entangled with this house and lacked the independence that would have allowed him to turn down commissions. Nor could he develop his strong points or let his work mature, always having instead to adapt himself to immediate needs and deliver promptly what had just been requested. Most likely he had little influence on the selection of the libretti and took too little time to rework them, or else he lacked the confidence necessary to reshape their dramatic form. Admittedly, this practice can be said to have begun only with Mozart who, unlike other operatic composers of his time, participated in the decisions and responsibilities for the entire dramatic structure as well as for every single detail of his operas (except for *Idomeneo*). For it was customary at that time for a composer to receive a completed text that he had to set to music, sequentially, in the shortest possible time. Even *opera buffa*, whose compositional rules are not as rigid as those of *opera seria*, had its established models, typical resolutions, and musical forms fitting many dramatic intrigues, characters, and situations. That made it possible to compose entire operas quickly—incredibly quickly, from today's perspective. But ready-made patterns were inadequate to go beyond what had been done so many times, to express in music what was unique and special in each dramatic moment; transcendence demanded artistic individuality.

A new opera by Salieri, *La calamità de' cuori*, based on a text by Carlo Goldoni, appeared on New Year's Day, 1774. The *Historisch-Kritische Theaterchronik* of Vienna commented:

> Herr Marchese ***, the Abbate Casti, Herr Dominicus Poggi, Herr Pocherini and Herr Salieri are supposed to have corrected, patched and embroidered the verses of this opera by Herr Goldoni, yet the text did not manage to please. Some connoisseurs and music lovers maintain that the music is artistic, beautiful and harmonic, and does much honor to Herr Salieri. But others hold that the subject is too childish, and that the music, though beautiful, is too serious for the text. One particular incident is noteworthy: at the final rehearsal the conductor stood on the stage to arrange the scenery and props, while the dramatist was down in the orchestra pit distributing the music.[7]

Whether the latter incident was just an invention or actually happened is impossible to know. But the mix-up before the opening could not have been described better.

The text of this opera had already been set to music for the Venetian Opera by Baldassare Galuppi in 1752, and had then been produced elsewhere in Europe. It deals with a beautiful woman who is courted by four men: one is an innocent, one is a miser, and the remaining two are pursued by jealous and quarrelsome former loves. The beautiful lady cannot decide on any one of them, but finally demands that each provide proof of his love. The amorous men engage in a tournament, but the beautiful woman does not wait for the result, and announces her decision in favor of the ingenuous and generous one. The two jealous women are united with their former lovers, whereas the miser remains alone. It is a typical burlesque piece based on an ultrasimple and familiar pattern; as in rough woodcuts, the characters are sketched with only the essential traits, and no allowance is made for individual feelings or motivations. Everything depends on situation comedy and fast-paced confrontation, rather than on delicate transitions, empathetic scenes, or conflicting emotions.

The criticism that the subject was "too childish," and that

the music, "though beautiful," was "too serious for the text" accurately reflects the dilemma of this opera. Salieri was probably unable to write a sparkling, witty, lively text, or to compose appropriate music for a libretto that did not contain even the rudiments of satire. When the aging Salieri took a critical look at his operas, he commented on this work in a way that clarifies his dilemma. "The symphony at least has the merit of not being in contradiction to this type of opera," he says about the overture. The first quartet "seems" to him to have "the appropriate coloring" for its situation; individual parts "create a good effect if well sung"; and the short finale "ends the opera fairly well."

More than a year and a half elapsed before the next work was ready, but this time there were difficulties again. First there was the long wait for the commission, then everything had to be completed very quickly. The librettist was Giovanni De Gamerra, who was already trying to get an appointment as a dramatist in Vienna—an aim that he achieved only twenty years later. He had served in the army for several years, and then led an unsettled life with hopes of finding employment as a poet. His works tended to deal with terrifying situations, and presented dreadful crimes and romantic adventures in alternate doses of horror and melodrama. He wrote *Lucio Silla* for Mozart, surely the weakest libretto Mozart ever set to music, and one that became minimally suitable only when Pietro Metastasio had made changes in it. Gamerra tried to compensate for his lack of poetic gifts with eulogistic poems dedicated to the various Hapsburg rulers in Italy and Vienna, though Joseph II happened to be not very receptive to that sort of flattery. On the other hand, Gamerra had the virtue of disregarding conventional categories, and being open to the exploration of new trends in the spoken drama.

Gamerra's text for Salieri, *La finta scema*, also had little to do with traditional *opera buffa*. It deals with the lord of a castle who would like to marry Rosina, the daughter of one of his servants. She, however, has long been promised to another servant. Two families arrive for a visit: an impoverished marquis and the widow of a colonel said to have fallen in

battle, each with two children. The widow offers to marry
either the lord or the marquis. While they are all sitting at
dinner the colonel, who was supposedly dead but had only
wanted to test his wife, suddenly arrives with his soldiers and
threatens to destroy the whole castle. However, he is soon
calmed, and later appears to be quite rational. The lord of the
castle eavesdrops on his servants during a tryst and finds
himself betrayed; as punishment he imprisons Rosina and
decrees death for her lover, but the colonel intervenes in time.
Various ongoing minor courtships, involving the children of
the marquis and the colonel, come to nothing in the end.
Finally the colonel succeeds in arranging the servant couple's
wedding; he then takes them into his own service, since the
lord of the castle no longer wants them.

It is doubtful whether such a whimsical and bizarre plot
was seriously intended to be a *commedia per musica*. Certainly
there are no recognizable traces of satire. Yet Salieri was not
put off by the imperfect and wildly imagined text. As traditional
models were of no use here, he used a mixed style in which
he freely combined the most varied elements, and produced a
through-composed work rather than one consisting of distinct
segments. That meant a wealth of ensemble movements and
many expanded and multisectioned finales in which recitatives
are even inserted into individual arias. In his old age, Salieri
was still justly proud of this music. But there was no way of
improving the plot and the clumsy dramatic construction. The
third act is more or less relegated to tidying up loose ends;
instead of providing a climax and resolution, it contains only
a gradual winding down of the action. There was not even
enough material for a proper finale at the end. Could this not
have been reworked?

Salieri must have noticed the libretto's deficiencies; he was
a seasoned enough practitioner of the theater. But rather than
alter the text, he preferred to make do with it—presumably
under the pressure of time (as Mosel had already noted). He
thus threw away the chance of a minor success. Did he lack
the artistic self-confidence to say that the libretto was unsuitable
as it stood—that at the very least the end needed to be rewritten?

As Kapellmeister, did he feel that the theater management would not agree to a postponed opening? Did he make the wrong choice between personal reliability and artistic responsibility? At the time many works were created that proved unsatisfactory and were later forgotten; but then some composers refused to waste their talents on projects destined to fail because of incompetent theater management. Salieri evidently considered it his duty to comply with management expectations, perhaps out of falsely conceived modesty and gratitude toward his sponsors.

The work *Delmita e Daliso*, an "azione pastorale," also written by Gamerra and performed July 29, 1776, was another failure that was never seen again—though for quite different reasons. The story concerns an old Athenian sea captain who lives with his two daughters (Delmita and Eurilla) and an adopted son (Daliso) in rustic tranquillity, represented by shepherds' festivities in the opening scene. According to an ancient law, Athenians regularly had to choose a boy and a girl and send them to Crete as human sacrifices. The die is cast when Delmita is the one chosen; Daliso decides to fight the minotaur in order to save Delmita and free Athens from having to make the sacrifice. Just then the news is received that Theseus has already killed the Cretan monster.

As in his first pastorale, Salieri again wrote a through-composed work; in many instances the recitatives are accompanied by orchestra, and special attention is paid to the choruses. Salieri enjoyed this kind of composition, and this one showed how much he had learned from and was influenced by Gluck, whose example he continued to follow. Mosel gives a convincing account of the poor reception of this opera—no doubt based on the composer's own account:

> Indeed, it seems as if unfavorable events brought about the misfortune of this work—quite apart from the fact that the verse is very weak. The first set depicted an amphitheater in the country, where the people were to gather to watch the young shepherds wrestle. After the dress rehearsal, at which everything went off well, the set designer decided—without consulting librettist or composer—to fill the seats in the painted amphitheater with painted spectators peering out between the shrubbery that decorated the entire stage; together with the extras who portrayed the

people, this would have conveyed an appropriate illusion in any other situation. However, after the wrestling was over and the protagonist had been crowned, everyone went off-stage except for the mayor of the community, who remained behind with his two daughters to confide a secret to them, and who begins with these words: "Or che siam soli, o figlie" ("Now that we're alone, oh my daughters"). The audience, which saw those painted figures looking out among the bushes, not only began to laugh but laughed all the more when they noticed the singers looking around the stage, unable to guess or understand the cause of the interruption. It is rare that there is only a single mishap; thus, in the second act, *Daliso*, the lover of *Delmita*, appears dressed in armor with his visor closed, ready to fight the monster to whom *Delmita* has to be sacrificed according to the laws of the land; she flees out of fear of him, and he begins to identify himself to her with these words: "Non fuggir, non temer, son' io Daliso" ("Do not flee, do not be afraid, I am Daliso"). At this point he was supposed to open the visor, but could not manage it, and the more he tried, without success, the louder the audience began to laugh. At the end, once the minotaur had been overcome, the illuminated city of Athens was supposed to become visible in the distance; but the signal for it was given too late, and as the public heard one of the people on stage say, "Vedete come allo splendor di mille faci e mille festeggia Atene" ("See how Athens is celebrating in the glow of tens of thousands of torches"), without being able to see it, laughter broke out for the third time and reached its peak when the illuminated city became visible just as the curtain descended. Thus everything worked together to turn this opera seria into an opera buffa. *Salieri* finally joined in the laughter himself, for he had never expected much of a work he had set to music only after repeated and ardent requests, and that was performed by singers from the opera buffa.[8]

That same year Salieri also produced a major oratorio, *La passione di Gesù Cristo*, for one of the two annual concerts of the *Musikalische Societät der freyen Tonkunst der Witwen und Waisen*. This institution, a sort of pension or beneficent society for widows and orphans of musicians, had been started by Gassmann five years earlier. Salieri was an onlooker when the original organizational discussions and meetings were held in Gassmann's apartment, though he did not become a formal member until somewhat later, after earning his spurs as a composer. It was the first public concert association in Vienna and remained its only musical institution for many decades, one that was specifically dedicated to the oratorio. The concerts took place during Lent and Advent, and were performed exclusively by professional musicians. Mozart wrote of it:

> ... everyone connected with music donates his services—the orchestra consists of 180 musicians—no virtuoso who loves his neighbor declines

to play when asked by the Society—for by doing so one earns the favor of the emperor as well as of the public (March 24, 1781).[9]

Indeed, the emperor was a major benefactor of this society, as it saved him much expense in aid for the impoverished families of deceased musicians. There was a one-time payment of the considerable sum of 150 gulden, and annual membership dues of 12 gulden. The concerts, which took place in the Burgtheater, served as fund-raising events.

The actual administration of the society was always in the hands of the Hofkapellmeister, who also conducted the concerts. As it was Salieri's task to assist the aging and sickly Bonno, he must have conducted his own oratorio. Its text already existed, Metastasio having written it for Antonio Caldara in 1730, and it had been set to music more than ten times. The solo roles are those of St. Peter, St. John, and Mary Magdalen, with Joseph of Arimathea joining them in the second part; the choir consists of the disciples of Jesus. The oratorio has no plot, consisting entirely of shared memories and observations on the crucifixion, during which St. Peter keeps denouncing himself for having thrice betrayed Jesus. The choir sings once at the beginning, and then ends each part with a fugue. Salieri creates a highly spiritual impact by forgoing large dramatic effects in favor of concentrating on the feelings of the four confidants of Jesus. Metastasio commented that of all the musical versions (and this included renderings by such important composers as Graun, Jommelli, Holzbauer, Naumann, and Mysliveček), Salieri's was the most expressive. This was a great compliment coming from Metastasio, who was himself enough of a musician to make such comparisons.

Salieri appears not to have been very productive between the summers of 1776 and 1777, but then no new works were being written for the music theater during this period, because of the changed circumstances at the Vienna Opera. What seems surprising is that Salieri wrote no instrumental music either. As he had the patronage of Joseph II, it stands to reason that he was committed to Vienna and was loath to give up that security. Yet the future prospects of the Viennese theater were more uncertain than ever. It is unlikely that a twenty-seven-year-old composer, who was beginning to be known outside of Vienna, would simply wait and see what the future held for him without producing anything. Salieri was much too conscientious and responsible, and, in addition, he had to take care of a family that meant a great deal to him. His first daughter, Josepha Maria Anna, was born January 1777; seven other children followed. No doubt Salieri already had students, but that does not explain what may have seemed like creative inertia. Mosel notes tersely: "There was no new work by our master in 1777. . . ."[10]

Admittedly, it was impossible to produce any opera in Vienna at that time. In the spring of 1776, Joseph II put an end to the operation of the slowly declining and even already ruined theater; he gave notice to the *opera buffa*, the orchestra, and the ballet, and inaugurated a new era. Actors of the legitimate stage were paid by the court from then on, and performed at the Burgtheater, which had been renamed Deutsches Nationaltheater. At the same time, a general policy of "free use of the theater" was declared; visiting theater companies had free access to the "Theater next to the Burg" when no performances were scheduled. The Kärntnertortheater was made available for lease by visiting companies. In fact, theater managers kept trying to stage productions and make use of singers from the previous ensembles who had remained in Vienna; but they generally gave up after a few months, making way for other courageous individuals.

It was under such circumstances that the performance of Salieri's most recent work, *Delmita e Daliso*, had taken place, using singers from the former Italian Opera. The sloppiness that led to the disastrous performance was of course connected to the lack of direction and to irresponsible improvisation. It is hardly surprising that mediocre performances led to continuing apathy on the part of the public. On the other hand, the legitimate stage of the Nationaltheater was not only clearly supported and favored by Joseph II, it also became increasingly popular with the public, so that the differences between these competing ensembles became quite blatant.

At the same time, the emperor was beginning to consider establishing a national music theater. In contrast to Sweden, where Gustav III had created grand opera based on national and historic subjects, Vienna attempted to produce a type of "Nationalsingspiel" that had its origins in many earlier types of Northern and Central German *Singspiel*: one need think only of the works of such composers as Johann André, Georg Anton Benda, Johann Adam Hiller, Ignaz Holzbauer, Christian Gottlob Neefe, and Anton Schweitzer.

In order to do this, a site had to be made available in which *Singspiele* would be performed in the German language. But this did not mean that performances would be limited to works originally written in German. Translations of French *opéra comique* (and in rare instances of Italian *opera buffa*) were probably included in the plan from the start. After all, the intention was to encourage composers to become interested in the new form, and to flock to Vienna once the attraction of a German *Singspiel* in the Nationaltheater next to the Royal Burg had been established. A sufficiently strong orchestra, a choir, and solo singers had been assembled, and the emperor had been generous; yet this ensemble cost far less than the Italian Opera, in which the soloists probably earned twice as much as the average. Only new compositions were lacking.

And that remained the main problem until the halfhearted experiment ended five years later. No effort was made to promote the North German *Singspiel*. Works by composers of this genre were not even performed in Vienna so as to make them known and generate some discussion, and no new works were commissioned. Those composers who lived in Vienna merely waited to see which, if any, of their compositions would be chosen; here, too, there was no sign of active or commendable planning. The only composer to make a steady contribution to the *Singspiel* with five new pieces was its musical director, Ignaz Umlauff; the rest of the material consisted of whatever happened to come to hand. The program was filled with translated works, as many as ten opéras comiques by Ernest Modeste Grétry being performed. In this five-year period, only one important work was written in the new form, Mozart's *Entführung aus dem Serail*, and this occurred at a point when the entire enterprise was past salvaging.

Salieri was not involved with this new category of theater

for the time being. He was still assistant Kapellmeister of
the Italian Opera, but that was now discontinued. However,
his old friend and mentor Gluck had recommended him
for a new project being undertaken in Milan. Under the circumstances, he did what seemed the most obvious thing: he took
a leave of absence and went to Italy.

CHAPTER THREE

Italian Journeys and
an Epilogue 1778–1781

Before Salieri made his first journey to Italy in April 1778, only two of his operas had been performed there. His successes abroad had been confined to the north and northwest, as far afield as St. Petersburg and Copenhagen. And yet he had not lacked support in the south. At the beginning of 1772 Joseph II had written to his brother Leopold, grand duke of Tuscany:

> Gassmann's student, Salieri, the young man whom you know and whose music is so well-received, would like to find a theater in Italy for which he could write an opera buffa or seria to become better known there. Would there be an opportunity in the spring for him to write something for Florence? I think he would be found satisfactory. If you consider that a good idea, let him know directly, as I don't wish to be involved in this arrangement.[1]

The emperor even sent a score for consideration. In this way *La locandiera* was given at least one performance in Florence in 1775. Salieri was evidently considered a Viennese rather than a typical representative of the Italian opera—an opinion that was not entirely inaccurate.

Then Salieri received a commission that conferred a great honor on him, even if he was merely the second choice for it. The Teatro Regio Ducale in Milan burned down in February

1776, and was rebuilt shortly thereafter in a very imposing style through the committed and combined efforts of the Milanese nobility and the ducal Habsburg government. Gluck had been requested early on to supply a new work for the reopening. Gluck had especially close ties with Milan, where he had spent the initial and decisive years of his opera-composing activity and from where he had taken off on his meteoric career. Now, more than thirty years later, the Milanese wanted him back, to emphasize that Milan's new house definitely belonged with the best of the Italian opera houses.

Gluck received this commission for an *opera seria* at the beginning of July 1777, while he was in Paris preparing *Armide* for its premiere. Obviously this was a most unpropitious moment, the literary controversy over traditional Italian opera and Gluck's reform opera having come to a head. While the former gave priority to vocally melodious music, with simple harmonies and instrumentation, the latter depended on convincing dramatic expression. Gluck worked in a very concentrated and thorough manner, calculating that he needed at least a year for a new opera. And as far as possible, he had been planning his work on a long-term basis that made him refuse all disruptive short-term engagements. (He had not yet begun to work on *Iphigénie en Tauride*, though plans for it had existed for years.) For these reasons, and the fact that he was now in his late sixties, he rejected the Milanese commission, but recommended that Salieri be entrusted with it. It was a judicious suggestion; for though Salieri was not his student, Gluck had followed his work and given him friendly advice from the very first. Presumably he considered Salieri to be the most likely among the younger composers to inherit his mantle and carry on his work.

The amazing thing was that Milan followed the advice, although there was no hurry. A whole year lay ahead until the ceremonial opening of the new house, so that the choice of Salieri was not a makeshift solution. If Milan had not wanted to accept Gluck's recommendation, there would have been time to look for someone else.

Abbate Mattia Verazi, private secretary and court poet to

the elector of the Bavarian Palatinate, was selected to write the text. He was an experienced librettist who had written five opera texts for Niccolò Jommelli, and had also worked for Ignaz Holzbauer, Johann Christian Bach, and Johann Rudolf Zumsteeg. Now he wrote *L'Europa riconosciuta*, a *"dramma per musica"* in two acts, for Milan. In keeping with the festive occasion, it was followed by a ballet, the scenario of which Verazi wrote with Legrand, the ballet master. Salieri arrived in Milan in the middle of April; the premiere was to take place on August 3. This was the customary length of time for writing and rehearsing a new opera. No doubt Salieri came prepared, for there had been nothing pressing for him to do in Vienna.

The text deviates considerably from the well-known myth of the abduction of Europa by Zeus transformed into a bull, and her later fate in Crete. The abduction is treated as a completely demythologized and secularized prefatory action. Neither Zeus nor any other god is involved, and only a few of the names are taken from the ancient myth.

In this version Asterio, king of Crete, has heard so much about the beauty of Europa that he has abducted and hidden her. Her father Agenor, king of Tyre, orders his sons to look for her, to avenge the shame and bring Europa back. But the sons cannot find her and are afraid to return, fearing punishment by their father. Believing them to be dead, the father settles the succession to his throne: his niece Semele is to marry whichever noble warrior keeps his oath of vengeance and kills the first foreigner to approach Tyre. He will then reign with Semele. Agenor now dies. The news of his death reaches Crete, whereupon Asterio and Europa (who has become his wife meantime) leave for Greece in order to claim the throne. So much for the preamble; at this point in the story the overture begins, depicting a raging storm that destroys the Cretan escort vessels. Europa, Asterio, and their child manage to reach a deserted beach near Tyre. All of them fall into the hands of Egisto, who expects to receive the promised prize by capturing them. But Isseo, who had been Europa's fiancé and is now Semele's lover, wants to ascend the throne with Semele. He defeats Egisto and his followers in battle, and allows himself to be acclaimed by the entire kingdom. Asterio and Europa now appear, and everyone recognizes them. Isseo and Semele bow submissively to Asterio and Europa; the latter are so touched by this sign of fidelity that Asterio sets the crown on Isseo's head and inaugurates him as ruler of Tyre. Asterio and Europa then return to Crete.

Clearly, it was not a very convincing text. An implausible dramatic complication was added in which Egisto, who comes from a more distant region under Phoenician rule, is the only one not to recognize Europa. Despite the weak text, Salieri managed to make effective use of the opening. His overture featured a "tempesta di mare" with thunder and lightning that could not help conveying an exciting atmosphere, very different from the one at the opening of *Armida*. Forceful movements by the strings finally calm down on a pedal-point and are resolved in *calando* half- and whole-note values.

Choral scenes occur in both acts, not merely in the finale, and there are altogether five recitatives accompanied by the orchestra. But seen as a whole, the opera did not succeed in ridding itself of contemporary clichés. On the contrary, Salieri obligingly fulfilled all the conceivable wishes of a public for whom representation was more important than theatrical credibility. The occasion of the opera surely had much to do with it. Moreover, the weak dramaturgical concept suffered from an additional handicap: not only were the two leading female roles written for coloratura sopranos—who had to be given sufficient coloratura parts to sing—but the two main male characters, Asterio and Isseo, were sung by castratos, which meant there were no contrasts. All in all, this opera typifies precisely the sort of work that had inspired Gluck's reform; it was ironic that Salieri was its composer. Even Mosel wrote about it in unusually critical terms:

> Any non-partisan critic who looks at this opera will have to admit that apart from an expressive aria by *Asterio* in the Second Act (written for a soprano), this opera does not contain anything outstanding, and—strangely enough!—as far as the form of the songs is concerned, it has to be described as being more antiquated than many of *Salieri's* earlier compositions.[2]

However, the opening of the new Milanese opera house, known as the Teatro alla Scala on account of its location, was quite overwhelming; and the new building was of such beauty, functionality and scale that its splendor outshone everything taking place on stage. Besides, the management had spared no extravagance for the event: the orchestra consisted of seventy players and a harpsichordist, forty choral singers and one hundred extras took part, and even the ballet in the epilogue comprised fifty dancers. Mosel writes of this performance: "The music received much applause, and the work continued to be performed for a long time, despite the harsh criticism of the text."[3] But this can only have referred to the Milan house (no information exists on how many performances took place there), because as far as is known, this work was never produced a second time.

Salieri's next stop in Italy was Venice, where he had a commission for an *opera buffa* to be performed in the Teatro di San Moisè at the end of the year. The opera (*La scuola de' gelosi*) became the most frequently performed of his works, along with *Axur*; it was presented more than sixty times over the next thirty years, in cities ranging from Lisbon to Moscow, and from Naples to Riga. And it is strange to observe time and again how in Salieri's life enormous successes, suggesting a celebrated, fashionable artist, always follow closely upon works that could be described as mere mayflies. Paradoxically, the opulence of the just-completed Milan production contrasted strongly with the economy and simplicity of the intimate Venetian opera.

The librettist on the latter occasion was Lorenzo Da Ponte's close friend Caterino Mazzolà; he was a dramatist in Dresden from 1780 to 1796, and in 1791 he wrote the libretto for Mozart's *La clemenza di Tito*. His creation for Venice was a cheerful piece on the subject of jealousy, avoiding the boisterous and exaggerated humor as well as the complicated and grotesque confusions of many an *opera buffa*. Instead, his intentionally simple scenes from bourgeois life depend for their effect entirely on the sublety of the dialogue.

Blasio, a rich corn merchant, is so morbidly jealous of his

wife Ernestina that he locks her up, and would like nothing better than to keep her in chains during his absences. In contrast, there is a count who is constantly unfaithful to his wife. Both women suffer on account of their men: the countess, because she loves her husband; Ernestina, because her love for her husband has long been stifled by his unworthy treatment of her. The count would like nothing better than to introduce men to the countess, so as to free himself of her reproaches. The immediate object of his attentions is Ernestina, whose husband hardly knows how to keep the count, with whom he shares business interests, away from his house without offending against social customs. The count makes good use of his discomfiture, and the jealous husband frets inwardly as the time for his journey draws nearer. . . . His cousin, who is a lieutenant and a man of spirit, later counsels him to rekindle his wife's love by making her jealous, rather than locking her up, which only makes him appear ludicrous. Blasio, who really does suffer from his jealousy, decides to leave a portrait of a stranger where his wife will find it. As the lieutenant is a friend as well of the count and his wife, he also advises the countess to change her attitude, whereupon she encourages the count in his adventures instead of being jealous. And that of course makes the count suspicious. . . . The opera ends in the country, where everyone spies on everyone else, but where the two couples are finally reunited.

This is not a complete synopsis of the plot but an outline of the central events. The work is more of a character study than a comedy of stereotypes. It deals with ever-changing views of jealousy, whether expressed or concealed, that are depicted as a form of love sickness; yet there is not a single seduction scene—nor even a hint of one—in the entire play. Bourgeois and noble are brought face to face without any recognition of class differences; at most, some conventional forms of social intercourse are observed, but there is no sense of either superiority or inferiority anywhere. The lieutenant, who appears as an incidental figure rather than a mediator, contributes to the social leveling as well.

Salieri's music for *La scuola de' gelosi* is very light and well adapted to the fast-paced, lively text. He has not shied away from using lengthy recitatives that are sung at a normal speaking tempo, his intention being to simulate speech and render every word understandable. The music of the arias and ensembles is characteristically, yet economically, orchestrated; there is nothing radically new; in fact, the sound is quite conventional, though rich in its shading. The frequent tempo changes in the finale correspond closely to the dramatic situation.

Oddly enough, the opera is set in Milan, from where Salieri had just come. We do not know what sort of allusion the two authors were trying to convey to the Venetians. As was then customary, a grand ballet was performed at the end of the opera, which would be impossible to duplicate nowadays. Compared with the sumptuous Milan production, the ballet was rather on a small-scale, though it consisted of eighteen dancers. Its music was undoubtedly also written by Salieri.

Salieri did not stay in Venice longer than he had to, returning to Vienna as early as January 1779. His family— now augmented by another daughter, Francisca Xaveria Antonia—was waiting to see him. No basic changes had occurred meanwhile at the Burgtheater. The national *Singspiel* was still in existence, and the works of Ignaz Umlauff enjoyed particular success. But there was a dearth of other suitable composers, so that French works had to be used again; three compositions by Grétry were put on that season. As an insider, Salieri would have been well aware of these problems and their effects. Joseph II must also have soon noticed that few appropriate German-language *Singspiele* were available. But he was willing to continue financially supporting his theatrical experiment somewhat longer. What he could not, or would not, do was to decide to commission the best local or foreign composers and assemble the right librettists and musicians. This would have required financing of a different sort; and as co-regent of the Habsburg patrimonial lands with his mother, Maria Theresa, the emperor lacked access to such funds on his own. Moreover, it would also have involved long-term contractual arrangements that the court always tended to avoid. So again there was nothing for Salieri to do in Vienna except bide his time; meanwhile he participated in the chamber music gatherings held regularly by his imperial patron.

Everything was just as it had been the previous year, not only waiting for local commissions, but also the new Italian contracts. There were similar opportunities in the same cities. Another opera house was under construction in Milan, and Salieri was again asked to write an inaugural opera; Venice, too, offered another engagement. And once more the emperor gave his protégé the necessary leave.

But history never repeats itself, even if the basic conditions are the same. This time a *commedia per musica* was planned for Milan, with a text by Carlo Goldoni, who had been living in Paris since 1762. He sent the synopsis of his piece along with the first act, and Salieri immediately began to work on it. However, this time he first stopped off in Venice, where a new production of *La fiera di Venezia* was given under his direction at the Pergola theater. From there he went on to Milan.

Everything, however, was delayed in Milan: construction of the theater was behind schedule, and Goldoni, who had once again suffered a heart attack, could not send the other sections of the libretto in time. The delays brought new problems; on the one hand, the singers had been engaged only until the end of the season and it was impossible to extend their contracts; on the other hand, three productions were planned for the inauguration of the opera house. These were Salieri's *fiera di Venezia*, with its masques and balls, a veritable spectacle with magnificently colorful costumes, and new operas by Salieri and Giacomo Rust, respectively.

This commission was especially important to Rust, for he had just recently arrived from Salzburg and had not yet received any satisfying work. He had been Kapellmeister in Salzburg (and hence Leopold Mozart's superior), but he could not tolerate the weather there and had had to give notice for reasons of health. He also had a mountain of debts. In view of the deadline, the management of the new house decided to open with *La fiera di Venezia*, to follow it with the Salieri-

Goldoni opera *Il talismano*, and to do without an opera by Rust.

As Mosel writes:

> [The management] gave Kapellmeister *Russ* [sic] a gift, along with a written invitation for the coming year. But as the poor, honest maestro was most disappointed that he was not to produce a composition for this festive occasion, whereas an opera by *Salieri* had already been given, the latter suggested to the management that *Russ* be permitted to set the second act of the Talismano to music. This suggestion was approved and carried out, and had the utmost success.[4]

Though Salieri was glad when circumstances worked to his advantage, he was not the sort of self-promoting person who always insists that only his own works be performed. And this unselfish readiness to compromise was by no means due to Goldoni's work, which he might not have found particularly inspiring. On the contrary; he returned to this material almost ten years later and finished the entire work himself. It deals with a governor's daughter, who is adopted by gypsies as a child and who receives a talisman from an old gypsy that has magic properties and can transform its wearer. The plot centers around complicated love intrigues and, as in the old farces based on mistaken identities, excitement is created through disguises and deceptions. At the end, the governor is reunited with his missing daughter.

The ceremonial opening of the new Teatro della Canobbiana also included two elaborate ballets, which were performed by more than thirty dancers.

Immediately thereafter, Salieri proceeded to Venice, where he was to set Mazzolà's libretto *L'isola capricciosa* to music, but this undertaking failed, as the Venetian impresario suddenly died. Though a section of the opera had already been composed, it could not be used later, nor did it find a new sponsor; it was filed away, and is still missing today. However, Salieri did not lack work in this period. There were commissions from Rome, and he established contact with Naples. Verazi, the librettist of *L'Europa riconosciuta*, wrote from Mannheim asking why he had not heard from Salieri in so long; he too was apparently interested in further collaboration.

In the autumn of 1779, Salieri quickly composed a two-act comic intermezzo, *La partenza inaspettata*, for Rome. It is a rather foolish piece about a scholar who experiences censorship problems and his sister, Rosina Spazzina. She has a coarse fiancé, but is also interested in a naive merchant who has come down in the world. The crafty Rosina rescues the merchant from his creditors, and eventually even marries him. This simple farce was followed by another intermezzo, *La dama pastorella*, based on a libretto by Giuseppe Petrosellini. The story is similar to *Il talismano* except that the heroine, Eurilla, abandoned in a box as an infant and raised by farmers in the country, is really the daughter of a count. This time, however, the romantic relationships are somewhat more comprehensible. Salieri reports that this little opera "neither pleased nor displeased."[5]

All of the shorter comic operas that Salieri wrote in Italy are musically sound but innocuous. He composed them without any fuss, adjusting himself to time limits and what the occasion required. He adapted his music to suit the desires and capacities of singers, accepting the texts he was given without making changes. He was as surprised by his successes as by his failures, which were only to be expected, given these minimal circumstances.

After the production of *La partenza inaspettata*, but before leaving Rome, Salieri requested an additional three months' leave from Vienna. It was a mere formality, but as Joseph II could be rather fussy about such matters, a necessary one. Naturally Salieri explained the reasons for his request in great detail. A performance of his *Scuola de' gelosi* was to be given in Naples, and he had also been invited to write the music for Pietro Metastasio's *Semiramide*. As the commission came from the royal theater in Naples—that is, from the emperor's brother-in-law, Ferdinand I—there was little doubt that the leave would be extended. However, the matter was transmitted only verbally to the emperor; he was not shown Salieri's letter.

Perhaps the court officials added what they considered appropriate comments to the request; at any rate, His Majesty reacted somewhat gruffly, and Count Rosenberg-Orsini was directed to issue the following answer:

With regard to your request to His Majesty for permission to extend your stay in Italy, His Royal Highness has asked me to inform you that you are at liberty to remain there for as long as you like and as seems reasonable to you, indeed, that you may even remain there permanently if that is your preference. I regret that I am unable to convey more pleasant news and remain yours, etc.[6]

That was plainspoken, in the unmistakable style then current in Vienna. Maria Theresa always suspected that she was being taken advantage of by court parasites, by people who ingratiated themselves and then could not be dismissed, who had some useless position and lived off the court without doing anything. And Joseph II was even more mistrustful. Later on, when he became the sovereign, he actually had a section of the imperial castle sealed off with boards to save having to pay the guards. He had a horror of commitments that might cost money but bring nothing in return. Yet personally he could be very generous, and Salieri did belong to his most intimate circle, where such cold, formal responses were not at all customary. To make matters worse, this expression of royal displeasure first made its way to Rome; from there it had to be forwarded to Naples, creating further delay. It gave Salieri a terrible shock.

He did what he considered unavoidable, as embarrassing as it was for him: he asked the theater in Naples to release him from his contract. He then traveled straight back to Vienna, where, immediately upon arrival, he made his way directly "to the court." According to Mosel's authentic and vivid account:

... he did not go to the emperor's chamber as was his right but, as though to demonstrate his submission, waited in the corridor (the so-called inspection corridor), where the monarch attended to oral and written petitions every day at 3 P.M. ...

The emperor returned from an outing at three o'clock; as usual, he walked through that corridor, dealing with petitions in the manner and tone of an affectionate father, when he suddenly noticed Salieri and immediately approached him with the words: "Look who's here, *Salieri!* Welcome! I did not expect you so soon; did you have a good journey?" "A very good one, Your Majesty," Salieri answered timidly, "though to make amends for my mistake, for which I most humbly ask your pardon, I thought I should travel day and night the sooner to fulfill my duties at court again." "It was not necessary," the monarch replied graciously, "to exaggerate the matter that much, but I am happy to see you again. Go upstairs meantime, we shall play a few sections of your new opera that they sent me from Italy."[7]

There was no more talk of the emperor's displeasure, and the excursion to Naples was forgotten. Instead, Salieri had to face the unchanging reality of conditions in Vienna yet again.

To begin with, Joseph II sent Salieri to the national *Singspiel* to report whether any progress had been made in his absence. Salieri went there and was very impressed. Small wonder, for he saw the vaudeville *La Rosière de Salency*, a successful French piece by Charles Simon Favart; and it was in that production that he first heard Aloysia Weber, who later became Mozart's sister-in-law. It was her debut in Vienna, and she sang the title role. "A marvellous singer, who produces a tone and expression that go right to one's heart; who has an extraordinary range, and who executes the most difficult passages correctly and blends them into her singing, the way it should be done," as a contemporary notes.[8]

But the emperor had long been harboring a plan, and Salieri unwittingly gave him the necessary signal when he praised the national *Singspiel*. Mosel reports the following conversation:

> "Now you should compose a German opera," said the emperor. Salieri suggested having one of the five operas he had written in Italy translated into German. "Not a translation," the monarch countered, smiling, "an original Singspiel!" "Your Majesty," Salieri answered, "I would not know how to begin composing an opera in the German language; I speak it so badly . . ." "Well then," the emperor interrupted him, still smiling, "this work will help you to practice the language. First thing tomorrow I shall instruct Count *Rosenberg* to have a German opera libretto written expressly for you."[9]

Salieri's predicament must have been great, as the German language was a handicap for him. Of course he had learned German—Gassmann having hired a special language teacher for him—but he was not really sure of his competence in it. At the opera he dealt exclusively with performers who spoke Italian, which, after all, was the common language of musicians. For everyday purposes, even with his students, his imperfect German did not present a problem, but it was quite a different matter to have to write an opera in this foreign tongue. Had he not learned from Metastasio that proper declamation was the basis for all forms of song? How was he to create suitable musical melodies if he had not mastered the speech melodies; how was he to portray speech musically, find the appropriate rhythmic values, and differentiate between the principal and secondary stresses? Yet he could not possibly turn down the commission; were he to do that, he might as well request his dismissal at the same time.

The emperor wanted original German *Singspiele*; that was why an ensemble had been engaged and paid for by the court. In view of his ideas on managing the theater economically, Joseph II was quite justified in asking himself why employ a composer if he did not create what the theater needed. Actually, the emperor may well have suspected that Salieri was not the right person to compose a major exemplary work for the national *Singspiel*, but there were gaps in the program and daily demands that needed to be met. Why should Salieri not be able to do that? Salieri was quite aware that he served as a fill-in, and he did not find it easy to be saddled with lowered expectations from the start. Not to mention the difficulty of finding a suitable libretto—that, after all, being the crux of the *Singspiel*.

Nothing is known about how the text for Salieri's "musical comedy" *Der Rauchfangkehrer* came to be chosen. Did Salieri himself participate in the choice, or was it the management that—to put it bluntly—threw him this bone? At any rate, the libretto was not especially felicitous. It was ostensibly by Leopold Auenbrugger, a well-known Viennese doctor, whose two daughters, Francisca and Marianne, were highly esteemed for their pianoforte playing. Auenbrugger did not claim to have written the text, and Mosel denies that Salieri was aware of this fact, but Salieri must have known, as he was on friendly terms with the Auenbrugger family. The librettist had been one of Salieri's marriage witnesses, and Marianne Auenbrugger was his student. Perhaps Mosel merely wanted to protect Salieri, because he referred to the text as "unworthy of criticism in terms of the language and construction of the verse." In contrast, the actual plot seemed to him thoroughly acceptable: "If the verse in this Singspiel were improved, or actually rewritten on the basis of the subject and the music, this composition could yet find approval in our time."[10] But in truth, not only the language but the entire plot was inadequate, so there was not much left to rescue.

It is the story of Volpino, an Italian chimney sweep, who speaks only mangled German and is betrothed to Lisel, the cook. He rather brazenly intends to make some money by presenting himself to Lisel's employers as a persecuted Corsican marquis who is about to win a lawsuit involving large sums of money. He explains his plan to Lisel: "Music I'll use, and lies, to make her ladyship and the young miss love me; then each will want me as husband; so the two gentlemen will be in a pickle; then I'll make it clear: a good dowry they must give us so they can be happy in their love. Because they'll be angry, their ignorant servant will become very rich" (Act 1, scene 3).

The first act describes the circumstances of the young widow, Frau von Habicht and her stepdaughter, as well as those of their two lovers. While that is going on, Volpino directs an opera, *Die Entführung des Ganymed*, that is full of classical allusions:

> The story is familiar, anyway: when Ganymede was chasing Ida on the mountain, Jupiter had his eagle bring him to heaven and made him his cupbearer. In this dull version the poet has Ganymede and his followers come upon two shepherd huts, in which live two nymphs called Chloe and Daphne. The tame doe being raised by them for their sustenance is chased by Ganymede's retinue. Apprehensive and frightened, Chloe and Daphne intercept the chase. Ganymede, who is moved by their grace, falls in love with both of them. As each expects to be the one chosen by the love-sick Ganymede, who divides his caresses between them, Jupiter's eagle kidnaps him. (Act 1.)

This opera within an opera ends prematurely, when Lisel enters suddenly, surprises Volpino in the role of Ganymede with the two nymphs, and makes a loud jealous scene. The second and third acts deal hurriedly with Volpino's planned fraud, for which he poses as the two ladies' teacher of Italian and singing. It is all a contrived confusion that ends in a deliberately set chimney fire, the revelation of Volpino as a chimney sweep, and the reunion of the various couples.

The text clearly reveals the level of the Viennese national *Singspiel*, especially if one considers the disparity between this libretto and that of Mozart's *Entführung aus dem Serail*. Realizing their importance to good opera, Mozart was especially critical of his librettos. In this connection, he writes to his father on May 7, 1783:

> I have read through at least one hundred—probably even more texts—I hardly found any that would satisfy me; at any rate a great deal would have to be changed here and there, and if a poet were actually willing to do that, it might perhaps be easier for him to write something entirely new. And a new version is, after all, generally better.[11]

The humorous subtext of the libretto of *Der Rauchfangkehrer* contains reflections on the relationship between German and Italian opera, providing a critical commentary on the situation at the Nationaltheater. That would suggest that Salieri advised Auenbrugger on the text, in which case Salieri was informing Joseph II, in an elegantly indirect way, that he did not consider himself a suitable composer for the German *Singspiel*. Volpino at times behaves like a parody of Salieri with his linguistic problems, especially when he appears as the music teacher and sings two arias in Italian (Nos. 6 and 12), the former certainly being parodic coloratura. (He claims to be a student of Farinelli, one of the most famous castrati of his day.)

The characters of Frau von Habicht and her stepdaughter, "the young miss who's reached her majority," provide an even more direct reference to the *Singspiel*, for Frau von Habicht had only been "a German opera singer." "It is said I make mistakes in the Italian arias." Whereupon the "young miss" quickly replies, "That's my problem too. So I've decided to engage Volpino as my singing and language teacher as well." The role of the "young miss" was sung by Catarina Cavalieri, who studied voice with Salieri and had only just made her debut; she was to become the most celebrated singer at the Burgtheater over the next fifteen years.

The following scene between the two women and their gentlemen friends can only be understood in terms of the

situation in Vienna. The aria of Herr von Bär was sung by
Ludwig Fischer, the bass who later became the first to perform
the role of Osmin. He was considered one of the best basses,
"who sings the lowest notes with a fullness, ease, and appeal
normally found only in good tenors."[12]

Frau v. Habicht: Do you know what, Herr von Wolf! I've already
practiced and listened to singing today.
  The Young Miss: My delightful Bär! — I've also been singing.
  Herr v. Bär: The printed songs, I suppose. How do you like them?
  The Young Miss: They're full of feeling and beauty, only it's too bad
that they're in German.
  Herr v. Wolf: Perhaps they would please you more in French?
  Frau v. Habicht: That language is just as inept for singing as German.
Italian! Italian, that's what they should be in, the language that makes
music lively and can be understood when sung.
  Herr v. Wolf: Forgive me! That's not the fault of the language but of
the pronunciation, something that most of the performers of the German
Singspiel neglect to the point of giving offence. Only here (pointing to
both ladies) is there an exception.
  Herr v. Bär: That's right! The pronunciation and singing skills of
both their ladyships are better than those of any Italian singer . . .
  Aria by *Herr v. Bär*:
    T'would be amazing, upon my soul,
    No singer can sing every role.
      Each has his goal.
      One receives praise
      for his bravura lays,
      in song that swells
      he much excels;
      another climbs
      to falsetto sublime.
      And how this one hones
      his deepest tones.
      Where's the crescendo?
      How sounds the calando?
      Or the melting note that ties
      and the yearning one that dies?
      What of the gruppettos,
      tenutos, falsettos?
      The liscio staccato?
      The tempo rubbato?
      Where's syncopation
        and ornamentation?
      Where's portamento;
      the trill at the end-o?
    T'would be amazing, upon my soul,
    No singer can sing every role,
      Each has his goal.

The singing lessons Volpino gives to the two ladies are presented one after the other, during which one has to imagine improvised comic scenes:

> (He starts playing the pianoforte, Frau von Habicht sings the Italian text incorrectly, and Volpino teaches her the proper pronunciation.)
> Aria by *Frau von Habicht*:
>   Se più felice ogetto . . .

In the next scene the directions given are:

> (Volpino sits down at the pianoforte with the Young Miss beside him; he plays and corrects her mispronunciation and her singing.)
> Aria by the *Young Miss*:
>   Basta, vincesti, eccoti il foglio . . .

As the texts of both arias are taken from dramas by Metastasio,[13] one can conclude that these lessons resemble Salieri's training in declamation with the famous master. Both arias are virtuoso bravura numbers with difficult coloratura passages, and in this context they represent a parodic quotation of the traditions of *opera seria*. It must have seemed especially amusing to the audience that it was a former "German opera singer," of all people, who condemned the use of German in operatic texts but praised that of Italian, and that she herself could sing only in faulty Italian, and thus involuntarily parody the Italian *aria seria*.

The music suggests that Salieri was inspired by an altogether very silly and linguistically clumsy text to create a deliberate contrast of various styles. Yet everything is geared to the special capacities of each voice in this staging—Volpino once even has to sing in falsetto—and is attractively orchestrated and harmonized. It is evident that Salieri deployed all his skill, despite the bad libretto, and enjoyed considerable success with the work in Vienna. Elsewhere attempts, only moderately successful, were made to improve the text, no doubt on account of the appealing and original music.

Mozart, who had been in Vienna for almost two months, attended the third performance of this *Singspiel*. His confrontations with the archbishop of Salzburg, Count Hieronymus von Colloredo-Waldsee, had just come to a head, and he had confidently given his notice during an audience with the archbishop. He was still so full of rage, and so angry at a conversation he had had afterward with Count Karl Arco, that he hardly took in anything of the production. He wrote to his father:

> Everything edifying the Archbishop told me in the three audiences he gave me, especially in the latest one, and the most recent comment this wonderful man of God made to me, had such an excellent effect on my state of health that in the evening, in the middle of the first act of the opera, I had to go home and lie down—for I felt very hot—I was trembling all over and lurched on the street like a drunk; the following day, as well as yesterday, I stayed at home and spent the whole morning in bed because I took some tamarind water (May 12, 1781).[14]

Mozart appears to have seen the opera again sometime later. After a visit to Salzburg late in the summer of 1783, he was supposed to send the score to his father, and writes:

> I'm just writing to you in greatest haste to tell you that I bought the "Rauchfangkehrer" for 6 ducats and have it at home. . . . judging from your letter, you believe the "Rauchfangkehrer" to be an Italian opera. No, it is a German one and moreover a poorly written original piece, of which Doctor Auernbrucker [sic] of Vienna is the author. You will recall my telling you that Herr Fischer satirized it on stage (December 10, 1783).[15]

At the end of 1781 came an occasion when, for the first time, Mozart and Salieri might have been seen as rivals for the same post. This had nothing to do with personal animosities, and it was always clear that Salieri would be given preference. It concerned the position of a pianoforte teacher for Princess Elisabeth Wilhelmine of Württemberg, who—though only fourteen years old—had been chosen to become the wife of the Archduke Franz and was being raised in a Viennese convent. Franz was destined to become Holy Roman Emperor one day, as nephew of the childless Joseph II, so naturally only the best teachers were selected for Elisabeth Wilhelmine. Mozart entertained hopes of obtaining this post, which he expected to be well paid. He held no official position in Vienna yet, and was entirely dependent on students.

If Mozart was ever poor as a churchmouse, it was in this first year in Vienna. But why should he, of all people—a highly regarded pianist and composer, but still undeniably a stranger in the city—be awarded a position that required the careful consideration of the court? Emperor Joseph saw no reason to favor Mozart—not that he intended to slight him. On the contrary; he valued Mozart highly, and soon a very friendly and informal relationship developed between them. But there were others for whom Joseph II was responsible, to some extent. As Salieri could not pursue his duties as assistant Kapellmeister of the Italian Opera, since this type of opera was no longer being performed, the emperor preferred to give him other tasks that would justify his court salary. The emperor, as we have noted, was very strict about expenditures and an avowed enemy of all sinecures. And Salieri happened to have been in Vienna fifteen years longer.

Mozart wrote somewhat resignedly to his father:

> As for the Princess vom Würtenberg [sic] and myself, that's over and done with; the emperor wrecked it for me because he cares only for Salieri. The Archduke Maximilian recommended *me* to her; she answered him that if it were up to her, she would not have engaged anyone else, but the emperor had suggested Salieri, on account of the singing. She really regretted it (December 15, 1781).[16]

Salieri did have the advantage of being a most successful teacher of voice, the proof of which being Catarina Cavalieri's performances at the opera in the evenings. So Mozart had to give way in this instance; but it was not an injustice. Besides, Salieri only held the position for a short time—the time it took for Italian opera to become reestablished in Vienna in 1782.[17]

A commission from Munich now gave Salieri the chance to complete *Semiramide*, which he had begun when under contract to Naples. This came as a sort of epilogue to his Italian journeys. It is not clear whether Verazi acted as intermediary in this connection, but Salieri probably had no other contacts there. The libretto, by Metastasio, was being set to music for the fortieth time. Almost all the noted composers of the eighteenth century used this text, including Porpora, Hasse, Gluck, Gal-

uppi, Sacchini, Traetta, and Jommelli (the latter actually
worked with it twice). Even Giacomo Meyerbeer wrote music
for yet another adaptation in 1819; his version has legendary
Babylon for its setting, and calls for a lavish production.

The opera deals with three princes competing for the hand
of the Princess of Bactria (Afghanistan), who lives at the court
of Queen Semiramis. The latter, dressed in men's clothes, rules
as King Nino. A complicated intrigue develops because one of
the suitors turns out to be a prince with whom Semiramis had
once had a love affair at the Egyptian court. The two recognize
each other, but at first keep their identities secret. Even after
they have revealed themselves, the deliberately created mistrust
has to be resolved in order to bring about a happy conclusion,
at which two couples become united. The work ends with a
great tribute to Semiramis.

This was typically sumptuous *opera seria*, a celebration of
large voices, with pathos, passion, and pride, but with less in
the way of gentle and delicate feelings. There are many rich
bravura and coloratura parts; the role of Semiramis (performed
in Munich by Elisabeth Wendling, who had sung Elettra in
Mozart's *Idomeneo*) is especially full of the most difficult passages.
Two of the leading male roles are written for castrati; there
are only two smaller bass roles, in addition to those for sopranos.
That was customary in *opera seria*, and presented no problems
for the composer, there being far more arias than ensembles
in this type of opera (Salieri included one duet). The arias
abandon the strict *da capo* form in favor of somewhat freer
musical patterns and variations where the text is repeated;
there are also some short song forms. But Metastasio's *opera
seria* is changed only in its details; nothing fundamental is
altered. The deemphasizing of the *da capo* aria lent the orchestra
greater importance, but as long as the patrons continued to
support the ever-popular libretti by Metastasio, there was little
scope for fresh dramatic language in music. Entirely new
librettos would have had to be commissioned.

One can hardly accuse Salieri of having been idle since the
dismissal of the Italian ensemble in Vienna. He had made good
use of his time during these years, with trips to Italy, and had

also discharged his obligations to the national Viennese *Singspiel*. But this period was of little significance for his artistic development. Salieri had cleverly adapted himself to the prevailing taste wherever he was, and had not disappointed any of his various patrons. He had even written one of his greatest and longest-lasting successes, *La scuola de' gelosi*. But he had not continued on the daring new course he had begun in the realm of heroic grand opera with *Armida*. Only in this first work had he admitted that Gluck was his mentor; after that he had timidly reverted to the old conventions, as though on that occasion he had been too courageous. He should have realized that *Armida* was successful and admired precisely because of its new dramatic language. With his musical comedies, except for the highly popular *Scuola de' gelosi*, and possibly also *La locandiera*, in which the musical language finds forms that correspond to the tempo of the plot, he had repeatedly discovered how difficult it was to find a suitable text.

Salieri had shown himself to be a multi-talented composer, with considerable experience in the different varieties of music theater. But he still lacked a clear direction, a vision of his future musical course, and decisiveness and rigorous standards in his choice of libretti. Moreover, he needed to pursue a consistent musical-dramatic concept if he wanted to distinguish himself from the many opera composers competing for commissions and the favor of the public. And yet he could count on reliable patrons like Joseph II, as well as musical friends who believed him capable of the largest and most difficult tasks. Given such support, there were no reasonable grounds for timidity on his part.

CHAPTER FOUR

Feast and Famine, Paris and Vienna 1782–1783

Salieri had scarcely returned to Vienna from Munich, where he had attended the successful premiere of *Semiramide*, when the fuss began over the prospective visit of Pope Pius VI. The latter was alarmed by the Josephine church reforms, and intended to use his personal influence to rescue Roman Catholicism. It was a matter of specific spheres of power, for Joseph II was about to establish a type of state religion that came close to being another Reformation. The most obvious signs of a reform that planned closer ties between church and state, as well as a loosening of the ecclesiastical ties to Rome, had been the dissolution of many monasteries and the confiscation of related church treasure to benefit a welfare fund. At the same time, an engaged devoutness was demanded from the church, in place of empty pomp, sanctimoniousness, or exaggerated monasticism.

The pope's visit was a unique event, an extravaganza; his arrival drew two hundred thousand spectators. As many as thirty thousand foreigners were said to have come to Vienna to attend the outdoor mass at Easter. Everyone wanted to witness this extraordinary visit and its ceremonial pageantry. It was a public festival, although the pope had serious matters to discuss with the emperor. As it happened, these negotiations turned out to be unsuccessful, which could have been foreseen at the time; indeed, monasteries continued to be dissolved even during the visitor's presence in Vienna. However, the curious populace was more intrigued by the custom of kissing the pope's shoes; for greater convenience, the shoes were taken to aristocratic homes where they were passed around among the upper nobility.

During these exciting weeks Salieri received a visit from a Venetian in his early thirties. He had been in Dresden and brought a letter of introduction from Caterino Mazzolà, the librettist of *La scuola de' gelosi*:

> My friend Salieri
>   Da Ponte, whom I value highly, will convey these few lines from me. Do all you can for him as you would for me. His courage and his talents deserve it. Besides, he shares my way of thinking and is indeed my other half.
>
> Yours, Mazzolà.[1]

Lorenzo Da Ponte, a priest by profession, was an extremely well-educated, amiable man, and a witty conversationalist. He was without employment, income, or ties of any kind, and wanted to seek his fortune in Vienna. He wrote elegant poetry, and hoped he could work as a librettist at the opera. In coming to Salieri, he found himself in good hands, especially with Mazzolà's recommendation.

Soon after his arrival, Da Ponte also called on old Pietro Metastasio, to whom he introduced himself with a poem. Metastasio then presented him to those gathered at one of his regular large receptions, the best way of becoming quickly known. Of course, no one present could have foretold that they were witnessing a most significant moment, one that heralded a new chapter in the history of opera, following Metastasio's unchallenged reign of over half a century. Without Metastasio, Italian opera could hardly have been as dominant as it was, for Italian literature had produced no one else anywhere near his stature. However, as the librettist of Mozart's three great works, *Le nozze di Figaro*, *Don Giovanni*, and *Così fan tutte*, Da

Ponte would very shortly add three unsurpassed masterpieces to post-Metastasian Italian opera. With these works he developed a type of realistic, topical libretto for music drama that was based on the contradictions of society (and there was to be no musical successor to Mozart in this category for a long time). The encounter between the two librettists turned out to be their only one; Metastasio died some days later at the age of eighty-four.

At first Da Ponte relied completely on Salieri, who could not only provide him with access to the theater but, even more important, to Joseph II as well. The time was most propitious, as the national German *Singspiel* was beginning to show signs of weakness, creating new opportunities for Italian opera. A court theater had also to serve for official ceremonies and state visits, which prohibited any overly superficial comedies. The emperor did not like such official events, and avoided them as much as possible. But when the visit of Grand Duke Paul of Russia was scheduled for late autumn of 1781, the emperor arranged for a new production of Gluck's *Iphigénie en Tauride* to be put on in German. However, it was to be followed by his *Alceste* and *Orfeo ed Euridice* in Italian. Furthermore, in April 1782, an Italian "dramma giocoso" was once again performed at the national *Singspiel* theater, a clear sign that German opera would not last much longer. Even Mozart's *Entführung aus dem Serail*, produced on July 16, 1782, had no effect on this development, though it proved to be a sensational success and was soon repeated on several European stages.

By the end of that summer, the first approaches were made to Italy concerning new appointments of male and female singers of Italian works—no doubt at the instigation of Joseph II. Thus the end of the season terminated the experiment with the national German *Singspiel*, while announcing the reestablishment of Italian Opera. Salieri, who was reinstated as Kapellmeister of the Italian Opera, was even able to begin work in November on a new production of *La locandiera*. This was a makeshift solution, because no usable *Singspiele* existed; moreover, it was an advance notice of coming changes.

Salieri was now significantly involved in the programming,

and he adroitly put his institutional advantage to good use. But anyone who believed that Salieri would now continuously produce new works of his own in "his" house was grossly mistaken. For Salieri—surely to everyone's surprise—was shortly to follow a different course, which took him to Paris. Meanwhile he was content that the Italian Opera reopened with *La scuola de' gelosi*, his most successful production to date, which had been performed in over twenty European theaters in less than five years. It was part of the repertory in Vienna for a long time.

Of course, there were important reasons why Salieri had to depend on an older work; but if there was not to be a new opera, then at least one of his earlier ones could be performed—that was his right as musical master of the house. However, his current attention was on work that was destined to be performed elsewhere. He was in the process of completing the opera *Les Danaïdes*, a piece that he could not acknowledge publicly just yet. This secrecy was part of the long early history of the work, in which Salieri's mentor Gluck played the most prominent role.

When Gluck arrived in Paris in 1778, for the last time, to rehearse *Iphigénie en Tauride* for its premiere, he found a letter waiting for him. It was from his old comrade-in-arms (librettist of the first of the three so-called reform operas), Ranieri de' Calzabigi. Enclosed with the letter was the libretto of a new opera based on the familiar story of Hypermestra. Nothing is known of Gluck's reaction, or what he thought of this text, but it was not rejected. It is likely that Gluck gave it to either François Gand-Leblanc du Roullet or Baron Louis Théodore Tschudi during his ten-month stay in Paris, for a French version to be prepared.

Roullet, a Commander of the Order of the Knights of Malta whom Gluck had known for many years, was one of the composer's most influential supporters and friends in Paris. Tschudi was a diplomat and belletrist who had contributed to the *Encyclopédie*, and had written the text of Gluck's *Écho et Narcisse*. Gluck kept in close touch with both of them while he was in Paris. He probably could not spend much time on the new drama, as he had to concentrate all his efforts on *Iphigénie en Tauride*, which had its first triumphant performance in May 1779; immediately thereafter, for performance in September, he composed the little idyll *Écho et Narcisse*, which proved to be the biggest failure of his life.

Gluck had already experienced great controversy, even rancorous criticism of his work; now he grew so discouraged over this see-sawing of approval and rejection that he decided at once to return to Vienna. Even Queen Marie Antoinette could not change his mind; in fact, he swore never to write another opera. Doubtless he had become more sensitive; perhaps he was also no longer as ready to engage in battle, having in the summer experienced a slight stroke that had not otherwise affected him.

Nothing was heard of the Hypermestra material for a long time. Gluck's comments on his plans for operas or trips to Paris vacillated a great deal over the following years; Paris remained a loaded word: "Nothing is going to come of my going to Paris again as long as the words 'Piccinnist' and 'Gluckist' are in use, for thank God I am well now and don't want to lose my temper in Paris again," he noted on March 31, 1780. Two months later he wrote, "I will scarcely let [myself] be talked into becoming the object of criticism or praise by the French nation again, for they are as contrary as red roosters; if it were to happen it would have to be very convenient, as being lazy is now my only pleasure" (April 29, 1780). It hardly seems possible that Gluck was still thinking about Hypermestra. But on June 30 he was more conciliatory: "If the silly comments that are made about music and presentations in Paris were to go out of fashion, I might perhaps decide to go to Paris again and whistle a tune for them, only I no longer trust them; once burned, twice shy." Gluck must have received the French libretto for the Hypermestra story, no doubt already entitled *Les Danaïdes*, by January 1781 at the latest. But even at this point he still held aloof from Paris: ". . . my return to Paris will be difficult to carry out, you are right, a dignified man can't deal with the rabble any longer, but I would gladly see my friends once more" (January 3, 1781).[2]

All of these letters were addressed to Franz Kruthoffer, secretary to the Austrian ambassador in Paris, who kept Gluck abreast of theatrical events. Yet Roullet and Tschudi probably counted on using *Les Danaïdes* as an incentive for Gluck to write another opera for Paris. They must have been unaware that his state of health might prevent this. Gluck himself occasionally still dreamed of journeys as far afield as England. In June 1781, however, he suffered a second stroke that paralyzed his entire right side and made writing impossible. Meanwhile, Tschudi had begun negotiating with Amelot de Chaillou, the relevant minister; he raved about the opera *Les Danaïdes* and promised Gluck's complete recovery after a second cure in Baden.

However, Gluck had quite another plan in mind. He meant to secure a suitable, formally agreed-upon commission, ensuring his honoraria (considerable, in view of his great renown). But he intended not to write the opera himself, and entrust it to Salieri instead. He would then delay revealing the change in composers, though that came close to being a deception, until the fait accompli was accepted by the Paris Opera. It is not known when the plan was put to Salieri or when he began to compose. But he had known since 1779, when Calzabigi told him about it during his brief stay in Naples, that the libretto was in Gluck's possession. Salieri must have been very close to Gluck, whom he saw frequently in Vienna; why else would Gluck have helped Salieri obtain such an important contract— for the second time since the inaugural opera for La Scala in Milan—providing him with opportunities he would never have acquired on his own? After all, *Les Danaïdes* was a subject requiring an elaborate production—surely too much of a risk to assign to someone completely unknown in Paris until then.

Matters tended to drag on, but Gluck had a very skilled partner in Roullet, and carefully placed rumors did the rest. In August 1782 a letter of Gluck's was discussed by the Comité de l'Opéra; in it he offers to produce an opera, *Les Danaïdes*, for 20,000 livres (the honorarium for music and text), and promises to bring it to Paris himself in October 1783. But Amelot was already better informed, and he reported that

Gluck had written only the first two acts of the opera, the rest being by a different composer. Gluck thus could at best be paid 10,000 livres, for under these circumstances he, Amelot, was somewhat doubtful of its success. But Amelot suggested that if the first three or four performances did prove successful, the other 10,000 livres could then be paid; Gluck, he thought, ought not to be dissatisfied with this arrangement.

The truth was supposed to come out only bit by bit, so the participants kept inventing new pieces of information to be revealed. A further letter from Gluck was considered by the Opera committee in January 1783, this time saying that Gluck's health would most likely not permit his coming to Paris; in that case, Salieri would bring the opera, and the fee would be reduced to 12,000 livres. The committee could therefore no longer be in any doubt that Salieri was the sole composer of this opera. The next fabrication was that during the composition Gluck had worked with Salieri (perhaps Gluck had used such words himself) and had helped him on his way to an immortal career, a claim that would be borne out by this work. Evidently efforts were being made to find the right terminology. It was then said in April that the first two acts were by Gluck, while the third had been composed by Salieri under the famous composer's dictation.

Now a performance date had to be decided upon, as even Joseph II, who was quite willing to give Salieri a leave of absence, wanted a precise schedule. Since the Italian Opera had just been reestablished in Vienna, Salieri could not easily be spared. The period after Easter 1784 was agreed upon; Salieri was to be in Paris in March, but had to send the score beforehand. He seems to have been somewhat wary lest difficulties might arise at the last moment, and thus arrived in Paris at the beginning of January to sign a firm contract and to begin promptly to work on the preparations.

Naturally, the three years of confusion had not taken place without public knowledge. The anti-Gluck faction was as aware of the internal affairs of the Académie Royale de Musique as were Gluck's supporters, and it was an essential part of their strategy to discuss everything in public—not that either side adhered closely to the truth on these occasions. And the deception as to Gluck's authorship had even been confirmed —and the facts corrected—in German newspapers months before the opening. Salieri himself was no doubt interested in not letting things go too far, and he unburdened himself to Cramer, who thereupon fashioned the following announcement:

> (Excerpt of a letter from Vienna, August 18, 1783) . . . Something else from the forty-five-minute digression about *Les Danaïdes* by Salieri. He is going to produce this opera in Paris in 1784 at Eastertime. He has to put up with the fact, as conditio sine qua non, that the Paris public has been led to believe Ritter Gluck composed the first acts and that he [Salieri] only made a minor contribution to the last acts. But the whole thing is by him; Gluck merely offered some ideas for it. Salieri assured me that unless his life were threatened he would not be able to compose another such opera so soon again.[3]

All of this was surely a hard test of Salieri's probity and modesty. On the other hand, the more a work is gossiped about publicly while shrouded in mystery before it even opens, the more curiosity it arouses and the larger audiences it draws.

It might be overstating matters to say the public's expectations were feverish, but it was clear to everyone that an exceptional evening at the opera was in store. Indeed, the costs of the production—the singers, the ballet, the orchestra, sets, and costumes—as well as the demands made on the entire personnel, required that the rest of the season's program be planned around it. However, such enthusiastic attendance was anticipated that the opening night ticket sales alone were expected to cover the monthly salaries.

But there was yet another event in the offing that suddenly made French theater the most important subject in the world. Paris became the place where everything happened, the showcase of sensations. The day after the premiere of *Les Danaïdes* at the Opéra, Beaumarchais' play *La Folle journée ou le Mariage de Figaro* was to be performed publicly for the first time at the Comédie Française. This almost legendary piece had been exciting people for three years. Though banned, it had circulated among the nobility; and while King Louis XVI had rejected it, Queen Marie Antoinette supported it. It was an unprecedented attack on the aristocracy, yet was presented so wittily that no one could resist it, so that finally public performances had to be permitted. The coincidence of two such outstanding theatrical events was not pure chance. Beaumarchais, who was a most prudent advertising manager for his enterprises, might even have exerted some influence on the setting of the date at the Comédie. At any rate, it showed an understanding between Beaumarchais and Salieri that was soon to lead to a fruitful collaboration, with spectacular results.

Anyone who was of any consequence attended the first night of *Les Danaïdes*, including Marie Antoinette. She had previously had some of the scenes performed at the court in Versailles, and took a lively interest in this opera. In fact, she was one of Gluck's most important supporters in Paris; she had lent her name to the announcement of the opera and was surely aware of its background, having received Salieri several times at Versailles. Luckily, all went well; the work even became an enormous success, not least on account of the impressive representation of Hell at the end.

Yet what is it actually about? The opera deals with King Danaus and his fifty daughters, especially Hypermestra, and is based on an ancient legend that had been dramatized in a tetralogy by Aeschylus. It was one of the most frequently used themes in drama and opera in the seventeenth and eighteenth centuries. The story is as follows: King Danaus has banished his twin brother Aegyptus, who had fifty sons, out of envy and fear; this has caused a long family feud, about to be formally ended by celebrating the union of the daughters of Danaus and the sons of Aegyptus.

The opera opens with the arrival of the ships bearing the fifty brothers led by Lynceus, who is promised to Hypermestra; a ceremonial oath is taken at the altar of Juno, followed by a merry dance. The second act takes place in one of the subterranean chambers dedicated to Nemesis, where Danaus explains to his daughters that Aegyptus is dissimulating, and really wants to depose and murder him. Danaus therefore orders his daughters to stab the sons of Aegyptus to death on their

LES DANAÏDES,

TRAGÉDIE LIRIQUE

en cinq Actes

MISE EN MUSIQUE

PAR

Salieri

Eleve

DE GLUCK.

*Representé pour la premiere fois
par l'Academie Nationale de Musique
le Lundi 19 avril 1784.*

Prix 30ᵗ

A PARIS.

Chez DES LAURIERS Mᵈ de Papiers, rue St Honoré à côte de celle des Prouvaires.

Les Danaïdes, title page of the first edition

ACTE PREMIER

Le Théatre représente le Bord de la Mer; un Temple des preparatifs des Sermens de la paix et de l'humen; les filles d'Egyptus descendes de leurs Vaisseaux.

SCENE I.

Danaus, Hypermnestre, Lyncée, les freres de Lyncée, les Danaüdes, peuples et Sacrificateurs.

Les Danaïdes, beginning of Act 1

Der Rauchfangkehrer, autograph of Fräule's Metastasio aria

wedding night. Hypermestra refuses, and Danaus threatens her; left alone, she laments her fate. The mass marriage is celebrated in the third act; only Hypermestra refuses to drink from Lynceus' nuptial cup. She goes outside while Danaus tries to calm the confused Lynceus. The wedding celebrations continue.

In the fourth act, Hypermestra pleads with her father, but Danaus remains firm. Hypermestra rebuffs Lynceus, though she loves him, which he cannot understand. But she is unable to reveal what she knows. Then the signal for the murder is given, and Hypermestra tells Lynceus to flee. In the fifth act, Danaus asks Hypermestra whether she has stabbed Lynceus; she denies it. Danaus is about to search for the missing Lynceus with his daughters when Lynceus attacks the palace with his soldiers and forces his way inside. At the very moment that Danaus wants to kill Hypermestra, Lynceus rushes in. Danaus is killed. The earth trembles, thunder rolls, Lynceus flees with Hypermestra and his soldiers as lightning destroys the palace and it collapses. The final scene is in Hell, with a shore along a sea of blood. Danaus is chained to a rock, his bloody entrails are being eaten by a vulture. As the fettered Danaïdes are persecuted and tortured by demons, snakes, and furies, the theater resounds with their screams and a fiery rain falls steadily down.

The first review appeared in the *Journal de Paris* the day after the opening, and contained a detailed description of the plot. The comment on the music was that the public did not seem to notice any disparity in the various sections, so that Salieri deserved to be placed alongside Gluck. The *Mercure de France*[4] stated:

> Those who expected to see a terrible spectacle were amazed to discover more festivities than horrors in it; those who anticipated the grand effects of tragedy did not discover enough to touch, or of sufficient variety to interest them; others who were concerned with differentiating between the passages of the music written by Ritter Gluck and those of his disciple, readily recognized in the spirit of the composition the great, forceful, lively, and genuine form that characterizes the ideal of the creator of dramatic lyricism; at the same time they also noticed an independent style in certain details, especially in the recitative and the

phrasing of the arias, revealing a remarkable talent that warrants the greatest hopes for our theater. Finally, those of the spectators who came without any preconceptions or special theory, who allowed their perception to be entirely determined by the natural impressions of the situations, were vividly struck by the novelty, the richness, and the unexpected variety of the spectacle.

But the real critique of the music of this opera only appeared on May 22 in the *Mercure de France*. It states that the overture "by far outdoes unimportant symphonies that do not portray anything, that do not herald anything, that are shaped in the usual form of sonatas, all of them patched together out of three or four pieces"; instead, it is described as being completely in the tradition of Gluck's *Iphigénie en Aulide*. As for the recitatives, ". . . the plain and so-called accompanied recitatives are blended together"; Salieri "from time to time interrupts both of them with *a tempo* passages for voice, that are not formal arias and are only intended to convey the sense of the words, the situation and the feelings of the characters of his piece." As for the arias, the article comments: "The composer has managed to combine the declamation with the arias, without encroaching on the development of his theme and the unity of the whole work. He shows taste in his use of repetitions that are necessary to the arias and help to round them out but that can, if misused, become weak in their effect and hamper the progress of the plot. The accompaniment makes its contribution by supporting the general character of the arias and strengthening their most expressive parts."

Thus, in "Hypermestra's pathetic aria" in the second act

the repetition of the words: mon père! . . . has heart-piercing notes, strengthened in a remarkable way by the crescendo of the instruments that seem to blend their voices with that of Hypermestra as she attempts to soften Danaus' heart. This aria could perhaps be cited as an example of the range and true proportion considered appropriate for a passionate aria occuring in the middle of an interesting scene. . . . The first aria by Danaus: *Jouissez du destin propice* seems to us, in its conception as well as its execution, to have been composed by a master. The subject of the aria is in the classic tradition and recalls the strophes of Anacreon and Catullus, where the idea of death was conceived in wanton images. We feel that the composer has done full justice to this intention. The theme of the aria is sung in a pleasant and light manner; the somber expression of the second idea is linked to it in a delicate and natural way. The accompaniment projects spirit and passion. These two contrasting characteristics are blended in the aria with a skill and success that seems to us to deserve the attention of all discerning people; yet we must admit that in performance this aria never achieved the effect we would have expected from it.

Seldom was a chorus interwoven so closely with the action of an opera, instead of merely representing the crowd. The fifty sons of Aegyptus and the fifty Danaides are on stage for long stretches as active personae; even in the final scene the Danaides become the victims of Hell. Though the entire complement was not brought on stage in Paris, thirty-five of Danaus' daughters and thirty-nine men were used. Thus the choruses were also given special praise: ". . . almost all of them have character, melody and excellent harmonic effects; some are full of imagination, grace, and feeling."[5]

The title Les Danaïdes, for a subject that had in numerous other theatrical or operatic versions generally been called Hypermestra, was chosen deliberately. It focused on the incredible massacre by the Danaides and their punishment in Hell. Danaus believed himself betrayed, and did not hesitate to encourage his daughters to commit a horrible deed to maintain his authority. Hypermestra tries to change her father's mind, but she does not argue with him. Her "refusal," hesitant at first, becomes more decisive when she sees the fiancé whom she is supposed to kill. Yet her humanity lacks the strength to avert the murderous plan. Calzabigi, the opera's original librettist, had clearly recognized this limitation in the Hypermestra character. However, Salieri masterfully managed to underscore the timidity and hesitancy of this character without any loss of interest in the fate of Danaus and his daughters. The point of the opera, after all, is not the rescue of Hypermestra and her fiancé Lynceus, but the monstrous crime. Nevertheless, and without jeopardizing this dramatic idea, Hypermestra as protagonist constitutes a most brilliant role that belongs with the best in tragédie lyrique; in its conception, the big solo scene gives a foretaste of Cherubini and Spontini.

The premiere did not put an end to the confusions surrounding the work. Tschudi, the co-translator of the libretto,

had died some days earlier. On the opening day Gluck sent
Roullet a letter surely intended for immediate publication:

> I would ask you, my friend, to include in the *Journal de Paris*, an
> explanation that I must give and give herewith, that the music of *Les
> Danaïdes* is by Mr. Salieri and that I have no share in it except for some
> advice for which he asked, and that my respect for him prompted me
> to give him the benefit of my experience.[6]

But Roullet delayed its publication for a few days, as was
noted to his discredit in the *Mémoires secrets*. He did not disclose
this surprising news to the general public until the sixth
performance, maintaining all that time the fiction that Gluck
was the work's creator. Upon its publication, however, Salieri
immediately published an expression of gratitude to Gluck in
the *Journal de Paris*:

> The statement by Ritter Gluck that I have just read in your newspaper
> is a fresh token of the goodwill shown to me by this great man, who by
> bestowing his friendship wants some of his renown to reflect on me. It
> is true that I wrote the music for the opera *Les Danaïdes* myself, but I
> wrote it entirely under his supervision, guided by his light and inspired
> by his genius. . . .
> I would be guilty of untruthfulness as well as ingratitude if I failed
> to admit the honor of having been allowed to add his name to mine on
> the title page of this work.[7]

But that explanation still did not set matters entirely straight.
For it was misleading to list Tschudi and Roullet as the authors
of the libretto, when all they had done was prepare its French
version. No mention was made of Calzabigi's being the work's
rightful librettist. The latter may have been even more disappointed that Gluck had simply passed on to Salieri a libretto
that was written for himself. Calzabigi did not ignore this
disregard of his intellectual property, and set out the correct
facts for the *Mémoires secrets*, which resulted in a counter-
explanation by Roullet—a controversy that dragged on in the
press into the fall.

Salieri was anxious to go home. He was quite ready to
depart at the beginning of May when he was surprised by the
news that Paris had already requested an extension of his leave
from Vienna. The reason was that he was supposed to make

certain changes in Gluck's *Armide*, which was being prepared as a gala performance for the visit of Gustav III, king of Sweden. Salieri complied, and used the opportunity to visit Marie Antoinette once again. He dedicated the score of *Les Danaïdes* to her, and received a gift of 3,000 livres.

Thus Salieri returned to Vienna a rich man. Of course, he would have given some of his honorarium of 12,000 livres to Roullet for his work on the libretto. But the score of *Les Danaïdes* was printed immediately—as was customary in Paris—and brought him additional income. If one is to believe Cramer, who conducted an exhaustive correspondence with him, Salieri was left with 8,000 livres of his opera fee. He therefore returned home with more than 12,000 livres, the equivalent of 4,000 florins.

The work proved that Salieri was the sole legitimate heir to Gluck in the category of *tragédie lyrique*, and not his student, as stated on the title page of the printed score. He had accomplished this in the very city where Gluck had worked most determinedly to bring about his operatic reform. And he was the first native Italian to come out decisively in favor of musical progress.

In Paris, debate over musical styles was greatly simplified by the terms "Gluckists" and "Piccinnists," though this contrast referred primarily to their followers and not to the composers themselves. But what about Vienna? How did Vienna refer to the "Gluckist" trend, represented by Salieri? Was it possible there to speak simply of the German *Singspiel* and the Italian opera? If that were the case, Gluck's reform operas, performed in Vienna in their Italian versions, would simply belong with those of the Italian faction. The term "Italian" opera would then be too imprecise to differentiate between various types of opera. And since we have become accustomed to thinking in terms of competition between Mozart and the Italians in Vienna, where would that leave his Italian operas? Was Salieri the head of a group of Italians in Vienna whose ideas differed from those of Mozart? It is perhaps more realistic to speak of "traditional opera," representing the established patterns of *opera seria* and *opera buffa*, and to contrast this with an entirely

new trend. In the latter, the old *opera seria* was replaced by
Gluck's reform opera, and the old *opera buffa* was replaced by
a new form of the *commedia per musica* or *dramma giocoso*
(musical comedy in a revised "stilo misto").

Librettists were just as crucial to the advancement of the
commedia per musica as to Gluck's reform operas; this was
where Italian librettists who lived in Vienna played an important role. Calzabigi, for instance, had a decisive influence on
the new opera esthetic—as Gluck acknowledged time and again.
There was also Da Ponte, and not long thereafter Giambattista
Casti, who made significant contributions as well. It was they
who first managed to transform the older, stereotypical operas,
and to develop a musical "comedy of character" that enabled
music drama to become part of the modern theater.

Salieri participated in the process, and was an influential
supporter of that modern development. In most discussions of
the differences between him and Mozart, he is generally portrayed in an unfavorable light. But these differences were
confined to daily theatrical business, and were not fundamental.
That is what enabled Salieri and Mozart to use the same
librettists, though with varied success.

What applied to Salieri also held true for Joseph II, who
was not, as oversimplified theories keep insisting, an advocate
of Italian music. For which type would it have been? Did he
not act on his own authority in experimenting with the German
Singspiel? As for the Italians, was it not largely due to Joseph
that those who first made modern music theater possible were
summoned to Vienna? He became Mozart's supporter as well,
even obtaining commissions for him in critical situations. And
in patronizing Salieri, he acquired an agent who was important
to the development of music theater.

The extent to which the emperor valued Salieri's advice
was shown by the appointment of the inexperienced Da Ponte
as an opera librettist at the Nationaltheater, once the Italian
ensemble was established. Such an appointment cannot have
been based solely on the recommendation by Mazzolà. Da
Ponte must have impressed Salieri, and thus the emperor, with
his amiable yet vivacious manner. Moreover, their choice must

surely have been guided by Da Ponte's polished and witty verse. It had nothing serious or pedantic about it; it was light and sophisticated, yet mocking, and revealed a classical influence as well.

Da Ponte was born in the Jewish ghetto of Ceneda in Venice, in 1749, and was actually called Emanuele Conegliano. When the boy turned fourteen, his father Geremia and the whole family converted to Catholicism; at this time Emanuele received the name of his godfather and became known as Lorenzo Da Ponte. He was ordained as a priest at twenty-four after an excellent education, and became a professor of fine arts at the theological seminary of Treviso. Da Ponte soon lost this position on account of some provocative poems in which he showed himself to be an elegant and gifted satirical poet. The situation was aggravated by his very free life. He lived with a woman friend, there were love affairs, not to speak of envious acquaintances and even enemies. Eventually a formal charge was made against him for "adultery, cohabitation, and dereliction of priestly duties." It ended with Da Ponte being banished from Venice for fifteen years, although he had fled in the interim. His was clearly an unsettled life of irregular adventures.[8] But he was an educated person with a talent for clever verse. During Maria Theresa's reign Da Ponte would not have stood the slightest chance of an appointment in Vienna; under Joseph II, it was offered to him without prejudice, though largely on account of Salieri's intercession.

In his memoirs Da Ponte describes his first audience with the emperor, at which he thanked him for the appointment, which had already been arranged:

> Never before had I spoken to a monarch. Though all assured me that the emperor was a sovereign of the most benevolent sentiments, who received everyone with the utmost kindness, I still could not appear before him without experiencing the greatest shyness. But the smiling expression on his face, the pleasing sound of his voice and especially the overt simplicity of his behavior and dress, quite contrary to what one expects of a king, not only gave me courage again but left me no time to notice that I was facing an emperor. . . . As he was most curious to find out everything, he asked various questions about my homeland, about my studies and the circumstances that had brought me to Vienna. I answered all his questions as briefly as possible, which seemed to please

him. Finally, he asked me how many dramas I had written; whereupon
I told him frankly: "None, Your Majesty." "Good, good," he replied,
"then we shall have a virgin muse." It can be easily imagined how
enthusiastic this ruler made me feel when I left him. My heart was full
of a profusion of the most pleasant sensations, of joy, reverence and
admiration.[9]

Da Ponte as a writer for the theater—that was a daring
decision. But as he had evidently impressed Salieri and the
emperor, it was for Salieri that he had to write his first text.
Given his inexperience, he began by studying the enormous
collection of libretti owned by another Italian in Vienna.
Reading through the librettos was a very sobering experience:

> I had the courage and patience to look over between eighteen and
> twenty of these jewels. Poor Italy, what a lot of rubbish! There is no
> continuity, there are no characters, interest, scenery, no gracefulness of
> language or of style, and although they were created to make people
> laugh, no doubt everyone would instead have been driven to tears. These
> pitiful pastiches contained no verse that might have provided a charming
> conclusion, no lively ideas, no delicate, ingenious words that would
> encourage a desire to laugh. It was an absolute flood of foolish, simple-
> minded expressions, silliness, and nonsense.
> Now, I knew that it had to be easy to write better ones, and hoped
> that in mine one would at least find some pleasant jest, some witticism
> or an amusing idea here and there; that the language would be neither
> unseemly nor coarse, that one would be able to read the arias without
> aversion, and that the entire contents would be lively, full of interesting,
> ably created characters and unexpected events. Even with the best of
> intentions, I could not have written dramas as bad those I had read. But
> I knew from experience that in order to write a good play, it was even
> more important that it please, especially if it was also to be acclaimed at
> its performance.[10]

Da Ponte's criticism of contemporary librettos was quite
justified. Even today, one can only be amazed at the texts that
inspired composers to accomplished, sometimes even magnificent music. On the other hand, his own texts are also of an
incredibly varied caliber; Mozart was fortunate to have received
the best of Da Ponte's texts, to which he could lend his own
dramatic talents. One cannot entirely dismiss the fact that Da
Ponte was an astonishingly skillful adapter of existing texts and
other people's material, but not such an original inventor of
suitable theatrical plots. It is most instructive, therefore, to
learn how Da Ponte went about his task, and what were the

problems of adaptation for the music theater, especially since no other librettist has left such reflections on his activities:

> As my first text was to be set to music by Salieri who, truth to tell, is a most educated, knowledgeable man, I gave him several subjects to choose from. Unfortunately he preferred the one that was least suitable to being given a certain grace and theatrical interest. It was "Rich Man for a Day" (*Il Ricco d'un giorno*). I went to work courageously; but I quickly noticed how much more difficult it is to execute something than merely to conceive it. I encountered an endless number of unexpected difficulties. The material did not contain the desired number of characters, nor enough different and varied events to work out a plot sufficiently interesting to be entertaining for about two hours. The dialogues were too dry for me, the arias too forced, the expression of the feelings too mundane, the plot and action too lifeless. Finally, it seemed to me that I no longer understood anything, and could neither write nor create verse, nor embellish it, and that I had grasped Hercules' club with the hand of a child. Eventually the first act was more or less ready. It only lacked a finale. The finale has to be very closely connected with the rest of the opera, and is a sort of comedy or short independent drama; it requires a new introductory passage and must be certain to arouse interest. It must bring out the talents of the Kapellmeister and the art and power of the singers; and as the high point of the opera it must produce the greatest effect. Recitatives are entirely excluded from it, everything is sung and the songs have to be worked out in various tempi: the adagio, allegro, andante, amabile, armonioso, the strepitoso, arcistrepitoso, and the fortissimo with which the finale always ends and is known as chiusa or stretta. I do not know whether it is called that because the entire strength of the drama is gathered there, or because the brain of the poor poet who has to write it is hard-pressed, not once but over and over again. According to theatrical tradition, all the singers must appear on stage in a finale, even if there are three hundred of them—whether they appear singly, in twos or threes, in groups of six, ten, or sixty, to sing solos, duets, terzettos, sextets, or large choruses. And if the context of the drama does not allow for it, it becomes the task of the librettist to find a way to make it possible, even though it is contrary to all common sense, Aristotelian rules, or existing regulations; if it then turns out to be difficult to do, all the worse for him.
>
> After this account it cannot be difficult to picture the predicament in which I found myself with the finale of the first act. At least ten times I must have been on the point of burning whatever I had written, and of asking to be excused. Finally, after much biting of my nails, rolling of my eyes, scratching of my head, and much calling on the goddess Lucina and on all the saints and all the midwives of Pindus, I finished not only the first finale but the entire opera. I then locked it into my desk and did not take it out for two weeks so as to read it through with a clear mind. It now seemed even more vapid than before. Still, I had to give it to Salieri, who had already written the music for some of its scenes and who asked me for the rest of the opera every day. I went to see him looking downcast and handed him the libretto without saying anything. He read it right away in my presence, and said: "It is well written but it has to be seen on stage before it can be judged properly. It contains

some very good arias and whole scenes that I very much like, but you will have to make some minor changes for me, more on account of the musical effect than for other reasons."

I left him feeling as happy as a king, and just as one always believes what one wants to believe, I began to hope that this text might not be as bad as I had found it earlier. But what did those minor changes consist of? They involved the slashing or lengthening of the greater part of the scenes, the insertion of new duets, terzettos, and quartets and the like; it meant changing the meter of half of the arias, inserting choruses that had to be sung by Germans, shortening all the recitatives and hence the whole content, coherence, and interest of the opera, if there had ever been any. I believe that when the opera was staged, no more than a hundred stanzas were left of my original version.[11]

The draft and the final text can no longer be compared, but one must not take all these details literally. Da Ponte did not write this part of his memoirs until thirty years later. *Il ricco d'un giorno* contains only one duet, quintet, and sextet respectively, as well as two terzettos; hence the revisions hardly amounted to an "insertion of new duets, terzettos, and quartets." But Da Ponte has very vividly described the difficulties of a dramatic text that has to achieve its full effect through the music. For instance, it was in this opera that the lengthy and complex finales at the end of the first and second acts were provided with a lively plot development. But in the third act there was merely a minor dramatic problem to work out, a coda consisting of two numbers. And that was surely due to mismanaged dramatic planning. On the other hand, many of the arias and scenes in this opera worked out very well; they clearly reveal Da Ponte's feeling for carefully observed dramatic moments, for the presentation of individually differentiated characters in place of one-dimensional types, and for witty colloquial speech in his verses. The plot is as follows:

Two brothers—one of whom is extremely miserly and the other exceedingly prodigal—inherit a large fortune that is paid out to them by Berto the notary. Both of them love Emilia, the notary's daughter; she has long since chosen the prodigal son, and is encouraged by his sister Doralice and her maid. The prodigal has a servant, Mascharone, who skims what he can from all the expenditures. He even engages a host of merchants, jewelers, artisans, and servants who create unnecessary expenses. Doralice convinces Emilia to cure her lover of his spending mania before the wedding by pretending to entertain the courtship of the miserly brother. This leads to a complicated to and fro between the women and the two brothers.

In the second act, both brothers try to serenade Emilia, but their efforts are interrupted by a violent storm. Emilia grows confused because the prodigal does not seem to improve at all; on the contrary, he becomes more and more disastrously drawn into mischief by his servant, Mascharone. Finally Mascharone organizes a game of cards, in which he cheats, but loses. He has to pay up with all of his acquired loot, and is taken away. At last the prodigal realizes what has been going on, and asks the notary to administer his money. His miserly brother renounces Emilia, having received a sharp lesson in the demands a woman would make on him, and Emilia can then marry the reformed prodigal.

Da Ponte's libretto already contains many characteristics that would mark his later work: there is a relentless realism that does not divide society into "good" and "bad," but shows the most diverse characters against the background of disintegrating morality. Mascharone is a servant who becomes his master's radical antagonist; scenes of casual and natural conversation are set against complex theatrical situations, where large ensemble scenes are made possible by the skilful use of a dramatic chorus. There are allusions to current events, such as a reference to *Il rè Teodoro in Venezia*, by Giovanni Paisiello, a successful play that had just had its premiere in Vienna, and there is mention of the first ascent in a balloon by the brothers Montgolfier.

On the other hand, this first effort for the theater is still full of awkwardnesses and repetitions that reveal Da Ponte's lack of experience. Perhaps it was his misfortune not to have a partner blessed with great theatrical instinct who would test the minutest details for their dramatic effect, as Mozart would have done. Instead, he was working with a composer who believed in a division of labor with the librettist. Salieri did suggest various changes and adjustments on this occasion, but they could not compensate for the libretto's weaknesses. Yet

Da Ponte surely does Salieri an injustice when, in his memoirs, he blames him for everything that led to the work's eventual failure. As it turned out, there was enough time to work on the text in peace. While Salieri had doubtlessly finished composing the greater part of this opera in the summer of 1783, he decided to postpone its production; the date for the opening performance of *Les Danaïdes* had been settled meanwhile. Naturally, this took precedence over everything else, and so Salieri first of all attended to his six-month-long commitment in Paris.

He returned to Vienna at the beginning of July 1784, and could give his full attention to the more or less finished *dramma giocoso, Il ricco d'un giorno*. There was still no hurry, as three other operas were also ready to open, and Salieri could take his time to work with Da Ponte and make whatever further changes he wanted in either the music or the text. Apparently he no longer considered any alterations necessary. The premiere did not take place until the beginning of December.

Salieri must have been completely surprised by the work's failure. It barely managed to survive for six performances, and by the end of January it had to close. Of course, a variety of circumstances must have been responsible. Perhaps there were differences between the adherents of Da Ponte and those of Casti, especially as Casti was always prone to make fun of his competitors. Perhaps the music, and indeed the whole treatment of this work as music theater, was unusual; no doubt it was all this and more. Da Ponte reports:

> The main role in this opera was written for Storace, who was then at her peak and literally idolized by the Viennese. Unfortunately, she was indisposed and the role had to be given to another singer, who was as suitable for it as if a dove were to play an eagle. It was a great setback for the opera. But that was the least of it. . . . Brunati decided to write a review of it and to publish it on the evening of the first performance. He did indeed write it; and in the belief that he would be doing the Abbé Casti a favor, he asked him for permission to distribute the review himself at the performance.

Then he continues, in an apparently self-critical vein:

It goes without saying that the libretto was bad, and the music itself was not much better, as Salieri, who had just returned from Paris and whose ear was still filled with Gluck's and Lays' music, with *Les Danaïdes* and the ensuing uproar, had written totally French-sounding music, drowning in the Seine the lovely popular melodies for which he was so abundantly gifted. But in order to learn of the complete malice of my persecutors, it is sufficient to say that though so many things contributed to the opera's failure, there was an attempt to make people believe that I alone was responsible for it; for whereas in comic operas the text is seen as a frame holding a beautiful painting in place, in this instance it was maintained that the text was of such great importance that the success of the opera was entirely dependent on it. Not only Casti's followers, my own enemies, and all those who were vying for the position of court poet at the royal theater shouted insults at me, but even the singers, with Salieri himself in the lead, expressed themselves most unfavorably about me. Among other things, they said that they failed to understand how they could have presented such rubbish, and even less how the Kapellmeister could have set it to music; and the latter, actually a shrewd and not unintelligent man, made a serious vow that he would rather have his fingers cut off than ever have to set one of my verses to music again.[12]

Luckily Salieri did not keep his vow. . . .

Writing his memoirs as an old man, Da Ponte tended to see himself as persecuted by enemies and malicious people everywhere, and he may have exaggerated a little. He was also suddenly measuring his libretto against the elaborate ones he had himself criticized so harshly when trying to learn from the work of others. That was self-pitying instead of self-critical, and ultimately unjust to himself. And if Salieri intended to avoid any further collaboration, his judgment was not much better—even if the threat was only a temperamental outburst in a fit of angry disappointment. As to his having written music in the "French" style, and having "drowned his lovely popular melodies in the Seine," that is historically and factually incorrect.

First of all, the opera's dramatic events are emphasized by a spectrum of the most varied orchestral colors. Smaller forms predominate, but are arranged within the larger musical context, giving the chorus tasks of a proportion unusual in a comic opera. In this work, as in *La locandiera*, Salieri tried a light *parlando*-like tone that assigns great importance to the text. There are fully eighteen arias, as well as great variety in the formal dramatic and orchestral development. Arias are even often interrupted by short insertions. Thus much musical liveliness is created, above all in the richly arranged ensemble sections, and in the finales of the first two acts in which the chorus and all seven vocal soloists participate. Salieri tried specifically to respond to Da Ponte's novel dramatic tone and find a corresponding musical language. However, the music lacks memorable highlights, the kinds of melodies that one tries to whistle in the street the following day.

This opera makes one thing clear: a work that is performed successfully—for whatever reasons—is soon taken up elsewhere, whereas it has always been difficult for a failure to recover from a bad start. Salieri's relatively unimportant opera *La fiera di Venezia* created an effective atmosphere of street scenes and masques that aroused enthusiasm time and again, though it has little musical substance. *Il ricco d'un giorno*, which belongs among Salieri's better compositions in terms of its musicality, disappeared into the archives after its flawed and troublesome premiere, and was never produced anywhere else.

The fiasco sent Salieri straight into the other camp, to the poet Casti, and his next work more than compensated for all the disappointment.

CHAPTER FIVE

Salieri and Mozart 1784–1786

Giambattista Casti was no more an experienced librettist than his competitor Lorenzo Da Ponte, but that did not prevent him from trying to succeed Metastasio as royal court poet. Like Da Ponte, he was an ordained but nonpracticing Italian priest who made his living as an *homme de lettres*. Still, while they had a similar background and ambition, Casti's career turned out to be very different from what his habits, interests, and literary work would suggest. His life was characterized by constancy, uprightness, and determination, whereas Da Ponte—although not by nature an adventurer—was always driven to seek new projects, all the while keeping an eye out for further opportunities. Of the two, Casti's works were the more provocative; but he possessed a certain suppleness that prevented him from making undignified compromises or experiencing sudden setbacks. He held himself in check, never giving offense by the way he conducted his private affairs; and though a sharp satirist, he was never one to fight a losing battle.

Casti was born in Acquapendente (Latium) in 1724; his family lived in Montefiascone, a small hilltop town in a picturesque setting of lush vineyards overlooking Lake Bolsena. Little is known of his home, but the family appears to have been

well-to-do. Montefiascone was an old cathedral town with a
Catholic seminary, where Casti was accepted at the age of ten
and received the traditional classical education. He must have
possessed a versatile intellect, for at sixteen he was already
employed as a teacher of *humaniora*. His title of professor was
of little significance, although it did imply his ordination into
the lower ranks of the priesthood. In practice it meant that he
taught rhetoric and poetry using the classical texts. In those
days, Catholic seminaries were not simply theological establish-
ments, but also the best schools for comprehensive all-round
education; this explains why Italy's best minds were developed
in such institutions.

In contrast to Da Ponte, Casti did not endanger his future
career by indulging in literary excesses. He kept a low profile,
at least in Montefiascone, relieved by frequent excursions to
Rome, about a hundred kilometers away. That helped him to
bear the intellectual rigidity of the small town, for in Rome he
was in touch with a literary community that had already been
much influenced by France and the Enlightenment. There he
became a member of the Accademia degli Arcadi, made his
contribution by writing anacreontic verse, and had access to all
the literary salons. Distance helped him to lead a decidedly
double life. In 1759 Casti obtained a canonry in Montefiascone,
which doubtless gave him still greater independence. His liaison
with the young Marchioness Lepri enabled him to make a trip
to Paris with this famous beauty. He settled in Rome in 1762,
though he did not remain there long.

In that period Casti made a name for himself as a writer
of uninhibited erotic verse that, it was said, would have made
even Petronius blush. But there seems to be no truth to the
occasional allegations that he was forced to flee or was excom-
municated because of it. Otherwise he could scarcely have
presented himself at the Florentine court, or shortly thereafter
have obtained the official position of court poet to the grand
duke of Tuscany, who was a brother of (and successor to)
Joseph II—a connection that later proved exceedingly useful.
In Florence he also met Count Rosenberg-Orsini, who, as head
steward of Maria Theresa's household and her good friend,

was influentially placed at the court of the Grand Duke Peter Leopold. Casti's own acquaintance with Emperor Joseph II dated back to one of the latter's visits to Florence in 1769. Casti knew how to show himself to best advantage without any specific purpose in mind. He scarcely gave the impression of being a court sycophant, and that was probably the best route to success.

He joined Count Rosenberg on a journey to Vienna in 1772, an occasion he used to meet with Joseph II again. In the autumn of that year he accompanied Count Joseph Clemens Kaunitz to Berlin to visit King Frederic II. Count Kaunitz was the son of Prince Wenzel Anton Kaunitz, the state chancellor who controlled Habsburg politics for decades. The following year Casti traveled with Count Rosenberg to Trieste, where he met Giacomo Casanova. Vienna had by then become the center of his activities, with the undoubted approval of the grand duke. Their good relationship was also borne out by Casti's continuing to receive his salary as court poet. At first the poetic yield was extremely small—some verses and a few *novelle galanti*.

Casti's extensive travels through Europe over the following years were undertaken without specific tasks, diplomatic or otherwise. They were the educational journeys of a man who kept his eyes open, closely observed events at foreign courts, and kept a cool head as he accumulated experiences, impressions, and adventures. He was not taken in by anything, nor did he react to circumstances impetuously or spontaneously. Stoic philosophy informed his intellect as well as his life.

In the spring of 1776 he set out on a long voyage across northern and eastern Europe. He traveled through Stockholm and Talinn to St. Petersburg, where he spent about two years at the court of Empress Catherine II, returning to Vienna by way of Warsaw. After a year's interval, probably devoted wholly to assimilating his Russian impressions, he undertook another extensive tour, this time to Spain and Portugal. In Italy, on the way home, he became so ill that he spent almost a year in Milan and at Lake Como, recuperating. During this period he completed the *Poema tartaro*, a satiric epic in twelve cantos. Using scarcely altered names, he described the scandalous goings-on at the court of Catherine II—the sexual excesses of the empress, the intrigues and favoritism, the corruption, the terrible cruelties inflicted upon a completely deprived society—all under the guise of a civilized European court. However, Casti dared to go still further by projecting the czarina's future into the fate of his heroine Cattuna; Cattuna's son overthrows her and puts her into prison, where she suffers from remorse and terrifying visions. But her successor is soon overthrown as well; Cattuna is banished to Siberia, where, as an old and powerless woman, she meets a former lover. He, however, prefers to enjoy himself with a young serf girl.

Of course, the prophecies of this poem were entirely imaginary, yet they were not all that remote from later events at the Russian court; after all, half of Catherine's successors fell victim to assassination. Other European rulers were also subjected to the satiric knife of the epic, with the exception of Joseph II—but presumably that was owing less to flattery than to genuine conviction.

By September 1783, Casti was back in Vienna, where he tried unsuccessfully to obtain Metastasio's position as court poet. The post remained vacant, and he was confined to writing librettos, competing for work with Da Ponte. He wrote the text for *Il rè Teodoro in Venezia* for Giovanni Paisiello, later following it with *Il rè Teodoro in Corsica*. These two works deal with a self-appointed king, who is deposed and finds himself in severe financial straits. Meanwhile Casti had become the protégé of Count Rosenberg, then the director of the court theater. This inevitably led to friction between Casti and Da Ponte, who was the emperor's favorite.

Perhaps this will also help to explain the controversy between Mozart and his ostensible rivals among the "Italians." What appears likely is that Mozart—who collaborated with Da Ponte, and sometimes sought and received the emperor's support—found his chief adversary in Count Rosenberg, Casti's sponsor, who had considerable but not insurmountable influence. As for Salieri, he worked first with Da Ponte, then with Casti, finally with Da Ponte again, seeming to have maintained a stance of neutrality. At any rate, he cannot be considered part of the Rosenberg faction any more than he was an active anti-Mozartian, despite current musicological simplifications.

Da Ponte got back at Rosenberg by making the pointed comment "non casti amici di Casti," playing on the rumor that Casti had managed to mitigate Rosenberg's decreptitude either by serving as his procurer, or by composing verses that were sometimes downright obscene. But Casti was experienced enough also to retain the goodwill of Joseph II. He presented his *Poema tartaro* to the emperor, who was as amused by it as he was concerned that its publication might have political repercussions. After all, the czarina was his most recent ally. While he valued Casti personally, he felt it advisable to keep him at a distance. That was probably one of the reasons why Joseph II did not appoint Casti court poet; he might have been seen as an accomplice in an insult against the czarina.[1]

However, Casti continued to be welcome in Vienna as a librettist. He wrote *La grotta di Trofonio* in 1785 for Salieri, and in the following year he even produced a small opera, *Prima la musica e poi le parole*, for an official celebration given by the emperor in Schönbrunn. Thus, there was no visible disagreement between him and the emperor. To be sure, Casti was an independent man without any ties in Vienna. And he was certainly fond of travel, always as the guest of diplomats, aristocrats, or wealthy merchants. It was considered a friendly arrangement implying no obligations. People basked in the company of this amiable and witty *abbate*, who liked to read his romantic novels at gatherings and was acclaimed everywhere.

Casti used these travels to observe the courtly life that was the main theme of his poetic endeavors, and for which he had created a unique form of the satiric epic arranged in stanzas and cantos. In January 1787, he journeyed to Italy, accompanying the rich banker and art collector Count Josef Fries; the following year he was in Constantinople, with intermittent stays in Venice and Milan, where he had good friends. Meanwhile, he had written another libretto for Salieri, *Cublai, gran kan de Tartari*, in which he tried to adapt the motifs and methods of his *Poema tartaro* to the opera stage.

News of the death of Joseph II in 1790 reached him in Florence, though he did not return to Vienna until the summer of 1791—again with the hope of becoming court poet, this time to Leopold II. But the early and unexpected death of the new emperor spoiled his plans. His long-cherished desire did not materialize until Leopold's son Franz II ascended the throne. Casti immediately began a literary project that he wanted to turn into his major work, a big epic called *Gli animali parlanti*. It describes the creation of a large animal kingdom in which the lion is king. The kingdom becomes corrupt in the second generation, and declines into a long and bloody civil war in which the non-mammals gradually obtain power. At the end a great peace conference is about to be held on the island of Atlantis, just as the catastrophic earthquake occurs that submerges Atlantis and all the conference participants in the sea.

It was a barely disguised version of events preceding and during the French Revolution—a description of the moral decay, political grievances, and power intrigues at the court. In fact, it was an analysis of the uses of power by the *ancien régime* and all those European states Casti had come to know during his long travels. This time, even the Austrian Council of War in Vienna was not spared satiric treatment. And the church also received a lively "acknowledgement" through the behavior of the various night birds; in fact, the pope could recognize himself in the character of the crocodile. Casti worked on this poem of almost twenty thousand stanzas in twenty-six cantos until shortly before his death.

Casti led a peaceful life among his friends and patrons once he was back in Vienna. He wrote a few works for the theater, but these were only published posthumously. He was a witty and satiric conversationalist who followed political events with interest and commented on them in his extensive correspondence, especially with his Italian friends. Given this, his preference for a quiet private life must have aroused the suspicion of Emperor Franz II, who had a "nose" for Jacobins. Casti was accused of professing Jacobinism, and, as he disliked being involved in controversy, he requested leave to travel to Italy.

However, the court's agreement to his request by no means mitigated the seriousness of the accusations. As he set out on his journey, his luggage was searched by the police in Graz, and numerous manuscripts and letters were confiscated. Casti never saw Vienna again. In 1798 he went to Paris, where in 1802 he was able to finish his long animal epic. He prepared an edition of his complete works before he died unexpectedly of biliary colic in 1803, at the age of seventy-eight.

Having skipped ahead somewhat in our story, we now return to Salieri's failure with the first opera Da Ponte wrote for him. We have seen how at that time the composer had sworn never to collaborate with the librettist again. Salieri, in fact, had then turned to Da Ponte's chief competitor, Casti, for a text. Of course, Salieri soon forgot a vow made in an angry mood. Once Nancy Storace recovered from the sudden loss of voice that had precluded her participation in *Il ricco d'un giorno*—and therefore made her partly responsible for the fiasco—Da Ponte wrote a short cantata for her called *Per la ricuperata salute di Ofelia*. Salieri joined Mozart and the tenor Alessandro Cornetti in setting it to music, and it was published at the end of September 1785. Cornetti also taught singing but had composed very little; it is ironic that he was chosen as one of the collaborators, as his school was known primarily for conserving the voice as much as possible.

This joint composition shows that Mozart and Salieri were quite able to work together harmoniously, especially when it involved a singer like Storace, who was extremely important to both of them. She was to sing Susanna in Mozart's *Le nozze di Figaro* in 1786, and being the mainstay of Salieri's Italian Opera ensemble, she was about to perform Ofelia in his new opera *Prima la musica e poi le parole*. Indeed, the title of Da Ponte's cantata deliberately alludes to the Casti-Salieri opera.[2] So despite any dispute between them, Da Ponte actually publicized Salieri and Casti's new production—all of which goes to show that theatrical intrigues should not be taken too seriously.

Unfortunately, intrigues and disagreements tend to be perpetuated by confused records. One example generally cited as proof of the supposed rivalry between Mozart and Salieri

involves the latter's *La grotta di Trofonio*. It is always presented
as a work competing with Mozart's *Figaro*, an idea that dates
back to the memoirs of one of Mozart's good friends, the Irish
singer Michael Kelly;

> There were three operas now on the tapis, one by Righini, another by
> Salieri (the Grotto of Trophonius), and one by Mozart, by special
> command of the emperor. Mozart chose to have Beaumarchais' French
> comedy, "Le Mariage de Figaro," made into an Italian opera, which was
> done with great ability, by Da Ponte. These three pieces were nearly
> ready for representation at the same time, and each composer claimed
> the right of producing his opera first. The contest raised much discord,
> and parties were formed. The characters of the three men were all very
> different. Mozart was as touchy as gun-powder, and swore he would put
> the score of his opera into the fire if it was not produced first, and his
> claim was backed by a strong party: on the contrary, Righini was working
> like a mole in the dark to get precedence.
> The third candidate was *Maestro di Cappella* to the court, a clever
> shrewd man, possessed of what Bacon called crooked wisdom; and his
> claims were backed by three of the principal performers who formed a
> cabal not easily put down. Every one in the opera company took part in
> the contest. I alone was a stickler for Mozart, and naturally enough, for
> he had a claim on my warmest wishes, from my adoration of his powerful
> genius, and the debt of gratitude I owed him for many personal favors.
> The mighty contest was put an end to by His Majesty issuing a
> mandate for Mozart's "Nozze di Figaro," to be instantly put into rehearsal;
> and none more than Michael O'Kelly enjoyed the little great man's
> triumph over his rivals.[3]

Insofar as there is any truth in this frequently cited story,
it relates to the way in which Kelly characterizes the composers.
As for the actual chronology of the events, Giuseppe Gazza-
niga's *Il finto Cieco* was performed on February 20, 1786; it was
followed by Vincenzo Righini's *Demogorgone*, which premiered
on July 12 of that year, ten weeks after *Figaro*. The production
history of Salieri's *La grotta di Trofonio* goes back to 1785. It
must have been first performed that summer in Laxenburg,
the emperor's summer residence; otherwise the publication of
Da Ponte's *Ofelia* cantata at the end of September 1785, with
its allusion to Salieri's work, would not have made any sense.
The opera had its official opening at the Burgtheater on October
12, 1785, when Mozart was only just beginning to work on
Figaro.

Kelly's memory is much better when it comes to recalling

the summers the Italian Opera spent in residence at Laxenburg; he provides a vivid account of the very hospitable treatment there:

> The palace is only a few miles from Vienna, and nothing can be more magnificent; it is surrounded by forests full of all kinds of game; the park, gardens, and grounds, [are] truly beautiful, and in the centre of a rich and luxuriant country. The theatre was very pretty, and very well attended; for all had their *entrée* to it gratis, including the surrounding peasantry.
>
> Italian operas were performed three times, German plays twice, and German operas twice in each week. . . . Each performer of the Italian Opera had separate apartments allotted to him, and his breakfast was sent thither. There was a magnificent saloon, in which we all met at dinner. The table was plentifully and luxuriantly supplied, with every delicacy of the season; with wines of all descriptions, as well as all kinds of fruits, ices, etc.; and every night, after the spectacle, an excellent supper. In the mornings I had nothing to do (there were no rehearsals), but to amuse myself. The emperor and his court often went heron hawking—an amusement he was very partial to. Prince Dietrichstein, the Master of the Horse, was very friendly to Signora Storace, and did her the kindness to send her one of the court barouches to view the chase. I always accompanied her on these excursions.[4]

As Kapellmeister, Salieri would have been part of this group. But if no rehearsals were held in Laxenburg, then his new opera must have been rehearsed in Vienna before June, and the stay in Laxenburg, or else the ensemble went to Vienna from time to time where the opera season was still on. At any rate, the premiere at the Burgtheater was well prepared, and the opera became one of the greatest successes of Salieri's artistic career.

This was not likely to be on account of the libretto. Casti had selected a subject from classical mythology and turned it into a sort of fairy tale; but the plot is somewhat schematic and much too obvious. The piece is set in the "philosophic period in Greece" (as is pointed out in the "*argomento*"), which is to say, the time of Aristotle and Theophrastus. The story is as follows:

Aristone has two daughters, Ofelia and Dori, who are allowed to choose their own husbands. Dori chooses Plistene, who is very lively but certainly not intellectual; Ofelia, on the contrary, prefers Artemidor, a somewhat pedantic student of philosophy who talks of nothing but Plato and Socrates. Aristone feels it would suit their temperaments better if his daughters exchanged suitors. A quartet characterizes the differences between the two couples. A second scene shows Trofonio, the "philosopher and magician," in his cave with a chorus of spirits, during which the secret of his grotto is revealed. The cave has two entrances: one of them changes a serious mood to a cheerful one in anyone using it, and vice versa. The other entrance, however, lifts the magic spell. Artemidor and Plistene enter the cave, one after another; accordingly, their natures are changed. Once they return to their wives, they immediately begin to quarrel with them.

In the second act Aristone, whose advice has been confirmed by these quarrels, once more suggests an exchange of partners, which is again turned down. The suspicion arises that a magic spell has been used. The two men go to Trofonio once more, and are changed back to their original temperaments. Trofonio informs the audience of his true intentions: "I have let these overwrought youths know my real design for the good of mankind. They did not adopt a middle course, as wise men would have done, but reached for extremes in their youthful exuberance. One of them wanted to dazzle all wise men with his wisdom, the other wanted to taste every pleasure."

Now the two women, who also have come to Trofonio, have to be instructed. A spell is cast over them as well, causing fresh confusion when they are reunited with their husbands. Then Aristone visits Trofonio, who explains his magic. The women return to the grotto once more to have the spell removed. Then everyone is reconciled. In the epilogue, Trofonio wants to show Aristone the magic doors, but the latter declines. Trofonio next offers to foretell everyone's future, but they want nothing more to do with the magician. Aristone urges them to leave, and Trofonio returns to his cave.

The repetition of the magic spell was not a very skillful dramaturgical device, but its weakness was overcome by the wealth of musical ideas Salieri contributed. His music, entirely devoted to contrasting the characters, is based on a brilliant orchestra with engaging parts for the brasses. The most comic effects are used, in contrast to the rather gruesome invocation of the cave spirits, powerfully scored for Trofonio. Salieri effectively blended various styles, including accompanied recitatives and *arioso parlando*, making this an exceedingly popular work in which many numbers always had to be repeated. It is known that about thirty productions, often in translation, took place throughout Europe in the space of ten years. At the same time, it was the first comic opera to have its score engraved (by Artaria in Vienna), proof of the high esteem for the differentiated treatment of the orchestra. Salieri had more than made up for the bad experience of *Il ricco d'un giorno*.

In December 1785, while still working on *Figaro*, Mozart was again invited to perform at one of the Advent concerts of the Tonkünstler Society. The direction of these concerts was now in the hands of Hofkapellmeister Giuseppe Bonno, who had succeeded Gassmann. But as Bonno was old and sickly, Salieri usually replaced him, and so must have had considerable influence on the choice of program. An orchestral work was generally performed in addition to the traditional oratorio, and for this occasion Mozart chose to play his new Piano Concerto in E flat major, K. 482. His performance was scheduled between the first and second parts of *Esther*, by Karl Ditters von Dittersdorf. Most likely Mozart conducted his own concerto from the pianoforte, as was the custom. The great acclaim obliged him to repeat the slow movement—a sure sign of recognition as a composer, not merely as a pianoforte virtuoso.

Though Mozart carelessly neglected to join this pension society, he was often asked to participate in its concerts during Salieri's administration of them. In the eleven years he spent in Vienna, Mozart contributed his own works five times, a record matched only by Haydn and Dittersdorf. That fact reflects a considerable degree of esteem, for these concerts were intended primarily to increase the society's treasury, and therefore had to be planned with a particularly appealing program in mind. Although it is frequently maintained that Mozart was not accepted by the Viennese, that his works were no longer performed, and that he was eventually consigned to oblivion, he continued to attract audiences to the very end of his life. In fact the Tonkünstler Society's Lent concert in 1791 opened with a Mozart symphony, probably the now-famous Symphony in G Minor, K. 550, for which Mozart had specially written a new orchestration using clarinets. At this event, Salieri conducted an enormous orchestra of over one hundred eighty musicians. Eighteen months earlier the Clarinet Quintet in A major, K. 581, had received its first performance in the same place. Indeed, Salieri could only admire Mozart as a composer of instrumental music, as did all of Mozart's other contemporaries, including Joseph Haydn. In this area the two men could never have seen themselves as competitors, for Salieri wrote practically no instrumental music.

But what was the picture when it came to opera? Mozart was not really considered an operatic composer, but he had quite obviously been trying to write and obtain commissions for operas ever since his arrival. As long as it involved the national German *Singspiel*, there was no conflict of interest. Salieri did not consider that within his competence, especially as he was the Kapellmeister. Once there was only the Italian ensemble to write for, Mozart aspired to compose for Italian librettos as well, and in the autumn of 1785 he was actually permitted to work on *Le nozze di Figaro*. Apparently the emperor himself had given his consent; this may have been contrary to the wishes of Count Rosenberg, who favored Casti, whereas the *Figaro* libretto had been adapted by Da Ponte. Mozart's choice of Da Ponte was not a problem for Salieri, who at the time had no interest in collaborating with the librettist after the recent fiasco with *Il ricco d'un giorno*. This was Salieri's personal judgment; it did not mean that he wanted to harm Da Ponte, who had Joseph II's support as the official dramatist, and who worked with various composers. Salieri had become mistrustful of Da Ponte's ability, but had no objection to others continuing to work with him. There is not the slightest evidence that Salieri's cooperation with Casti, which had resulted in a great success, was a sign of an exclusive preference.

Another factor virtually ruled out any competition with Mozart in the realm of opera. Salieri had become known for a

Plate 1
Archway of Salieri's birthplace in Legnago, which today is in the
"Museo Fiorini."

Plate 2
The "Museo Fioroni" is mainly dedicated to the memory of
Antonio Salieri.

Plate 3
Florian Leopold Gaßmann, Salieri's mentor and teacher

Plate 4
Lorenzo Da Ponte, librettist for Salieri and Mozart

Plate 5
Salieri's silhouette by Hieronymus Löschenkohl

Plate 6
Playbill for the opening night of *La grotta di Trofonio* and the title
page of the piano score for *Axur, König von Ormus,* a German
transcription by Christian Gottlob Neefe

Plate 7
Pierre Augustin Caron de Beaumarchais

ANTONIO SALIERI

Plate 8
Salieri around 1815

ant. Salieri
nat. a Legnago 19 Ag
1750

Fr. Rehberg ad viv del
Vienna 6 febr. 1821

Antonio Salieri

Alla Signora Angelica Catalani

Vienna 16 febr. 1821

D.D.D. Fr. Rehberg

Plate 9
Salieri at age 71

Plate 10
Christoph Willibald Gluck

Plate 11
Emperor Joseph II

D. Pellegrini pinxit   F. Bartolozzi sculp.

J. B. CASTI,

Cui mixo carmine dicere verum

Nihil vetuit

Morto in Parigi nell 1802 all' età de 83 anni

Plate 12
Giambattista Casti, Salieri's librettist

Plate 13
Mozart at the piano, an unfinished portrait by Joseph Lange

Plate 14
Emperor Franz II (in Austria, Franz I, Emperor by succession)

Plate 15
Ignaz Franz Edler von Mosel, Salieri's first biographer

Plate 16
Monument on Salieri's grave in the Matzleinsdorfer Cemetery
in Vienna

quite different type of work. Having dared to introduce himself alongside Gluck in Paris with *Les Danaïdes*, he could now consider himself the legitimate heir to that towering operatic reformer. Moreover, his works were performed all over Europe. In contrast, Mozart was a complete outsider; aside from a few operas in his youth, he had composed only two major operatic works up to this point in this life. One was *Idomeneo*, a work that had been performed only in Munich; the other was the *Entführung*, an extraordinary piece now being produced everywhere. Yet on the whole, this genial composer appeared to concentrate primarily on instrumental pieces. In the five years he had spent in Vienna, he had already composed twelve pianoforte concertos and performed them himself, not to mention numerous other works, especially chamber music.

But there was a specific instance in the relationship between the two composers when, as Kapellmeister, Salieri made a decision that annoyed Mozart. The issue concerned some insertions Mozart had written for a production of Pasquale Anfossi's opera *Il curioso indiscreto* (July 1783). It was quite customary for composers to rework individual numbers in new productions of older operas. Each new production had to make allowance for the soloists' vocal capacity and expressiveness, and create the most advantageous bravura opportunities for their individual timbres. Once the soloists changed, the best of arias could easily fail to bring out the special talents of a singer, perhaps even produce an unfavorable effect. Even in those days, people went to the opera primarily to hear the great stars, and expected to be treated to the full range of their gifts. Hence new numbers, especially bravura arias, were written for specific performers by composers familiar with them. No copyright regulations existed at that time to prevent such attempts to improve the chances of the work's success.

Mozart's contribution to the Anfossi production consisted of two new arias for Aloysia Lange and a rondeau for the tenor Valentin Adamberger, both former members of the national German *Singspiel* company. It created a provocative situation: Adamberger was the only German male, and Aloysia Lange one of several German female singers to have been

engaged by the Italian ensemble. Lange was considered a most
capricious singer, and had often made herself unpopular. Now
she was competing in an Italian opera with the newly engaged
prima donna Nancy Storace, and wanted to hold her own with
a special bravura aria. Trivial incidents of this sort affected
Mozart because Aloysia Lange had become his sister-in-law,
and because his insertions for her turned out to be the only
successful numbers in the opera. In a letter to his father he
comments:

> Lange was here to rehearse the 2 arias and we consulted on how to
> be smarter than our enemies—for I have enough of them and Lange is
> fed up as well because of Storaci the *new singer*. . . . the opera il curiosi
> indiscreto by Anfossi, in which Lange and Adamberger appear for the
> first time, had its first performance on Monday, the day before yesterday.
> Only my two arias met with success. And the second one, a bravura aria,
> had to be repeated. Well, I want you to know that my enemies were so
> unkind as to spread this rumor beforehand: *Mozart wants to make changes
> in Anfossi's opera.* I found out about it. So I let Count Rosenberg know
> that I would not deliver the arias unless the following were printed in
> the scores, in German as well as Italian (July 2, 1783).[5]

Apparently Count Rosenberg, as director of the court
theater, criticized Mozart's insertions, and perhaps accused him
of arrogance toward Anfossi. At any rate, the following note
(formulated by Mozart?) was included in the libretto:

> *Note.* As the two arias by Mr. Anfosi [sic], on pages 36 and 102 were
> written for someone else, and as such did not measure up to the great
> talents of Madame Lange, Herr Mozztzrt [sic] wrote some new music to
> please the said Madame Lange. Everyone is so informed herewith, so
> that honor be given to whom it is due, without in any way damaging the
> reputation of the already well-known Neapolitan.

This was an unusual procedure, and scarcely calculated to
calm tempers, for it publicized the intrigues at the theater and
underscored Mozart's contribution. Even a review in faraway
Berlin (in the *Litteratur- und Theater-Zeitung*) contained the
following reference: "Mad. Lange sang at the Italian Opera
for the first time today, and the public proved, despite all
cabals, how much it values her talent . . ."[6] It makes one realize
what Kelly meant when he described Mozart as "touchy as
gunpowder." At any rate, the theater management must have

been very much annoyed, especially since they probably guessed
that the opera would not be much of a success without Mozart's
insertions, and that they could therefore not afford to reject
them.

In what way was Salieri involved in this rather petty story?
He clearly sided with Count Rosenberg and the sensitive Italian
singers, and in a fit of overzealousness even tried to outdo the
director of the theater. Mozart comments on this in the same
letter:

> . . . I submitted the arias, which did both my sister-in-law and myself
> an inexpressible honor—and my enemies were quite disconcerted! Then
> Herr Salieri used a ploy that will not harm me as much as poor
> Adamberger. I believe I wrote to you that I also composed a rondeau
> for Adamberger. At a short rehearsal, before the rondeau had been
> copied out, Salieri took Adamberger to one side and told him that Count
> Rosenberg would not approve of his adding an aria, and as a good
> friend he therefore advised him not to do so. Adamberger—angry about
> Rosenberg and unreasonably arrogant—did not know how to take his
> revenge and said stupidly—All right—*to show that Adamberger had already
> acquired fame in Vienna and did not need to gain esteem through the music written
> for him, he would sing only what was in the opera and never in his lifetime insert
> any arias.* What was the outcome? That he was not well received at all,
> as was to be expected! Now he regrets it, but it is too late. For if he were
> to ask me today to give him the rondeau, I would not do so. I can very
> easily make use of it in one of my own operas. The worst of it is that
> the prophecy made by *his wife and by me* turned out to be true, namely,
> that Count Rosenberg and the management *know nothing about this* and
> that it was just a ruse of Salieri's (July 2, 1783).[7]

The entire affair was insignificant, yet Mozart's temper
flared up. In his letter he uses the expression "my enemies"
three times—a term that seems somewhat excessive in this
context. For nothing is known of any real enemies of Mozart,
and whenever he makes such references in his letters—and
they occur frequently—it always involves angry, but rather
vague, exaggerations. That is what happened here. As Kapellmeister, Salieri found he had to resolve a conflict involving a
singer who was about to make his debut. And because of a
statement in a single letter—the only extant document—Salieri
has ended up characterized by musicologists as a professed
opponent of Mozart. In cases of this sort, the reader must form
his own conclusions.

Two and a half years after this business, a situation arose

that might have been interpreted as a little contest between the
two composers—and may even have been deliberately planned
as such. Its initiator was the Emperor Joseph II, who maintained
a very friendly relationship with both composers. Salieri still
belonged to the intimate circle of chamber music players who
met regularly with the emperor, and could consider himself
his protégé. Mozart, on the other hand, held no official position
at court but had the personal esteem of the emperor, who was
fully aware of his musical stature. The contest was occasioned
by a rare court festivity in honor of the governor general of
the Netherlands. The normally uninhabited orangery at the
Schönbrunn Palace, which was kept heated to protect its exotic
plants, was made ready for a "spring festival on a winter's day."
(Fortunately, it also turned out to be one of the warmer days
of an already very mild winter.) The festivities were organized
around a German play and an Italian *opera buffa*, performed
one after the other. The register of court events describes the
festivities in elaborate detail:

> Tuesday the 7th. February. His Majesty the Emperor decided to give
> a party today in the orangery at Schönbrunn, as was done last year, in
> honor of the Governors General of the Austrian Netherlands, Her
> Highness the Arch-Duchess Maria-Christine and Duke Albert of Saxony-
> Teschen, and invited 41 courtiers and their ladies;
> They arrived after 2 o'clock in the afternoon, some in their coaches,
> others in carriages drawn by four to six horses, on the Burgplatz next
> to the Schwarze Adler, and gathered in rooms on the first floor of the
> Amalische Hof where they drew lots to determine their order of
> departure, and then proceeded in that order at three-thirty from the
> Burg to Schönbrunn, each coach preceded by two grooms . . .
> Upon their arrival at four o'clock, dinner for eighty-two was served
> by the royal lackeys, at a table in the center of the orangery.
> The imperial wind instrument chamber players performed while they
> ate.
> After dinner, His Majesty and all his guests made their way to a stage
> that had been erected near one end of the orangery, while the table was
> cleared away, and both sides of the space beautifully illuminated;
> thereupon His Majesty and his guests went to another stage constructed
> at the opposite end of the orangery, where a German play interspersed
> with arias was performed.
> When it was over the whole party moved back to the theater put up
> at the other end, where an Italian Singspiel [sic] was immediately
> performed.
> At the conclusion, at 9 o'clock, all the guests were taken back to the
> city in the order in which they had arrived, in coaches and carriages,
> each preceded by two grooms with lanterns.[8]

Both pieces reflected current conditions in the theater, caricaturing certain excesses and abuses in its daily operation. The emperor himself had specified the rules to be observed by the two ensembles of the court theater, the German *Singspiel* and the Italian Opera. The text for Salieri's contribution, written by Casti, clearly shows that Italian opera (at least north of the Alps) always signified court opera or aristocratic theater.

Salieri's work, *Prima la musica e poi le parole*, parodies the preparations for a new opera—the unsatisfactory collaboration between composer and librettist, the engaging of female singers, and the first rehearsals. Casti's text deals with a Count Opizio, who orders a new opera that must be written, rehearsed, and performed in four days. There is also a prince, who is willing to contribute one hundred sequins if a certain female singer participates. The librettist considers the task impossible, but the music is already completed and needs only a text. The composer claims that no one is interested in the libretto anyway. The poet insists that the music reproduce the expression of the words; the composer counters that his music is suitable for any emotional expression.

A prima donna then appears, who introduces herself by listing the European theaters in which she has appeared and the roles she has sung. Eventually, she even offers to perform a perfect imitation of a famous castrato role (Giulio Sabino, from the opera of that name by Giuseppe Sarti). To help her do this, she assigns the nonspeaking roles of children to the poet and the composer. To look like children, they have to move about on their knees, while the prima donna sings the famous aria. The following scene is concerned with culling rhythmically suitable verses for the music from another drama. Then comes the problem of writing a role for an additional soprano—for whose engagement the rich prince has agreed to pay one hundred sequins—since no one wants to forgo any of the money (the composer demands nine-tenths of the fee as his share).

Composer and librettist begin their work at the harpsichord, and end up with a libretto that contains a role for both a prima donna and a second *buffo* soprano. This second singer appears in the next scene, where she and the poet wait for the composer together. She does not like the music lying on the harpsichord and tosses the sheets on the floor. When the composer finally arrives, the singer is very angry with him for having made her wait so long. She introduces herself by saying that she can sing anything; as proof, she first sings an aria depicting madness, then one in which she stutters. The final scene depicts a rehearsal at which the two sopranos quarrel with each other while performing their roles; it all becomes a cacophonous comic medley of four voices as the librettist and composer throw in their own comments. Harmony is restored only at the end, when all join in a *tutti* for the benefit of the audience.

Parody works best when it comes closest to the reality it mocks, and in this respect Casti's libretto has to be considered entirely adequate, certainly not inferior to the other work, Gottlieb Stephanie's *Der Schauspieldirektor*. But above all, Casti's libretto created an opportunity for some exceedingly comic scenes that could not fail to impress the audience. For this opera about opera portrayed the firmly established patterns of *opera seria* and *opera buffa* represented by each of the singers, and thus permitted Salieri to weave elements of both categories together as tightly as possible. The music is therefore full of contrasts and surprises that are effectively accompanied by varied instrumentation. Moreover, it also provided a chance for lengthy quotations, as the prima donna actually sings and caricatures a shortened version of an aria from the Sarti opera. It is a typical bravura aria for a soprano castrato, a part that had been sung in Vienna by Luigi Marchesi a mere six months earlier. And Nancy Storace, who had the role of the prima donna, had carefully observed and listened to her model, so that she performed a brilliant parody not only of Marchesi's voice but also of his very feminine gestures. Everyone in the audience immediately recognized Marchesi, with all his traits, his vocal mannerisms, and his typical movements. The art of the castrato tended to be severely ridiculed in any case, despite its significant vocal contributions. Of course Salieri's little opera had to remain an occasional piece, for it depended on the recognition of such allusions and on that absolutely unique casting; it cannot be separated from its historic context.[9]

Gottlieb Stephanie was the librettist of Mozart's *Entführung aus dem Serail*. His work for this occasion, *Der Schauspieldirektor*, illustrates how plays are mostly put on by independent theater companies at their own expense. It points out that companies can only maintain themselves by improvising a great deal, that responsibility for poor quality lies with the public, which values artistic merit less than dramatic effects, spectacles, and stars. It also argues that despite the prima donna system, opera suffers when a libretto is not up to the standard of the music. When it comes to drama, the expectations are different. There the same ensemble has to perform comedies, tragedies, ballets, and comic operas; all these categories (with the exception of ballet) are successively demonstrated in *Der Schauspieldirektor*.

Mozart's collaboration on this piece was strictly limited to the segment of the play featuring the German *Singspiel*, generally performed by singing actors, so aside from the overture, his contribution consisted only of four sections of *Singspiel* in the final sixth of the text. Salieri, on the other hand, had to compose an hour-long opera. This very unequal contest accounts for the difference in honoraria. Salieri received 100 ducats from the emperor (the regular fee for an opera), whereas Mozart received only half that amount. Anyone familiar with the works and their history will not see this as the affront to Mozart it is always claimed to have been. Mozart would scarcely have had the time to compose a lengthier piece, in any case, for this little interlude interrupted the demanding work on *Le nozze di Figaro* which was to have its premiere three months later. In musical terms, however, *Der Schauspieldirektor* is by no means an unimportant work, for the comic confrontation between two quarreling female singers displays the breadth of Mozart's talent. At the same time, it allows him to demonstrate all the turbulence and richness of color of his orchestration, while always permitting room for breaks in mood and sudden nuances—a remarkable foretaste of the sound of *Figaro*.

Neither Mozart nor Salieri have left any comments on this shared evening of opera. There was no cause whatever for any jealousy, contention, or rivalry. Not even the casting of their two productions could generate envy, for each had obtained exactly the types of male and female singer that he needed. In addition to Aloysia Lange, Mozart could even call on Catarina Cavalieri, a student of Salieri's who has often been quite unjustifiably described as the latter's confidante and mistress. It made for considerable contact between the two men, but this dual performance does not appear to have caused any difficulty between them.

It was a somewhat different matter when it came to *Le nozze di Figaro*, an opera whose length required the utmost attention from audience as well as performers. Moreover, it demanded the best available casting, so the rest of the season had to be planned around this production. That could not be done without causing considerable friction, from the theater management down to the lowliest participant. Aside from the little-documented references to intrigues in connection with this opera, the reports by Da Ponte and others are much too inexact to allow a reliable reconstruction of events. What concerns us here is only whether and to what extent Salieri was caught up in these intrigues, and what his relationship was with Mozart at that time.

As indicated earlier, there is a reference in Kelly's memoirs to "a cabal of three of the principal singers not easily put down," with Salieri in the background. It is not clear what this was about. Later, in connection with the emperor's prohibition of the use of *da capo* arias, Kelly does give three names:

> One morning, while we were rehearsing in the grand saloon of the palace, His Majesty, accompanied by Prince Rosenberg, entered the saloon, and addressing himself to Storace, Mandini and Benuci, said, "I dare say, you are all pleased, that I have desired there shall be no more encores; to have your songs so often repeated, must be a great fatigue, and very distressing to you." Storace replied, "It is indeed, Sir, very distressing, very much so"; the other two bowed, as if they were of the same opinion. I was close to His Majesty, and said boldly to him, "Do not believe them, Sire, they all like to be encored, at least I am sure I always do." His Majesty laughed, and I believe he thought there was more truth in my assertion, than in theirs. I am sure there was.[10]

Indeed, the three singers in question had principal roles, but why should they have been dissatisfied? Did this opera provide too little opportunity for brilliance and bravura? Did they feel they had to exert too much effort for an unsuccessful work? Did they have confrontations with Mozart during the rehearsals? We know nothing more specific. And what of Salieri's part in these cabals? Da Ponte refers mainly to the intrigues of Count Rosenberg, which perhaps involved not only Mozart but Da Ponte himself as well. Nor does the Mozart family's correspondence really yield any information. Leopold Mozart refers to the forthcoming premiere in a letter to his daughter Maria Anna:

> It will be amazing if he succeeds, for I know that he has remarkably powerful cabals opposing him. *Salieri* and all his followers will again try to move heaven and earth. Herr and Madame Duscheck [sic] already told me that your brother has so many cabals working against him because of his special talent and skill and because he is so highly regarded (April 28, 1786).[11]

But Leopold Mozart's "knowledge" is not based on communications from his son, since the most recent reliable letter dates back to the end of February or the beginning of March. It is more likely to have come from accounts by Josepha and Franz Xaver Dussek, who by then had been in Salzburg for more than two weeks. Indeed, what Leopold Mozart says about Salieri amounts only to supposition when examined more closely. "Salieri . . . will *again* . . . move heaven and earth" suggests a repetition, but nothing is known of an earlier intrigue. The comment in this letter is therefore too vague to be a reliable source.

However, there is a noteworthy item in the Mozart literature that has had a particularly malignant effect on Salieri's reputation, and has been uncritically exploited time and again. In his book *Leben des K. K. Kapellmeisters Wolfgang Gottlieb Mozart*, which appeared in 1798, Franz Niemetschek writes with reference to *Le nozze di Figaro*: ". . . how much the whole faction of the Italian singers and composers feared the superiority of Mozart's genius, and how true is what I noted earlier on the occasion of the *Entführung aus dem Serail*."

What he had written about that opera was: "The clever

Italians soon realized that such a genius could prove dangerous to their Italian jingling before long. Envy now set in with all the venom of Italian poison!" He then continued: "This cowardly alliance of undeserving people devoted its entire energy to hating, denigrating, and disparaging the art of this immortal artist until his untimely end."[12]

Though Salieri was not mentioned here either, any reader was bound to associate him with the Italian composers, since he was the only one permanently affiliated with Vienna. Who else, people asked themselves, could it have been? However, Niemetschek, literally blinded by his anti-Italian feelings, cannot really be considered an authentic source. And yet, because this comment was quoted verbatim in the Mozart biography by Georg Nikolaus von Nissen (Konstanze Mozart's second husband), published in 1828, it has been adopted into the annals of Mozart research.

But is there any truth to Salieri's supposed cabals during the rehearsals of *Figaro*? It is fairly certain that there were conflicts with Count Rosenberg, mentioned not merely by Da Ponte and Kelly, but also referred to in contemporary newspapers. There is no proof, however, that Salieri himself played an active part. His contemporaries most likely assumed him to be part of an "Italian faction" headed by Count Rosenberg, whereas Salieri would have tended to avoid such confrontations—if only to safeguard his standing with Joseph II, at whose insistence Count Rosenberg had agreed to the production of Mozart's operas.

At the time Salieri was working on two new operas for which he had received commissions from Paris; as he noted himself, he did so "with the greatest of pleasure, because this debated type of music (*the only truly commendable one*) is generally better performed and more appreciated in Paris than anywhere else."[13] One of these operas, *Tarare*, was also written by Beaumarchais. This was one instance in the relationship between Mozart and Salieri when a shared librettist may have caused some contention between them.

CHAPTER 6

Success with Beaumarchais: "Tarare" 1786–1787

It is difficult to pinpoint how long Beaumarchais had been working on the opera *Tarare*. He mentions the project as far back as 1775, but it probably did not take shape until 1784. Perhaps he actually thought of writing a libretto for Gluck, whose achievements in Paris with *Iphigénie en Aulide* and *Orphée et Euridice* might have encouraged such high hopes. But there is no record that he offered this text to Gluck, or that the latter suggested Salieri instead (an idea that simply duplicates the *Danaïdes* story). At any rate, the text had made such progress by the summer of 1784 that Beaumarchais was able to read from it before an illustrious gathering shortly after the memorable premieres of *La Folle journée ou le Mariage de Figaro* and *Les Danaïdes*. He commented at that time that he now had to find a composer who was worthy of undertaking this great venture.

Salieri and Beaumarchais must have come to know each other personally that summer, at the very latest. The commotion over *Les Danaïdes*, Salieri's obvious connection with Gluck's opera dramaturgy, and perhaps even a familiarity with other works by Salieri, must soon have convinced Beaumarchais that he could work with him. The piece was to be called *Tarare*, meaning "larifari" or mischief, and it was intended to make history. The reading before a distinguished group was supposed to arouse curiosity and produce gossip, which is why Beaumarchais most likely read only excerpts. However, Salieri took the text back to Vienna and worked on it over the next two years—not consistently, because other responsibilities kept interfering, but in all seriousness.

In his biography of Salieri, Mosel refers to the changes Salieri wanted made in the text. He wrote about them to du Roullet, who answered:

> Yesterday I visited Beaumarchais; he has received your two letters, is charmed by them, considers them full of wit and reason, and has firmly decided to accept your wishes. He told me that your letters have greatly increased the esteem in which he holds you and have further augmented the opinion he holds of your merits and your genius.[1]

Beaumarchais returned the altered text promptly.

Did Mozart know that Salieri was also composing a Beaumarchais opera when he first received the libretto for *Le nozze di Figaro* in February 1785, and that Salieri was actually collaborating with this author who was so surrounded by scandal? Mozart was certainly no close friend of Salieri's, but he could easily have found out about it. Michael Kelly, who spent a great deal of time with Mozart, recounts the following anecdote in his memoirs:

> One evening, Salieri proposed to me to accompany him to the Prater. At this time he was composing his opera of Tarare, for the Grand Opera House at Paris. At the back of the cabaret where we had been taking refreshments, near the banks of the Danube, we seated ourselves by the river side; he took from his pocket a sketch of that subsequently popular air which he had that morning composed. *Ah! povero Calpigi.* While he was singing it to me with great earnestness and gesticulation, I cast my eyes towards the river, and spied a large wild boar crossing it, near the place where we were seated. I took to my heels, and the composer followed me, leaving "*Povero Calpigi,*" and (what was worse) a flagon of excellent Rhenish wine behind us . . . The story was food for much laughter, when we were out of danger. Salieri, indeed, would make a joke of anything, for he was a very pleasant man, and much esteemed at Vienna; and I considered myself in high luck to be noticed by him.[2]

Might it not have been Kelly who told Mozart of Salieri's composition—if only by repeating such an anecdote?

By the time Da Ponte was enlisting the support of Joseph II for *Le nozze di Figaro*, the emperor, Salieri, and Mozart were all aware of the unusual situation of two Beaumarchais operas being worked on concurrently in Vienna. It is reasonable to assume that Joseph, who had a feeling for such matters, had in fairness given his consent to both of his protégés. Mozart was permitted to have a performance in Vienna, and Salieri received leave to go to Paris. To be sure, Mozart was not setting an opera libretto to music, but a play that Da Ponte—the very man who happened not to be in Salieri's favor just then—was struggling to convert into an opera. Salieri, however, was able to work on a piece that had originally been conceived as musical drama.

Mozart worked at what was almost suicidal speed. In the seven months it took him to write *Le nozze di Figaro*, he also completed the music for *Der Schauspieldirektor*, three pianoforte concertos, the *Maurerische Trauermusik*, and at least eight other works. In contrast, it took Salieri almost three years to complete *Tarare*. Of course, during that period he also had to finish *La grotta di Trofonio* and the two operas *Prima la musica e poi le parole* and *Les Horaces*, in addition to his duties as Kapellmeister.

Salieri undoubtedly stayed in Vienna for the premiere of *Le nozze di Figaro* (1786), and may even have remained a few extra weeks, as his wife, Theresa, gave birth to their sixth child, Elisabeth Josepha, on June 19. After all, Salieri, who led a model family life, was about to be separated from his domestic bliss for a whole year. He probably set out for Paris at the beginning of July, an assumption that makes sense if one consults the opera schedule. It seems that Salieri's *La grotta di Trofonio* was performed June 26 and 28, and that these were his farewell performances.[3] After that, the opera was performed only once a month until the end of the season. (The program schedule is a sure index of Salieri's presence in Vienna; his influence naturally decreased in his absence.)

While Salieri had only completed certain sections of *Tarare* to take to Paris, his other opera, *Les Horaces*, was finished.

Gluck, who had always been a reliable counselor and friend, had advised him to write *Les Horaces* first, as the other opera would take much longer because of its unique theme and treatment. Gluck had made his suggestion in July 1784, when the management of the Paris Opera had commissioned the two works. Now, three years later, bidding Salieri goodbye, he said encouragingly (and this has to be reproduced verbatim, the way Salieri himself transcribed it): "Ainsi . . . mon cher ami . . . lei parte domani per Parigi . . . Je Vous souhaite . . . di cuore un bon voyage . . . You are going to a city where one values . . . foreign artists . . . e lei si farà onore . . . I have no doubt . . . ci seriva, mais bien souvent."[4]

Indeed, all went well. The rehearsals of *Les Horaces* progressed smoothly, there were no special difficulties, the orchestra was cooperative, as were the singers, and everyone predicted a great triumph. And why not? Salieri had given ample proof of his ability with *Les Danaïdes*, which had become a box-office success in the preceding years. And now came a work based on one of the most famous plays by the great Pierre Corneille, with a libretto by the talented Nicolas François Guillard who, among other things, had written the French text for Gluck's *Iphigénie en Tauride*.

Les Horaces is based on material dating back to the founding of Rome, which Livius had described as being one of the best-known stories of antiquity. In Corneille's version, Romans (the Horati brothers) and Albanians (the Curiati brothers) have long been struggling for supremacy. Camille, the sister of young Horace, loves Curiace and consults an oracle that predicts the end of the dispute for that very day. The elder Horace announces an agreement under which three Roman and three Albanian warriors will fight to decide the victory. The populace enthusiastically agrees. But when the three young Horati brothers and the three Curiati brothers are chosen as opponents, everyone deplores their tragic fate, especially Camille. Horace Senior remains firm in his decision, and young Horace and Curiace arm for battle. The general revolt that ensues necessitates asking the gods once more whether some other warriors might be chosen. When the choice of the warriors is confirmed and the first news of the battle is received, Camille believes her love for him will save her fiancé. The Curiati are reported to have defeated two of the Horati; only young Horace is supposed to have survived, by fleeing. The older Horace curses his son, but then he learns that the latter only pretended to flee, and has meanwhile defeated the three Curiati. Young Horace is led in in triumph, along with the bodies of the Curiati. On seeing her dead fiancé Camille vilifies her brother Horace, who is so proud of himself and his country that he stabs Camille to death.

The opera was performed on December 7, 1786, with this ending, which aroused universal displeasure. Following Salieri's account of the event, Mosel tells of small mishaps during the performance of the first two acts, and continues:

> The third [act] was listened to with the same indifference, and as the scene in which young Horace murders his sister (though taken from history) was loudly criticized, the opera not only ended without applause, but with unmistakable signs of disapproval.[5]

The ending was quickly altered in time for the second performance, with Camille now stabbing herself instead, but this made no difference. Salieri found out how quickly one can lose one's credit in Paris, for the opera was discontinued after three nights.

Of course, the subject and libretto were primarily responsible for the opera's reception, but Salieri's music had to take some of the blame as well. In Corneille's work the conflict between love and duty to the state was clearly resolved. The fourth and fifth acts focus on the consequences of Horace's having murdered his sister: must he pay for it with his death, or shall he be forgiven because he is also the savior of his country? The contentious argumentation of Corneille's tragedy finally places the good of the state above all else, and that ideal could not be translated to the operatic stage. Critics immediately seized on this as their main objection to the work, which doomed it to failure from the start. They rightly questioned why a work by Corneille had to be transferred to the operatic stage at all. La Harpe even spoke of the ridiculous obsession that mutilated the best of French theater in an attempt to turn it into opera, and he was not expressing merely his own rejection of the Gluckist trend. Even the well-meaning *Journal de Paris* found the subject too cold and monotonous. For indeed, the whole work was now centered on Camille, but not firmly enough to develop her role into that of a great tragic female figure. Despite all condensation, the plot stuck too closely to Corneille's work.

As for the music, Salieri did not create the melodic emphasis that the theme of Camille's love deserved—the premonitions, hopes, fears, and finally the curse on the heroics of men who are prepared to sacrifice everything to their victor's pride. Instead, Camille frequently sings the text in recitative or *arioso* form, without being able to hold the audience with a single grand scene. Thus musically lovely details are wasted because they are not part of the dramatic development. The *Mercure de France* put it succinctly: "We believe that the composer is capable of far better things; if he is working on a new piece, he should remember that he has to live up to a fine reputation, that of the music for the Danaides."[6]

The opera received only scathing reviews, but they were deserved. Salieri was even rightly accused of transgressing the rules of prosody. Even those willing to overlook such trifles had to be aware of the absence of musical effects in those scenes that required them. The *Journal de Paris*, certainly well disposed toward Salieri, could not ignore that either. Beaumarchais expressed himself politely: "A truly beautiful work but a bit too gloomy for Paris."[7] Of course, that was supposed to point to *Tarare*, and in a way, to promise that the latter piece would show Salieri from quite a different angle.

Beaumarchais was surely not a librettist to wait and see what the composer was going to do with his material. He left nothing to chance, certainly not the success of a piece that he not only planned but brought into being using every means at his disposal. He believed that, if necessary, one had to invent difficulties and adverse circumstances simply to overcome them. He was a man whom nothing attracted more than the impossible. Yet he was by no means a gambler who wanted to stake all or nothing just for the excitement of risk; he was rather an impetuous man who pursued success, who constantly wanted to prove to himself and to others that he had pursued his goals more effectively than his opponents had. Never at a loss, he always managed to float like a buoy, and his unlimited self-confidence inevitably made him go for all or nothing. He intended *Tarare* to be a complete reform of opera, far surpassing anything Gluck had done. But that required unusually close collaboration with the composer.

Beaumarchais waited until *Les Horaces* opened. Then he invited the disappointed composer to come stay with him, which Salieri did that same December. Beaumarchais provided such a comfortable atmosphere that Salieri praised it decades later in a letter to his host's daughter:

> I went to live with your famous father and your admirable mother, who showered me with much good will and kindness. The two of us used to sit at the piano in the afternoon and play sonatas for four hands. Two hours later, M. or Mme Beaumarchais would come into the room and say: "Come to dinner, children." We would dine, then I would read the papers, go for a walk or to the Palais-Royal, or else to some theater. I came home early. If M. Beaumarchais was not at home, I went up to my room on the second floor and went to bed. Sometimes my servant was drunk. I slept in a room where each day I had the divine pleasure of working as dawn was breaking. Around ten o'clock M. Beaumarchais would come to see me, and I would sing what I had written of our grand opera; he applauded, encouraged me, instructed me in a fatherly manner. It all seemed so peaceful . . .[8]

But what did Salieri actually know about his amiable host? Everyone talked about Beaumarchais, and incredible tales circulated about him. They were not the sort of exotic fantasies that surround a mysterious adventurer; most of the stories had taken place in public in Paris, and people kept being entertained, surprised, or challenged by his doings.

Beaumarchais, born in 1732 as Pierre Augustin Caron, came from a background of honest craftsmen, and was the son of a poor clockmaker. At twenty-one he attracted attention by inventing a novel balance spring for clocks, and defending his invention in the Royal Academy of Sciences against an imitator. Throughout his life he never shied away from lawsuits, and made it his specialty to involve the highest authorities in his interests.

Naturally, he was attracted to the royal court, and managed to get there in a roundabout way. He persuaded the royal princesses (Mesdames de France), who were forced to live in the deadliest isolation, to let him become their unpaid music teacher. He was able to do this because he was an accomplished harpist, and played the flute and viola as well. Before that he had impressed the Marquise de Pompadour with a clock inserted into a ring, which he himself had fabricated; and he was already being invited to the gatherings given by her husband, where he made extensive contacts in high society. The most useful of these was probably with the important financier, Pâris Duverney, who soon allowed him to participate in his financial schemes. Later he even made Beaumarchais one of his heirs, which led to lengthy litigation. Beaumarchais became a wealthy man, purchased titles that he needed to give him status among the aristocracy, and owned a lovely house in the rue de Condé. He was married twice, each time ending as a widower. A nasty rumor had it that he had murdered his wives. His first wife's connections entitled him to call himself Caron de Beaumarchais.

Beaumarchais was a fearless citizen who knew how to expose the corruption of the royal law courts. He came to be known primarily through his numerous lawsuits, which he conducted by involving public opinion in his brilliantly written defenses, or *Mémoires*. With these he established his reputation as a celebrated and sought-after writer, and used them to elevate his private affairs into important matters of state. Though he could not always claim success in his litigations—at times he even had to endure prison and the loss of his civil rights—his litigious pamphlets were always successful. In one instance he was able to sell six thousand copies in three days.

At times Beaumarchais acted as a secret agent on behalf of both Louis XV and Louis XVI, by first forcing himself upon them and then attempting to make himself indispensable. In one instance, he traveled across most of Europe on behalf of Louis XVI to prevent the publication of a libelous pamphlet on Marie Antoinette—which he himself may well have written. In this connection he spent a few weeks in Vienna in 1774 under a pseudonym, but he carried on so that for most of that time he was under arrest and subject to deportation. He was also involved in other affairs of the foolish French king, but never to his financial disadvantage.

Indeed, one of Beaumarchais' greatest coups was to influence his country to adopt a favorable policy toward the English colonies' movement for independence in America. He achieved this by founding a company, Hortalès & Cie., that used state funds to obtain arms for the rebels, shipping them in its own vessels. Very little risk was involved in this venture, since the state paid for any losses. Though Beaumarchais was one of the leading bourgeois of the *ancien régime*, the image he presented to the public was that of a poor, put-upon Figaro who confidently defends himself against harassment by the aristocracy. In fact, he worked both for and against the *ancien régime*, and since he understood how to manipulate finances, he became extremely rich.

However much time he devoted to his business enterprises, he presented himself first and foremost as a writer. He established his reputation with *Le Barbier de Séville*. Its sequel, *La Folle journée ou le Mariage de Figaro*, not only became a literary triumph but a moral victory over thoroughly corrupt social conditions as well. The latter play has rightly been called the "stormy petrel of the French Revolution." Beaumarchais fought for five years to have this play performed, continually drawing both public and aristocratic attention to it. Finally the curiosity of the royal couple got the better of their political wisdom, and the dazzling premiere was allowed to take place.

All this occurred before Salieri went to live with him in 1786, to complete *Tarare*. But what was Beaumarchais up to while Salieri was staying with him? Salieri's later recollection of that period in his correspondence portrayed the man in whose house he spent those agreeable days as an *homme de lettres*, an esthete preoccupied with the theater, literature, and music, who led a peaceful family life. But in reality Beaumarchais was then mainly interested in quite a new venture, which was supposed to combine effectively literary and business interests. He had established his own publishing house, the "Société littéraire et typographique," to bring out the collected works of Voltaire in seventy-one volumes. Unfortunately, it turned into a ruinous misadventure.

As most of Voltaire's writings were forbidden in France, their publication presented a risky undertaking for which extensive guarantees needed to be obtained from the government in a resourceful and diplomatic way. Of course the printing could not be done in France, but Beaumarchais solved that problem by taking a twenty-year lease on the Margrave of Baden's fortress at Kehl, with all its buildings, meadows, and fields, and hunting and fishing rights. He obtained a printing license that also exempted him from censorship, bought English type, and set up a printing press and paper manufacturing plant, and he provided interim financing for the entire enterprise out of his own pocket. An edition of fifteen thousand copies was printed, but there were only two thousand subscribers for a work that was supposed to cost 365 livres, the annual wage of an artisan.

As if all this were not enough, Beaumarchais participated in the "Compagnie des Eaux de Paris," a lucrative business run by the Périer brothers that provided water for Paris by pumping, filtering and selling water from the Seine. And finally, on the day of the premiere of *Tarare*, he bought a large lot across from the Bastille, on which he later built an ostentatiously palatial house. The bourgeois had made it to the top at the very moment of the outbreak of the French Revolution; he had acquired a "box at the theater" that was bound to make him suspect in the eyes of the have-nots.

One wonders whether Salieri was aware of any of this. Beaumarchais behaved as if the arrangements for *Tarare* were his sole concern, and orchestrated a regular fireworks of sensational events, delays, and surprises that can only be seen as a brilliant promotional stunt. In comparison with Beaumarchais' machinations, the intrigues at the Nationaltheater in Vienna amounted to nothing. And he had to have Salieri close by if he wanted him to be and remain a patient collaborator.

Salieri never commented on the goings-on, nor expressed any criticism of his librettist. Indeed, he played along willingly, though Beaumarchais took the leading role. In connection with some disagreements during a rehearsal, the Opera's director Antoine Dauvergne notes in a letter: "I have reason to believe that M. Salieri is one of those wily Italians who is in league with M. de Beaumarchais . . ."[9] On the other hand, a report on one of the rehearsals in the *Mémoires secrets* states that "M. Salieri accompanies him [Beaumarchais] all the time, but the musician is like an underling: he does not utter a word; M. Beaumarchais makes all the comments, even about the music."[10]

As part of his strategy, Beaumarchais first accompanied Salieri to the salons of the nobility and to his rich bourgeois friends. He tempted them by presenting individual scenes from the opera, accompanied by high-flown claims to the effect that it was unlike anything ever seen before, and would create a great furor. Then the first rumors leaked out from the theater that Etienne Lainez had refused to sing the role of Tarare—a conflict that was soon resolved. Next came the matter of a certain prop: Beaumarchais demanded that a bell be brought from Bordeaux, for an opera set in the Orient. There the singers complained that the costumes were not ready. And there were problems about the sets—Beaumarchais was unwilling to use sets from another opera. It was subsequently agreed to rehearse with the old ones, but that new ones would be made for the actual performances at a cost of 30,000 livres.

When the rehearsals were well under way, Salieri suddenly announced to the director that the opening date would have to be postponed by six months, as Beaumarchais was forced to leave for Germany (Salieri was surely just acting as a messenger). Was Beaumarchais bound for Kehl, where things were topsy-turvy at the printing plant? But aside from that, he had an additional reason for delaying the premiere: once again he was involved in a lawsuit, this time quite unnecessarily. The issue was a divorce, the famous Kornmann affair. However, on this occasion circumstances were not propitious; his opponents reacted very strongly, attacking him as a base and immoral creature, even calling him the "scum of the nation," so that this articulate man was almost struck dumb.[11] He had been busily spreading a comment by Count d'Artois, that if the Assemblée des Notables were meeting at the time of the opera's premiere they should recess; now, however, he feared that the work's success might be affected by the lawsuit. Hence he used every means to delay the opening, but the management and the relevant minister remained adamant. Beaumarchais had become a hostage to his own propaganda, and there was no turning back. All of Paris talked of the coming event—it even took precedence over the state budget, for the news that the king's brother and some of the bishops had praised the libretto of *Tarare* was of greater importance.

Even now Beaumarchais had more ideas for publicizing the occasion. Thus he demanded that the text of the libretto be printed only after the performances had begun. After some discussion, it was agreed that it would be generally available following the opening, and that the royal family alone should receive it beforehand. Then Beaumarchais forbade anyone to attend rehearsals, although thirty highly placed personalities, mostly noble ladies, were admitted. When the public dress rehearsal took place on June 4, 1787, the fifth act was booed, whereupon Beaumarchais, striking a "Roman pose" in his box (as reported), delivered a short speech and promised to make changes (that were probably not made). He prohibited any audience at the final rehearsal, so that all the tickets already sold had to be returned.

There was tension until the very last moment. Queen Marie-Antoinette had been advised not to come to the opening, as it was impossible to guarantee that court etiquette would be observed. Such crowds were expected in the streets that for the first time, wooden gates had been erected as a precautionary measure. Four hundred guards were posted in the streets around the Opera for additional safety. Beaumarchais could feel satisfied.

All the excitement surrounding this piece had been perfectly orchestrated. Gifted as he was for publicity, Beaumarchais had alerted the public that something extraordinary was to take place, without divulging too much at an early stage. He had released pieces of information one by one, like the bits of a mosaic; even the scenes read beforehand in society were only excerpts. The title *Tarare* did the rest. It was the name of the leading character, but it also suggested something not serious. Although the opera was set in Hormuz, on the outer edge of Persia, any fairly educated person knew better than to associate it with a real Asiatic kingdom, and that meant it probably dealt with serious matters. Just as in Charles de Montesquieu's work *Les Lettres persanes*, this politically disruptive opera needed the exotic setting as a device to reflect conditions in France. The libretto as well as the music made good on the expectations of something unprecedented.[12]

A lengthy prologue consisting of three scenes preceded the five-act work: "The overture begins with howling winds and a terrible upheaval of the elements. The curtain rises on a view of turbulent rolling clouds that part to reveal the unleashed winds; they whirl in a violent dance." Nature enters and "says commandingly":

> Enough of confusion in the universe; angry winds,
> stop unsettling air and sea.
> Enough, put your chains back on:
> Zephyr alone shall rule the world. (Prologue,
> Scene 1.)

This opening contains a synopsis of the whole plot, deliberately contrived by the intervention of Nature. Aided by the Genie of Fire, Nature turns cold, lifeless phantoms into characters whose actions after forty years in the world are described in this opera in an ironic interplay.

The first act begins with a dialogue between Atar, king of Hormuz—a sinister, cruel despot—and Calpigi, the chief eunuch, who enjoys a position of trust, although a European slave. Calpigi puts in a good word for Tarare, an important army officer whose virtue makes him popular with one and all. But Atar is jealous of Tarare because the latter is happy, whereas the king is not. Though Tarare once saved the king from death (and Calpigi as well), such achievements count for little with the moody king. Tarare is to be made to suffer, and hence the king commands that in Tarare's absence his house be set on fire and his beloved wife Astasie be captured and taken to the royal harem. The order has been carried out by Tarare's rival Altamort, son of the high priest and savage general of the army. As a reward, he is given the rank of vizier. Atar visits the terrified Astasie, who accuses the king of his crime in front of all the harem servants. Atar gives her a new name, Irza, and with threats he orders Spinette—a European slave, described as *intrigante et coquette*, who is Calpigi's unloved wife— to make Astasie ready for him.

Having shown the uninhibited and vengeful side of his nature, the next scene reveals Atar's perfidiousness and baseness. Tarare appears before him and complains that in the midst of peace he has experienced the horrors of war, his gardens have been laid waste, his slaves murdered, and his house burned. Atar offers him his palace, together with slaves and a hundred Circassian beauties just waiting for his commands (this disturbs Altamort, who is present). Tarare now laments the capture of Astasie and sings a moving aria ("Astasie est une déesse" [Astasie is a goddess]). But Atar answers quite unfeelingly, "What? A soldier crying over a woman? Your king no longer recognizes you. You may have lost the object of your passion, but here an entire harem awaits you." (Act 1, Scene 6.) Tarare, however, asks the king's permission to look for Astasie and avenge her. His wide-eyed innocence cannot be deflected.

At the beginning of the second act, the high priest announces that the country is threatened by the arrival of a group of savages. They are Christians, and that means that the temple as well as the throne is in danger and must be defended. The priest says that it is important to make the people think the battle is being fought under divine guidance. He suggests that a commander be chosen by a child soothsayer who can be appropriately influenced. The king suggests Altamort. The high priest warns against by-passing Tarare, as he is the idol of his soldiers. But the king wants to have Tarare killed as he searches for Astasie. He therefore suggests that the priests prepare a grand ceremony to deceive the people when a commander is proclaimed. The high priest agrees because he already sees his son as commander in chief: "When kings are afraid the priests rule; the Persian tiara is about to enlarge its sphere and who knows, perhaps my son will become ruler of the world one day." (Act 2, Scene 3.)

Meanwhile, Calpigi reveals to Tarare that Astasie is a prisoner in the king's harem; Tarare decides to rescue her, dead or alive. Then the priests' sacrificial rites begin. The soldiers and the populace swear obedience to the one chosen by the god Brahma and announced by the child soothsayer Elamir to be the commander in chief. But at the decisive moment the boy calls out "Tarare," and everyone is delighted. The high priest questions Elamir, who explains, "Heaven told me to say Altamort, but Tarare came out of my mouth." (act 2, scene 8.) (The word "Tarare," which means nonsense, is here used as a sort of pun.) Altamort is enraged, and begins to argue angrily with Tarare. The latter challenges him to a duel for that evening, outside the temple.

In the third act, Atar commands Calpigi to arrange a feast in the harem. Calpigi tries in vain to delay the feast so as to inform Tarare of it. The king learns that Altamort has been killed in a duel. Calpigi meanwhile has prepared a European-style feast, at which an interlude is performed that compares European monogamy with the advantages of the harem. Atar crowns Irza (Astasie) as the sultana, and homage is paid to her, but she thinks only of Tarare. The king thanks Calpigi for the successful feast and asks him to sing. In a barcarole, he describes his life: how he was born in Ferrara and trained to be a singer; how he married out of wantonness, was captured by corsairs, then sold as a slave, and finally was saved by Tarare.

On hearing this name, there is a general outcry; Atar is furious, Astasie faints and is taken away. The king follows her and leaves his coat and boots outside her door. The others flee. Tarare now appears, observed only by Calpigi, who quickly disguises him as a mute negro. The king returns and sees the negro. Having been repulsed by Astasie, he is again unpredictably wrathful. First he thinks of having the negro beheaded, then arrives at an even more devilish plan. He will punish

Astasie by letting the negro force her to become his bride—an idea that excites him. Calpigi is shocked, but simulates agreement.

The fourth act shows the desperate Astasie ("O mort! termine mes douleurs" ["O death, let my suffering end"]), whom even Spinette cannot console. Now Calpigi informs her that a mute negro is to be her new husband. She is so wretched that when she is alone again, she asks Spinette to impersonate her. This means that Tarare (who is disguised as the negro) will not be reunited with Astasie, whereas Spinette (in her role of Astasie-Irza) finds him attractive. King Atar now comes up with another fiendish scheme, and wants to have the negro thrown into the sea as food for the crocodiles. Calpigi tries to protect him by refusing the soldiers entry into the harem to take him prisoner, and then reveals the negro's identity: it is really Tarare whom they are arresting. Calpigi is now in great danger himself, and plays his last card: "So be it! Abuse of the highest authority will eventually rock everything to its foundations. The evil one whom all fear will finally begin to tremble himself." (Act 4, Scene 8.)

The fifth act shows the king inspecting a stake being made ready for Tarare. He commands the high priest to pronounce a death sentence on the intruder into the harem. Tarare is led in, and warns Atar that in killing him he is only punishing himself; his many crimes will one day unleash the anger of his people. Astasie has also been condemned to death. She and Tarare are united at the stake and embrace each other for the last time. Angered again, Atar demands that Astasie watch Tarare die. Now the soldiers rush in and request that Tarare become their general. They indicate that if he is put to death, they will punish the barbaric king. That is open revolt, so Tarare intervenes and urges them to restrain themselves: "A rebellious mob is simply disastrous for the state. Is it up to you to judge your masters? Are you being paid by traitors? In taking power into your own hands, you soldiers, have you forgotten that respect for the king [in later republican versions of the text the word "rois" or "king" became "lois" or "laws"] is the highest commandment? Put your weapons down, you madmen! Your king will discharge you." The soldiers go down on their knees, as does Tarare, who says to the king, "Majesty, they submit; I ask you to have mercy on them." (Act 5, Scene 6.)

Thus Tarare, about to be burned at the stake, is still obedient and willing to use his influence on the soldiers, though the king is a cruel and inhuman despot. But the king is beside himself as he realizes that he is still dependent on Tarare. His ego is so wounded that he asks those around him whether he is still their king. Most of them shout no. Calpigi points to Tarare, and the populace and soldiers joyfully agree to have him rule instead. Atar grows desperate and shouts at Tarare, "Monster . . . all of them have been bought . . . so take my place." And as he stabs himself to death, he says, "Death is easier for me than ruling over you . . . over this hateful nation." (Act 5, Scene 6.)

Calpigi uses the occasion to address the populace: "A single word can make up for all the injustice of his rule. He is leaving the throne to Tarare." (Act 5, Scene 7.) Everyone agrees enthusiastically, but Tarare does not wish to accept the honor, preferring instead to lead a private and peaceful life with Astasie. One of the soldiers then tells him that if he is unwilling to become king, they will take advantage of the chains that are still confining him, and crown him against his wishes. Tarare finally gives in, but wants to keep his chains as a symbol of his striving for the welfare of the state. Clouds gather over the proceedings. As in the prologue, a Fire Genie and Nature arrive together to declaim the quintessence of the work. The Genie speaks: "Nature! What an awe-inspiring and calamitous example this is! The soldier ascends the throne and the tyrant is dead." Nature answers: "The gods gave them only a throne without a destiny; their character did the rest." Nature and the Genie sing the concluding verses together:

> Mortal, whether prince, priest or soldier
> *Man!* your status on this earth
> is not determined by your rank
> but by your character alone. (Act 5, Scene
> 10.)

Beaumarchais also wrote a variant conclusion—"for times and countries where it would be considered a mistake if the opera did not finish with a celebration"—in which the opera ends with an homage to Tarare and Astasie sung by the chorus:

> Your Majesty, we submit (our freedom)
> to your great virtue;
> rule over your people who love you,
> using law and justice."

Beaumarchais added a further comment: "I would prefer the first version, which is more philosophical and appropriate to the subject. The choice is yours; my task is completed." Salieri ultimately set both versions to music; the more "philosophical" first ending was the one used for the premiere. The alternate conclusion was used in the first scene of the "Couronnement de Tarare," the epilogue written for the performance of *Tarare* on August 3, 1790, to celebrate the "Fête de la Fédération."

It was indeed an extraordinary and unusual work, full of striking situations, sumptuous images, and a fanciful combination of characters. The subject was not taken from mythology or history. Beaumarchais had written a sort of experimental piece about a king who is motivated by despotism, inhumanity, and the abuse of power. This monarch does not shrink from any crime, be it murder, barbaric force, or the misuse of religion—he is a man whose excesses end in his own suicide. In contrast, there is Tarare, a courageous soldier and affectionate lover, who carries virtue and legality to impossible ends. He lives by his moral standards, but does not use them to obtain political power, for that would mean rebelling against the king, despicable as his rule is. Finally, there are the people, whose subjection is extreme and who make a choice only when it is unavoidable. There are also such strange characters as Calpigi, whose bizarre fate takes him from being a castrato in Naples to becoming the chief eunuch in a harem—a Christian serving an oriental despot. Or there is his wife Spinette, bound to him in an impossible marriage, who appears to have adapted quite well to life in a harem. Though both are comic characters, they are not intended merely to provoke laughter, for they have maintained an admirable humanity despite their horrible fate.

Beaumarchais had a premonition of what lay ahead, and based his sensational plays on the tremors he registered in the prerevolutionary conditions of the *ancien régime*. Without questioning the monarchy's right to exist, he had depicted the downfall of a tyrant, and the possibility of a more deserving candidate succeeding him. He had turned the impossible into something plausible and logical; and having opted for the people, had thus contributed what he considered beneficial to the political debate. Of course, the piece contained built-in protection for its author: though it could be read as a revolutionary statement, it could also serve as a warning against revolt, or as an emphatic expression of loyalty to the monarchy. It was a brilliant work that every spectator could interpret according to his own political inclination, while the crafty Beaumarchais straddled the fence. This was precisely what the now-sensitized society of Paris held against him. For some the piece was too revolutionary, for others too appeasing. But many found it interesting because of its ambiguity, which meant that the work continued to be highly popular under each of the following regimes. With relevant changes, it became palatable for revolutionary, Napoleonic, or Bourbon tastes.

The challenging innovation of this opera was also contained in the underlying concept of music theater that Salieri expressed in musical language. In a foreword entitled "To the Subscribers of the Opera Who Want to Love Opera," Beaumarchais professed his support for the further development of Gluck's opera reform.[13] He was certainly not one to be satisfied with existing forms of *tragédie lyrique*, and to abide by rules, conventions, and the demands of *bienséance* (propriety). Moreover, he wrote as a playwright, not a musician, which of course determined the nature of his views. He was concerned with what opera stood for in terms of the Enlightenment:

> The last century is characterized as an outstandingly literary one; but what does literature amount to among so many useful things? A superior

intellectual pastime. Ours is a century known for its science and philosophy, rich in discoveries, full of power and reason. The spirit of the nation seems to enjoy critical but happy circumstances; a bright and widespread light permits everyone to feel that progress is possible. People are inquisitive, move about, invent, reform; and from the great competence that characterizes the government to the superficial talent for composing a *chanson*, from the heights of genius that make us admire Voltaire and Buffon to the facile and lucrative business of criticizing what one is unable to produce oneself, I observe in all classes the desire to amount to something, to triumph, to spread one's ideas, knowledge, and pleasures, that can only be of universal benefit; and this is how everything grows, prospers and flourishes. Let us try, if possible, to improve this great Spectacle.

For Beaumarchais the text is most important, the music is merely "a new art of embellishing words"; it is only "a more powerful way of showing feelings or thoughts," but, as he promptly adds, "let us be careful not to misuse these means, not to become too extravagant in this type of coloration." Each word must be comprehensible, each sentence must be heard in its natural rhythm. He keeps warning against the use of "too much" music, whether it is in a dense orchestral movement, an extended aria, or simply the repetition of words dependent on music. Presumably he mistrusted the ability of the music to express beliefs, impressions, and emotions clearly. On the other hand, he wanted to transform opera into realistic music theater—even if that is not what he calls it. And it required a new type of libretto.

Beaumarchais' concept of a libretto was that of a generally interesting topical drama and the replacement of historic or mythological material with current subjects, whose multiple political, social, and philosophical aspects could be developed. He envisaged a theater in which tragedy, comedy, and other categories would be integrated. His type of theater also did away with typical overblown language, and instead employed a varied idiom that did not shy away from colloquialisms; it was direct, rapid, and tailored to a given situation. Simplicity of expression was more important than propriety. And instead of long monologues, Beaumarchais preferred to make use of dialogue in its many forms.

In his foreword to *Tarare*, Beaumarchais did not outline a

new esthetic of the opera, but introduced the special features of this particular work, and outlined the experiences and thoughts on which it was based. He included in it a self-defense, in which he took full responsibility for the work. He was prompted to do this because the disproportionate length of the libretto subjected its musical transposition to unusual restrictions, and a close working relationship between librettist and composer became an absolute necessity for Beaumarchais. But he was lucky in that—as he puts it—"Salieri is a born poet and I am somewhat of a musician." And he praises Salieri for "having the strength to eliminate for my sake a great deal of beautiful music that graced his opera, because it would merely expand a scene and make the action seem dull. But the strong color, the fast-paced and proud tone of the work, compensate him for this sacrifice."

Yet Salieri was willing to enter into close cooperation with a librettist who kept saying that "too much music is one of the biggest mistakes of our grand opera," and who provided in his libretto little opportunity for big arias or ensembles. He was ready to work with someone who had always been bored by traditional French opera, and who wanted to create something completely new. Salieri, the Italian raised in Vienna, was amenable to becoming a musical partner in an unprecedented attempt to revitalize French opera. This presupposed that his music would not interfere with the comprehensibility of the text; that he would aim for correspondence between musical expression and dramatic content; that he would not merely subject himself to Beaumarchais' requirements, but would adopt them as his own, and thus become the co-author of a *Gesamtkunstwerk*. As the admirer of Gluck who had been the first to follow in his footsteps, Salieri was the most appropriate person for this task; moreover, he had the advantage of being able to consult his mentor when he first began to work on the new opera. One can even say that the basic ideas for it were conceived under Gluck's tutelage.

The opera is completely through-composed as a kind of huge recitative lasting close to three and a half hours. The music is very lively, full of color, variety, musical density, and

power of expression, though it always serves as an interpretation of the text and never acquires an independent life of its
own. The entire opera is declaimed, nothing is merely spoken,
but the declamation moves from the simplest *parlando* to
dramatic song, with every conceivable transition and shading
indicated quite meticulously in the score. Cantabile sections
develop out of the recitative environment, as it were, and are
rarely longer than twenty beats, when they are interrupted
again and cut off by insertions. Tarare and Astasie have the
largest share of these quite simple, melodic, but unornamented
lyrical arias. The sections in which King Atar rages like a wild
animal about to pounce for the final kill provide little opportunity for the use of *arioso*, but most of the time he is contrasted
with the nimble-minded and witty Calpigi, a histrionic figure
who is anything but a *buffo* character. There are no stereotypes
in *Tarare*; both text and music bring out the individual personalities of the characters. The music, moreover, reflects personal
feelings as well as complex situations onstage. There is no
opportunity for a big love scene between Tarare and Astasie,
as they do not meet until their encounter at the stake.

It seems as if Beaumarchais wanted to avoid as far as
possible whatever the public took for granted. On the other
hand, Salieri turned the scene in which Spinette (as Astasie/
Irza) is attracted to Tarare (as the mute negro) into an
overscored *duo dialogué* showpiece that sounds almost like a
love duet. Salieri's music lends an ironic note to the work that
is in complete harmony with Beaumarchais. There is no room
for pathos; to avoid it, Beaumarchais even uses poorly chosen
verse and "unsuitable" expressions, and Salieri avoids any
untoward grandeur by keeping his recitative tightly controlled,
fast-paced, and open at all times to musical commentary and
emphases.

The choruses play an important role in all of the acts; often
they are simple but extremely effective segments. The ballet
grows out of the action, not merely as a concession to a ballet-
oriented audience, but as an integral component of the ceremony Calpigi arranges for Atar in the third act. A short
pastoral entr'acte by "European" choruses is inserted in this

ballet, which discusses the various ways of dealing with love. Thus the ballet loses its predominance, though it consists of several lengthy but attractively orchestrated parts. Calpigi's ballad-like barcarole, a strophic song with a refrain ("Ahi, povero Calpigi") that is taken up by the chorus, ends the ceremony when all express fear at the sound of Tarare's name. In this way music acquires a more independent role in the third act, which is twice as long as the other acts. The fourth act, which takes place in the harem, also has many lyrical sections in which declamation forms a transition to *ariosos*. At the end of the act Calpigi even sings an aria with an extended *da capo* (the one in which he foretells the tyrant's ultimate demise), and this is the turning point of the opera.

Salieri certainly found enough musical possibilities in this work. His main concern, as it had been Gluck's, was to avoid overemphasizing the music so as not to detract from the interest of the opera as theater. Nevertheless, Beaumarchais was anxious that the opera not be musically thin. Salieri understood this distinction only too well. He even wrote two overtures: one preceding the prologue, which presents the amorphous universe in which the characters of the opera are created; the other, "completely different from the first one" as he defines it, introducing the first act, and relating it entirely to the world of Hormuz.

Salieri avoided the pitfall of "too much music" by using richly varied and distinctive music to support and clarify the action of the drama without having it assume an independent weight of its own. The orchestra consisted of a normal complement of two each of flutes, oboes, and clarinets, four bassoons, two horns, two *clarini* (or trumpets), and three trombones. In addition, there were strings and percussion, the latter made up of cymbals and a bass drum, which lent an oriental tone. The brass section was generally reserved for Atar, whereas the woodwinds were used for Tarare and Astasie, but this was done unobtrusively without any schematization. Oboes were frequently given solos, clarinets lent an alluring darker coloring, and the effective use of the strings revealed Salieri's complete artistry in orchestration.

Beaumarchais and Salieri had not miscalculated. The opera made a powerful impact on the public. Surely this was not merely thanks to a libretto that contravened all conventions of opera, or to an unusually lively and exciting plot, but also to the music. This music, inspired by close observation of the dramatic events, determined the overall pace of the action. Its beauty did not develop through appealing cantilenas, but entirely as dramatic enhancement. Yet the music was scarcely acknowledged by unappreciative critics, who saw it as a negligible ingredient added to Beaumarchais' work, rather than an integral element of it.

The first-night audience remained very quiet and attentive during the performance. There was some occasional displeased muttering about the crude and violent behavior of Atar; and when Tarare demanded respect for the monarchy as one's highest duty, there were partisan demonstrations. But the performance concluded without any serious disruption. Individual sections of the music were much applauded, among them, naturally, the barcarole by Calpigi, the duet in the fourth act, and especially the choruses, which were so impressive throughout. There was great applause at the end, and calls for the authors. Beaumarchais was nowhere to be seen, and could not be found, so the actors let Salieri receive the ovations for a work the likes of which had never been seen before.

Tarare remained the biggest box-office success of the Paris Opera for decades. Thirty-three performances in the first nine months brought in more than a quarter of the Opera's revenue that year. The unusual popularity of this piece was not simply an expression of enthusiasm, but reflected its much-discussed novelty and sensationalism—soon parodied in numerous small Paris theaters. But reviews were generally disparaging, and referred to the work as a "dramatic monstrosity such as has never been seen before and may never be seen again."[14] Only the *Mercure de France* tried to do justice to the work, in a comprehensive discussion that took up almost forty pages spread over three issues. It is the only critique that gives the music its due, because "it is important for young people studying this model to learn to differentiate what one should copy from what one should avoid." Finally, the review tried to play Salieri off against Beaumarchais by telling the composer to note that "he may rest assured that the beautiful melodies will always retain their irresistible influence over the feelings of listeners; that they will always suitably express all passions, even the most violent ones; and that a beautiful song can never weaken the action if it occurs at the right place."[15] That is indeed the way in which Salieri's duly praised musical virtues, so unequivocally emphasized, must hold their own against Beaumarchais' dramatic-operatic intentions.

CHAPTER SEVEN

Shifting Winds 1787–1790

Salieri returned to Vienna in July 1787, having stayed in Paris just long enough to enjoy the great initial success of *Tarare*. The opera was performed six times in both June and July, after which it was given two to three times a month. By the end of the year he already received bonuses of 4,500 livres (about 1,500 gulden), the Paris Opera being the only one that not only paid an honorarium but also a percentage of the performance profits; moreover, the scores of the works were published.

Naturally French librettists competed for the attention of this successful composer, and brought him the most varied libretti, including a text based on Shakespeare's *The Tempest*. However, it all came to nothing in the end—presumably owing to a lack of time, but also on account of political events connected with the French Revolution. The only commission he did not want to turn down was for a cantata, *Le Jugement dernier*. It was originally given to Gluck, who had begun to write it during his last stay in Paris, but was unable to complete it. The cantata was commissioned by one of the numerous concert associations, the "Société des Enfants d'Apollon," and Salieri promptly began work on it.

During this time Salieri met with Gluck frequently, if only to seek his advice on the composition of the cantata. Mosel reports that Salieri had just [reached] "the part where Christ begins to speak," and had asked Gluck:

> whether he approved of his intention to write this part in a high tenor (*tenore acuto*), the work being intended for France, where this register is commonly used in the key and designation of contralto, and especially as it is more penetrating than any other. *Gluck* agreed with his idea and added, half-seriously and half-jokingly, "I shall soon be able to report to you with certainty from the other world in which key our Savior speaks." Four days later (on November 15, 1787) this great man was taken from the world![1]

Salieri was very much affected by Gluck's death. He owed a great deal to Gluck who, next to Gassmann—and especially after the latter's early death—had been the one to give Salieri crucial musical ideas and advice. Moreover, no one else, aside from Emperor Joseph II, had supported and promoted his musical career so consistently, especially by passing on commissions. Yet if in early years Salieri's work reflected something of the admired master's style, he by no means automatically accommodated himself to the expectations linked with Gluck's name. For Salieri was clearly developing an independent language for the music theater that was taking Gluck's suggestions in quite new directions. Gluck had primarily chosen classical tragedies for his reform operas, for which he had developed an integrated and contained style, and a lofty, pathetic, yet highly dramatic musical language. Salieri, on the other hand, became increasingly preoccupied with music theater that portrayed tragic and comic aspects concurrently, and also included satire; he blended all these elements together, using a varied musical style.

Salieri knew he had lost a true friend in Gluck, and saw it as his task to pay homage to the great composer. The Tonkünstler Society, to which almost all musicians in Vienna belonged, rejected the idea of having a memorial concert, as Gluck had not been a member, and had paid little heed to the affairs of the organization. The association's small-minded attitude thus prevented this tribute from being paid, although it would have reflected honor on the Viennese musicians themselves. Salieri therefore conducted a requiem for Gluck, by Niccolo Jommelli, in the parish church of the royal court; he also used the occasion to perform a *De Profundis*, which was the last work Gluck had written.

The success of *Tarare* had naturally aroused curiosity in Vienna as well. Emperor Joseph himself encouraged an Italian translation of the work, which Lorenzo Da Ponte as the official theater dramatist was ready to do. Any previous discord between Salieri and Da Ponte was long since forgotten—besides, the latter was not expected to write a new piece, only to undertake an adaptation.

According to Mosel, Salieri and Da Ponte

> . . . met every morning for three or four days, and worked on this task together, though with little pleasure as they were unconvinced of the good results of their efforts. "Music," said Salieri, "written for *French actors who sing*, always renders too little song for *Italian singers who act*. Moreover, when the poet was satisfied with his verses, the music—to quote *Gluck*—smacked too much of translation; and when the words were adapted to the existing music, to satisfy my ears, then *Da Ponte* was displeased with his verses. Out of concern that the two of us might work in vain, I decided rather to compose some new music for the material. I requested the poet to devise a new scheme for the verses based on the French original and suitable for the Italian Opera ensemble; he was to distribute the singing segments as agreed to by me, aside from which he could write the verses as he saw fit; I would take care of the rest."
> That is what happened. The work began anew, and poet and composer took the chosen path hand in hand. Wherever the latter could use a musical idea from the French version, he did so; where it was impossible, he composed completely new music.[2]

That sounds much easier than it was. And if one looks at the result, one has to conclude that nothing of the French original remained completely unaltered, and that more than half of it was entirely new. Indeed, the French declamatory style could not simply be translated into Italian, especially in view of the differences between the two types of performer. These differences required not only a change in the music, but a different text as well, which would do justice to the clearly differentiated recitative and *arioso* sections.

The structure of the plot remained the same, except for

the elimination of the prologue. However, the characters'
names were changed: Atar, king of Hormuz became Axur,
while Tarare was now called Atar; and Calpigi, the overseer
of the harem, became Biscroma. Even the title of the Italian
version was altered to *Axur, rè d'Ormus*. This put the emphasis
on the fate of the Asiatic despot instead of on Atar (Tarare),
the king chosen by the people, although the ending remained
the same. The new version is considerably more concentrated,
some of the contentious dialogue having been shortened, and
compares favorably with Da Ponte's transformation of *La Folle
journée* into *Le nozze di Figaro*.

Once again—as had happened with Mozart's *Figaro*—it was
Joseph II who wanted to see this Beaumarchais opera put on
in Vienna. He must have known what *Tarare* was about, and
had probably seen the score before asking Salieri to turn it
into an Italian opera.[3] It was not the emperor's desire that the
work be changed, or that anything "offensive" be eliminated.
He was thinking merely in terms of a translation, not a
reworking or a new version, as is shown in the following
anecdote recorded by Mosel in great detail:

> The emperor . . . wanted to hear whatever was completed at his
> usual afternoon concert. Accordingly, he had the originals fetched from
> the copyists, and requested the attendance of his musicians. . . . The
> emperor sat at the pianoforte and began to read: "Act 1, scene 1, duet."
> The musicians answered, "The French opera begins with a prologue."
> "They must have omitted that in the translation," His Majesty replied,
> "look for the first scene." "This version," said the musicians, "begins with
> a recitative in dialogue form." "In my copy," the monarch responded,
> "the opera opens with a duet that serves as an introduction, followed by
> an aria and then a short duet." "We cannot find any of that," they
> answered. Almost two hours went by, during which they searched and
> compared, without finding anything that corresponded entirely . . . Then
> the monarch laughed and called out, "It's enough to drive one mad!
> What in heaven's name have those two done? Go to *Salieri*," he com-
> manded the orchestra's director, *Kreibich*, who was always present at
> these concerts, "and tell him about the farce we went through here."

When Salieri met Joseph II some days later, the latter said:

> ". . . you almost drove us to distraction with your music two days
> ago. Tell me, why did you change your lovely French music to such an
> extent?" When *Salieri* explained the reasons for it, which we already

know, the emperor not only agreed completely, but after having heard
and praised the Italian version, he gave the composer a royal reward
for his efforts.[4]

It is unlikely that Joseph's motive for having this opera
performed was simply to give the Viennese public a chance to
see a successful French work by his protégé; rather, his
intentions were similar to those that permitted the performance
of Mozart's *Figaro*. Italian opera, it will be remembered, catered
to a largely aristocratic audience at the Nationaltheater. But
most of the nobility were not exactly supporters of Joseph's
reformist policies, especially since the emperor was seriously
and resolutely pursuing his plan to do away with their privileges.
What they opposed most strongly was the project to tax their
property; an extensive survey of all domains was already under
way. But Joseph's reforms also included provisions for the
equal treatment of the nobility and all other citizens under the
law. Any other ruler would have seen this ambitious program
as a way of concentrating power in his own hands, and
excluding individuals whose privilege was a threat. But Joseph
II was not a Sun King concerned purely with absolutism; he
considered himself an enlightened emperor of the people. His
missionary-like zeal was focused on doing his reasonable best
(as he saw it); he did not wish his legitimacy to depend on
hereditary rights, but on his usefulness and unconditional
support for the welfare of all his people. Convinced of this as
he was, it would have made him happy to be accused of being
an enlightened despot, or a despotic enlightener.

Despotic rule out of sheer caprice, despotism out of wantonness, abuse of power for one's own advantage—of which
many European rulers were guilty—all were anathema to
Joseph II. And surely this was what *Tarare* was all about. The
opera questioned the legitimacy of sovereignty; it dealt with
the failure of the church to fulfill its real duties, and with
priests willing to form alliances with secular power in order to
deceive the people. The work was a demonstration of utterly
corrupt and lawless despotism, and showed how legitimacy is
earned. This Italian opera, as didactic drama intended for the

nobility, suited the emperor's efforts at reform very well. There was nothing in it he considered objectionable.

That autumn Da Ponte was working on three opera libretti simultaneously: one for Vicente Martín y Soler's opera *L'arbore di Diana*, which was first performed on October 1, 1787; another the text for Mozart's *Don Giovanni*, which had its premiere in Prague on October 29; and finally *Axur*. Da Ponte's work for Mozart was not part of his duties as dramatist at the Viennese Nationaltheater. But writing three such different pieces at the same time was a most unusual feat. Da Ponte notes in his memoirs that he told only the emperor of the three-fold task he had undertaken, and when the latter expressed his concern, Da Ponte answered, "At night I shall write for Mozart and think I'm reading Dante's *Inferno*; in the morning I'll work for Martin and imagine I'm studying 'Petrarch'; and in the evening it will be Salieri's turn, and I shall remember my 'Tasso.' "[5]

Yet such a schedule did make for complications. Da Ponte left for Prague right after the first night of *L'arbore di Diana*, in order to be present at the rehearsals of *Don Giovanni*, in case any changes had to be made. But after a few days he received an urgent letter from Salieri, requesting his return to Vienna to work on *Axur*. That was an official order, so to speak. Da Ponte was therefore unable to remain for the premiere of *Don Giovanni*, which had been postponed by some days. However, there is no need to see Salieri's letter as a deliberate attempt to create difficulties for Mozart. The opening of *Axur* had been scheduled to celebrate the wedding of Archduke Franz with Princess Elisabeth Wilhelmine of Württemberg; it was to be a special occasion, as the archduke would eventually succeed Joseph II. In view of the extensive work required to create what was practically a new Italian opera, time was now of the essence, and Da Ponte was indispensable.

It was undoubtedly Joseph II himself who chose *Axur* for the gala performance, and the reason for the royal uncle's choice was obvious. He wanted to give his nephew and successor a piece of advice on sovereignty, and to provide a free lesson to the nobility who were involved, and would in future become more so, in government—even if many of them failed to grasp the work's significance on opening night.[6] The other court officials, such as Count Rosenberg-Orsini, who administered the royal theaters, would have preferred a ceremonial, decorative, and politically safe piece.

The opera was staged with care, in keeping with such an important event. Nothing was spared in new sets, especially the garden scene in the fourth act, which was filled with fountains and featured the most lavish lighting. No reviews of the production have survived, but the fact that the opera was given seven times in four weeks speaks for its success (there were twenty-eight performances by the end of the year). And it was this new version (and not *Tarare*) that immediately became popular throughout Europe in numerous translations. There were several German ones, one each into Russian and Polish, and in 1814 there was even a production in Rio de Janeiro, in Portuguese. Based as it was on an avant-garde transformation of French traditional opera, it was unlikely to gain a following outside of France, but Da Ponte had cleverly managed to give it a form that ensured its worldwide acclaim. And Salieri had composed music of an extraordinary caliber, a masterpiece in a completely new genre previously unknown in the Italian Opera repertory.

Da Ponte had meanwhile become an experienced librettist, undoubtedly having learned from Mozart what kind of opportunities the text must provide for the music. Hence, he tried to convert into action the many anecdotes that in *Tarare* are declaimed. At the very beginning, Da Ponte wrote a love scene between Atar (Tarare) and Aspasia (Astasie) that is suddenly interrupted by a fire in Atar's nearby house; during the ensuing confusion Aspasia is abducted. Beaumarchais, on the other hand, merely had a dialogue between the king and Calpigi (Biscroma in Da Ponte's version), in which the former envies the lovers and orders the capture of Astasie (Aspasia). This is only one of many such examples. Da Ponte's emphasis on stage action still left room for singing, even *da capo* arias, duets, and quartets, where Salieri blended traditional forms with completely free ones that depend entirely on the dramatic moment; he also added a number of insertions or breaks. The normal alternation of recitatives and arias was largely forgone in favor of a through-composed work that featured relatively few *secco* recitatives. Accompanied recitatives were composed in such a way that the transitions to song forms were quite organic. Salieri tried everything in this opera, from *parlando* recitatives to dramatic outbursts, undoubtedly influenced by his experience with French declamation.

Instead of ballet, which had been an indispensable element of the Paris production, Da Ponte used a harlequin interlude for the king's festivity that fitted in well with the constant interplay of tragic, heroic, and comedic aspects of the opera. This mix of different levels of style was more marked in *Axur* than in *Tarare*, where the brilliance of the work resulted from the fast-paced dialogue. Da Ponte gave Salieri far greater opportunity to use contrasting passages to develop characterization and create a varied dramatic effect. On the other hand, Da Ponte had to give up the lengthy argumentative and discursive elements used by Beaumarchais if he wanted to intensify the action on stage. To regard *Axur* merely as an attempt to popularize *Tarare* by adapting it to the Italian Opera (at the price of reducing its philosophical implications and the nuances of its dialogue) is to miss the exceptional importance of this work in the history of opera. It was a milestone in the transformation of the Italian genre into multi-leveled music theater. And with the French Revolution developing, even the Italian version was a cryptic political commentary on sovereignty and legitimacy, and on the *ancien régime* and its likely demise.

Though the Viennese adaptation eliminated much of *Tarare* that was too closely related to the situation in France and the ongoing debates there, it did not delete anything significant; it specifically preserved from Beaumarchais' text the perfidious behavior of the priests and the replacement of the king by Atar (Tarare). Hence, it is as incorrect to speak of a depoliticized Italian version as it is to refer to *Le nozze di Figaro* as a downplaying of *La Folle journée*. Whoever maintains that, or speaks of an opera dealing with universal humaneness or variations on love, has neither read Da Ponte's text nor listened carefully to the music. Today more than ever, opera has become such a mélange that, however eloquent the music and unambiguous its text, it has difficulty conveying its intended meaning to the public, or even to professional musicians, musicologists, and critics. In the case of Salieri, oblivion has created additional difficulties. Yet there is little doubt that if Mozart—who must have known the opera, though there is no record of it—had made one or two comments about it, the work would not have been forgotten.

There is yet another opera from the same period as *Tarare* and *Axur*. It was written in an equally tragi-comic vein, though it had a satirical element that was previously unknown on the opera stage. The piece was begun in Paris in 1786 and completed after the premiere of *Axur*, in 1788, but was never performed. *Cublai, gran kan de Tartari*, as it was called, had a libretto by Giambattista Casti and was based on an episode from the eleventh canto of Casti's *Poema tartaro*, a barely disguised version of the outrageous conditions at the Russian court. The plot is exceedingly simple, revolving around a single intrigue:

Cublai has entrusted the education of his feeble-minded son, Lipi, to Posega, the high priest, so that the prince will become a worthy successor to the throne. Cublai's nephew, Timur, has just arrived with Alzima, daughter of the king of India and Lipi's bride-to-be. However, Timur and Alzima have fallen in love during their journey. Alzima's first encounter with her feeble-minded fiancé is rather confused. Posega, who now has control over Lipi, anticipates that the latter's succession will consolidate the power of the clergy. But he is faced with resistance on the part of Memma; she is a European, and Cublai's favorite, with great influence on the ruler, which allows her to do more or less whatever she wants. She suggests that Timur instead of Lipi succeed to the throne, with Alzima as his wife. Posega sees his plans come to nothing, and tries to convince Alzima that Memma is having an affair with her lover Timur. But Memma's sway over Cublai is decisive. The latter decides to make Timur his heir, and to let him marry Alzima. He exiles his son and the intriguing priest to a pagoda, banishing them from his realm.

Casti's libretto does not rely on the story to carry the action, but on fast-paced dialogues into which lyrical sections (arias) are effortlessly woven. It gives the composer a wonderful opportunity to through-compose so that the often abrupt disintegration of dialogues, recitatives, and arias can be avoided in favor of dramatic scenic unity. Casti came up with excellent ideas whose satiric force put all other staged music theater in the shade. There is no insipid *buffo* farce, no pointless wit, no mistaken identities or contrived situation comedy; the work has a deadly serious side. For Cublai is always the unpredictable barbaric despot, harsh and rough, yet also weak-willed, and soft as putty in the hands of Memma, his European mistress.

The work is a sharp portrayal of social customs, but one that avoids giving any moral satisfaction by punishing or showing the downfall of this tyrant. There is no doubt that Alzima and Lipi would have made an unlikely pair—Alzima's arias are in a capricious coloratura form, while Lipi stammers childishly—but Lipi's banishment remains purely arbitrary, even if the simpleton childishly looks forward to his stay in the pagoda. The eventual successors, the lovely Alzima and the handsome Timur, scarcely promise anything better, and though love is praised by the chorus at the end, the happy moment does nothing to obscure reality.

This opera described the Russian Czar Peter I without much pretense of disguising his identity. In 1794 Casti wrote an extensive *argomento*[7] in which he tried to conceal the connection by presenting the underlying events as incidents from Chinese history, which he had culled from various history books; but this was probably just a smokescreen to make performance of the work someday possible. In 1788 performance was out of the question; the connection with Casti's *Poema tartaro*, the satiric epic on conditions in Russia, was all too obvious. Moreover, it was in that year that the Habsburg monarchy became involved in the dangerous war against Turkey as allies of Empress Catherine II. In view of the unpopularity of the war, such an opera could have had a negative influence on the attitude of the public toward the alliance.

There is no evidence that Salieri tried to publish the opera.

However, it is hardly possible that the busy Kapellmeister would have begun work on a piece—even completing it, though it might have still needed some revisions here and there— merely to have it lie in a drawer. And can one seriously assume that a composer who was on such good terms with Joseph II would have avoided telling his patron what he was working on? It is more likely that Joseph advised him, as he had done with Casti and his *Poema tartaro*, that for political reasons it was best to forget publication of the opera for the time being.

In any case, Salieri continued to enjoy the personal favor of the monarch. And in February 1788, some weeks after the successful premiere of *Axur*, he was given the position of royal Hofkapellmeister previously held by the sickly and aged Giuseppe Bonno. The latter died shortly thereafter, on April 15, 1788. The appointment came as no surprise to Salieri, as it had long been intended for him. It carried a salary of 1,200 gulden, excluding his duties at the Opera, for which he received 200 ducats (900 gulden). This appointment should not be seen in terms of promoting any rivalry between Salieri and Mozart. The latter had no reason to expect an official position, having been given the title of royal *Kammercompositeur* in December 1787, and awarded an annual honorarium of 800 gulden. There were no duties connected with the title, except to compose dances for the masked ball at the annual carnival. Salieri had now arrived at the height of his artistic career; *Tarare* and *Axur* were unquestionably his most important compositions. He now occupied a central position in Viennese musical life; not only did he administer the royal orchestra and all the concerts of the Tonkünstler Society, but he was also in charge of the Opera and the royal chamber music.

It did not make for a peaceful life. Right at the start of the new opera season, there were difficulties in connection with the famous singer Celeste Coltellini and her sister Anna, who had just been engaged. Celeste Coltellini was known in Vienna for her previous appearances, including in three of Salieri's operas, in 1785. It was not pure chance that at that time she had been given the role of the capricious soubrette Tonina, who, among other things, quarrels with the prima donna in

Prima la musica e poi le parole. Casti had cleverly written a role for her in which she played herself, even if it was a caricature—but actors are not offended by that. Now, in 1787, the Coltellini sisters arrived two weeks late, so that the entire program had to be redesigned and the first premieres postponed. An opera director has of course to deal with all sorts of problems relating to his singers, but the sisters' late arrival was a deliberate breach of contract that could not be condoned.

Count Rosenberg submitted a written report on the matter to the emperor, who was already at his war headquarters in Semlin, but still liked to be kept informed and to make decisions on all theatrical matters. Celeste Coltellini, anticipating some reaction, took the offensive by complaining that Salieri did not give her appropriate roles, and by insisting that only the emperor had the right to determine what should be done. She may have recalled that Joseph II himself had once chosen her for Vienna, and thought she therefore had rights that took precedence over others. She even sent what appears to have been a rather impudent letter to the emperor, although he was not influenced by it. He wrote to Count Rosenberg:

> In returning the letter from Coltellini, I am of the opinion that one should take the opportunity to get rid of her, and therefore to insist irrevocably on what has been indicated to her, namely to use the pretext that she herself was the first not to keep to her contract, having arrived after the theater season opened, to the detriment of the takings.[8]

Coltellini was in fact asked to leave only on July 31, after she had given many performances. There was no help for it, as famous singers were in short supply.

It was not so easy to arrange new engagements. The emperor, who in the best of times stressed economy, was even more unwilling to pay exorbitant fees during wartime, and had set the upper limit for first-rank singers at 1,000 ducats (4,500 gulden). Though the chance to perform in Vienna was coveted by singers, they received considerably better salaries elsewhere. The Opera faced difficult times on account of the war; many of the nobility were away in the army, and their families had retired to their country estates, unwilling to leave them unpro-

tected. Opera revenues were therefore severely reduced. As
for the singers, they were not exactly motivated to give their
best, and the atmosphere was very depressing. Other musical
events were also cut back to a minimum. Scarcely any concerts
were given, and even private salons planned few social activities.
It is known that Mozart suffered a great deal from these effects
of the war, losing many opportunities for income. The emper-
or's absence was keenly felt.

Unfortunately, Joseph II had a habit of making too hasty
decisions in dealing with difficulties. Thus, when he received a
financial report stating that the Nationaltheater had incurred
a debt of 80,000 gulden (no doubt due in part to the above-
described circumstances), he answered:

> I believe now is the time to decide to do without opera performances
> in the coming year, and hence to cancel all further engagements of
> members of the company who are in Vienna, and not to bring in anyone
> else from outside. We shall have to see whether just the German theater
> can be kept going and wait for a year or two, to put a new opera company
> together.[9]

Accordingly, at the beginning of August many members of the
Opera were told their contracts would be terminated at the
end of the season.

For the second time, Salieri was confronted with the closure
of the Italian Opera, of which he was Kapellmeister. Unlike the
previous occasion, when the courageous experiment with a
national *Singspiel* interrupted his activities, it was now owing
to financial problems, together with the pressures on the
emperor of politics and the war. The latter's usual concern
with theater and opera was overshadowed by fatigue and
sickness. He and many of his troops were suffering from fever
and unable to engage in decisive battles. Moreover, the ruler's
current political standing was disastrous, so that he had no
energy or interest left to deal with the problems at the Opera.
But what lay in store for the opera performers? They had to
continue working to the end of the season, and that was more
than half a year away. During this period new premieres had

to be prepared, and the program adhered to, so that the public could have their nightly entertainment.

Salieri contributed a new production, which was really a makeshift work. Nine years earlier he had written the music for the first act of Carlo Goldoni's comedy *Il talismano*, on the occasion of the opening of Milan's Teatro della Canobbiana. Now he had Da Ponte transform it into a three-act opera, and composed additional music for it. The piece is a conventional *opera buffa* with simple song forms, and with little evidence of having been written by the composer of such a novel work as *Axur*. Of course the libretto did not provide much opportunity for innovation; it relies heavily on the old comedy of mistaken identities, and only rarely makes use of the device of a talisman, which enables its wearer to change himself (and his voice) as he wishes. Despite all this, however, the opera managed to remain popular until 1800.

Salieri and others tried to avert the fate awaiting the Opera by enlisting the help of the public—especially of the nobility. In his memoirs Da Ponte actually mentions such a project, by which the Opera would become independent, financed by sponsors and subscriptions. He claims to have presented a fully worked-out plan to the emperor, who was touched by such initiative, and accordingly decided to allow the Opera to continue.

When the monarch returned from the battle front in early December, he was deathly ill, suffering from hemoptysis, and difficulty in breathing. Salieri had written a mass and a *Te Deum* for the safe return of the emperor, which could not be performed in view of this severe illness. There was no cause for paeans; on the contrary, Joseph's condition, though he tried not to show it, was cause for concern. In mid-December the emperor was able to attend *Don Giovanni*, but he was given a very cold reception by a dejected public and left the opera early. Perhaps that was why he now decided to continue the Opera, hoping to halt the general displeasure at the overall political situation.

The uncertainty of recent months had naturally had a devastating effect on the Opera's program. Normally at this point in the season a new production would be featured each month. That was impossible now, when no one knew what the future would bring. Aside from Salieri's *Il talismano*, on September 10, 1788, only one new opera was put on, *Il pazzo per forza*, by Joseph Weigl. The rest of the program was made up of the standard repertory. Salieri wanted to offer the public at least one more work that was unfamiliar to them. As nothing was available, he quickly contributed one himself—more out of responsibility to "his" house than out of artistic conviction.

As the official theater dramatist, Da Ponte had to write the libretto, and he chose the famous *Pastor fido* as his theme. It had been set to music innumerable times, and had always been very popular with the public. But haste makes for poor judgment. Da Ponte tried to simplify the complicated pastoral play, by Giovanni Battista Guarini, turning it into a four-act "dramma tragicomico." There being a lack of suitable singers, the casting required careful planning. Thus the role of the faithful shepherd, Mirtillo, had to be sung by a female soprano; moreover, the shepherd's role was written in a higher register than that of the shepherdess, Amarilli, whom he marries at the end.

There were other such incongruities, abrupt surprises intended to be funny and awkwardnesses that could hardly have inspired the composer. The music for the supposedly comic sections in particular fails to make sense; having to work under such pressure, the librettist and composer do not appear to have arrived at a common conception. One cannot lay all the blame on Da Ponte—as Mosel does—for Salieri implicitly agreed to the choice of text by setting it to music. In any case, the work was not one to solve the Nationaltheater's problems. It closed after three performances, and was never performed elsewhere.[10]

Da Ponte ended this unfortunate season with an improvised sketch, for which he created a framework using the Opera's best male and female singers. It was a sort of gala for the singers, and each evening featured a different combination of performers. They sang popular arias from operas by Cimarosa, Gassmann, Martín y Soler, Mozart, Paisiello, Piccinni, and

Salieri, among others. Even if no new works were offered, the company could at least present whatever talent it had.

Salieri must have been keenly aware of the attrition of personnel in the just-completed season—not only as the Opera's artistic director, but because most evenings he had to conduct. His own operas filled more than one-fourth of the program—especially *Axur*, which was repeated frequently. Once the new season opened (it was postponed until April 20, owing to the emperor's ever-worsening illness), Salieri could devote himself entirely to his duties as Kapellmeister. The problems of the Nationaltheater were resolved, at least insofar as the Opera's existence was guaranteed. And there was a specific plan for the season: the highlights of the program, which constituted almost a quarter of all performances, were to be three works by Domenico Cimarosa—presumably to link Cimarosa more closely with Vienna, now that he had left St. Petersburg. The second half of the season was to consist of two Mozart operas, *Le nozze di Figaro* and *Così fan tutte* (the premiere of which took place on January 26, 1790). Two of Salieri's works were also included, *Axur* and *La cifra*, which had its premiere on December 11, 1789. Thus, in these four operas, which together made up over half of the schedule, the audience had a chance to compare two Da Ponte adaptations of Beaumarchais texts.

La Cifra was another adaptation of an older opera, *La dama pastorella*, that Salieri had written for Rome in 1780 and had been quickly forgotten. The indispensable Da Ponte was once again put to the task of reworking the libretto, expanding a small intermezzo into a longer opera. It is about Eurilla, actually Olympia, a count's daughter given as a child into the care of a farmer. A Scottish lord is supposed to find the girl and then marry her. The opera opens with the lord on a hunt that ends in Eurilla's village. The discovery of the count's daughter is made more difficult by the mistrust of her adopted father, and by his real daughter, who would like nothing better than to live in a fine house in the town. She keeps calling attention to herself in the hope of being taken for the count's daughter. But Eurilla's refined manners convince the count that he is on the right track. Suddenly a small locked box is found, which the farmer had received when Eurilla was left with him. In addition to jewelry and gems, it contains documents concerning Eurilla's true origin. The opera ends with a chorus of praise for the nobility.

The story is obviously similar to that of *Il talismano*, although there are no magic tricks. Instead of the lost daughter growing up in a gypsy setting, here a rural atmosphere is contrasted with that of the aristocracy, the music for which immediately determines Eurilla's real background. There are dramatic moments in the first act, when the hunt is overtaken by a storm in the middle of the woods and the hunters are surprised by a wild boar. The courageous and iron-willed Eurilla kills the boar by firing four shots, while the others all flee. Naturally Salieri could not resist using all his musical skills to portray such a scene. The role of Eurilla was made to order for the newly engaged Adriana Francesca Del Bene (known as "la Ferrarese"). She was a singer whose voice manifested "astonishing depth at an incredibly high pitch,"[11] and who was capable of singing the most demanding bravura arias and the most difficult coloratura passages.

The undeniable success of this opera (not only in Vienna, but all over Europe up to 1800) was not due merely to this brilliant role. It lay rather in its naively romantic subject, which in some similar form has appealed to the emotions of the public from the Middle Ages onward, culminating in today's pulp novels.

In view of the Vienna Opera's financial difficulties, *La cifra* must have been planned with its aristocratic patrons in mind. It is true that under Joseph, all classes had the right to attend the Nationaltheater (if they could pay the high ticket prices), and public musical life had opened up to a bourgeois audience. But Italian opera was still largely the domain of the nobility, whatever their political convictions or views on class. While work was proceeding on the opera in the autumn of 1789, exciting events were under way elsewhere. In France a revolution had just broken out whose final outcome was still unknown, but which must also have encouraged the nationalist and separatist-inspired unrest developing throughout the

Habsburg monarchy. Yet here was an opera that could only be interpreted as a hymn to the higher culture and refinement of the nobility, and to its supposedly innate human dignity. For there was no other way to explain the rediscovery of Eurilla as Countess Olympia Clerval. And strange to say, the piece was by the same composer who had produced *Tarare* and *Axur*, in which the privileges of the aristocracy are challenged, and which proclaim that man's right to rule depends on his individual integrity.

Most likely, Salieri intended only to pay homage to the public of an Opera company whose existence was still shaky, and thus to ensure a much-needed success. He must not have realized that the work's political implications could be interpreted as a repudiation of *Tarare*. The fact that he was unaware of this shows that despite his politically important operas (including *Cublai, gran kan de Tartari*), Salieri was not very farsighted when it came to politics. This would not be particularly noteworthy in another composer, but it is significant in the man who composed *Tarare*. In that instance, Salieri had undoubtedly taken a risk.

Around the time of the premiere of *La cifra*, there were again some disagreements with Mozart, who was just beginning to rehearse *Così fan tutte*. In a letter to Michael Puchberg, Mozart writes:

> I invite you to come here (by yourself) at 10 o'clock on Thursday morning, for a small opera rehearsal. I'm just inviting you and *Haydn*. When I see you I'll tell you about Salieri's cabals that have all come to nothing meantime. (December, 1789)[12]

This does not necessarily refer to "imagined intrigues,"[13] though Mozart's comment should not be taken too literally, either. It might have referred to the matter of fixing a date for the Mozart premiere, since Salieri would not have wanted to set it too close to *La cifra* so as to ensure sufficient performances for the latter work. But more likely the issue centered around Adriana Del Bene, "la Ferrarese," who not only had to sing the role of Eurilla for Salieri, but was also to appear as Fiordiligi for Mozart. (Mozart alluded to this singer's stage name, "la Ferrarese," in the dramatis personae of his opera, noting of her and her sister, Luisa Villeneufe, who was to sing the role of Dorabella, "The ladies come from Ferrara and live in Naples.") Both composers were very demanding, and used similar methods to bring out the special characteristics of "la Ferrarese's" voice. The fact that this singer was crucial to both operas had to be considered when planning the season's program. Whatever conflict arose was normal in the day-to-day business of the theater, and should not be regarded as leading to deep-seated animosity between Mozart and Salieri. *Così fan tutte* was given a total of six performances by the time the season ended on February 11.

Joseph II died not long thereafter, on February 20, 1790, but his death had long been expected. His brief improvement in the autumn of 1789 had not concealed the fact that he was deathly sick. The heritage he left—the vast Habsburg empire that stretched from the Netherlands to Transylvania, from Western Austria (Freiburg-im-Breisgau) to Bohemia-Moravia, and that also included the Hungarian crown—was in a sad state. The empire was involved in an unresolved war with Turkey that did not even serve its own interests, but to which it was committed through its alliance with Russia. There was open revolt in the Netherlands, along with efforts by Hungary to gain its independence. As for internal reforms, the majority of these had either not been completed or had failed, as had the taxation of the nobility, for instance. The economic situation was catastrophic, and popular anger was such that people had not been afraid to heckle the dying emperor with satiric verses.

Yet to Salieri and Mozart, Joseph's passing meant the loss of a great patron. He had been a monarch who played an extraordinary role in cultural life, who considered that music and theater should at the very least be enjoyed by the court, and who even personally supported difficult works. His many internal reforms had also created a liberal climate that encouraged the arts and sciences, yet without his giving up the rights of an absolute monarch whose concurrent aim was to govern with a high degree of legality and avoid arbitrary acts.

For the time being, it was impossible to tell what the consequences of the emperor's death would be for the Vienna

Opera. One thing, though, was certain. A new administrator would be appointed, since Leopold II, the new emperor, was not expected to take theatrical matters into his own hands as his brother had done. Of course, he had other problems on his mind than the Opera, which he attended for the first time on September 20, 1788, for a performance of *Axur*. Everything was suspended for the time being, and the number of premieres and new productions was drastically reduced. Still, performances of works by Salieri and Mozart were given frequently in the new season. Salieri's operas *La cifra*, *Axur*, and *Il talismano* were each performed eight times. *Le nozze di Figaro* was seen on sixteen occasions, and *Così fan tutte* had five performances. This is proof, once again, that Mozart was not forgotten by his public, especially as *Figaro* had already been seen thirteen times in the previous season.

In all this time Salieri never abandoned his contact with Paris. He received suggestions for various librettos from there, and he himself was interested in further collaboration on a French opera, as he doubted that Italian *buffa* texts would do well in Paris. Thus he writes to Franz Kruthoffer in March 1789: "I have no doubt that I shall soon be going to Paris with a new work for the Théâtre de l'Opéra, which I've already begun to write."[14]

He had indeed found a libretto to be enthusiastic about, *La Princesse de Babylone*, by Désiré Martin. It had been sent to him anonymously in the late autumn of 1787, but in the interim the problems at the Opera at home had been more urgent. Then he had received word from the Académie royale de musique (as the Paris Opera was officially known) that this project could not be undertaken so easily, owing to the great expenditures it would involve. Yet he continued to work on the piece, and had almost completed the first act. In August 1789 the prospects for such a spectacular work did not seem any more auspicious, in view of the political events. Writing to the librettist, Salieri comments:

> The terrible news of Paris overcome by the greatest catastrophe robbed me of my courage and the desire to think about more entertaining matters. As things stand now, and we are led to believe that everything

has taken a turn for the better, and the news gives us hope for a happy outcome, one can once again begin to talk about libretti and music.[15]

Vienna was well informed of the events occurring in Paris. The *Wiener Zeitung* carried the latest developments daily (even if there was a delay in the transmission of news of from ten days to two weeks). So when Salieri speaks of the first dreadful news, he is apparently referring to the early acts of violence of July 14 and the storming of the Bastille, which were marked by personal assaults and vindictive murders. The new "hope" seems to refer to the work of the National Assembly and the comparatively orderly procedure of the abolition of feudal rights. Detailed reports were available of the meetings of the National Assembly, including excerpts of the most important speeches as well as the debates on the declaration of human rights that was adopted on August 26. Salieri evidently belonged to those observers of the French Revolution whose approval was marked by restraint, who were horrified by acts of violence, and who stood in great fear of popular uprisings.

Salieri suggested to Martin that they wait for more favorable conditions, or, if he preferred to work with another composer, to advise him of his decision. The project was in fact postponed for the time being.

Beaumarchais was still on the scene as well. Despite the ambiguity of his political attitudes, he continued to be active, though regarded with suspicion. He did not readily let pass the opportunity for big public spectacles. Extensive festivities were being planned for the first anniversary of the storming of the Bastille, which seemed an ideal opportunity for Beaumarchais to participate with a new production of *Tarare*. However, he planned to append an epilogue to the already overly long work, a "Couronnement de Tarare," to suit the new taste. He hoped the music for it would be written by Lemoyne or Grétry, but both of them declined a commission that they must have considered politically controversial.

Thereupon Salieri was asked to undertake the complementary composition himself, and he did so. Perhaps he saw it as an appropriate expression of what the Revolution had achieved up to then—a constitutional monarchy that was about to undertake far-reaching reforms. From his vantage point in Vienna, he was unable to discern that, so far, only the first act of the Revolution had taken place; that the turmoil among the people and the demands of the different groups and clubs would increase, and that it was far from certain who would eventually seize control. Moreover, he could not have known that Beaumarchais, who was always a bit of a braggart, was skating on very thin ice with the revolutionaries. When Salieri's music arrived in Paris, Beaumarchais wrote effusively:

> Neither you nor anyone else, dear friend, can picture the enthusiasm aroused by the great celebration to be held on the 14th [July]. Fifteen hundred workers are busy creating an embankment at the base of the tower of the Champ de Mars, where the event is to take place; it is feared that the work will not be completed because they are so careless; all the citizens of Paris are coming to the site; even the Mont Morencis, who are, after all, the coal merchants of our harbors; men, women, priests, soldiers, all are hoeing the ground and pulling the wheelbarrows. I heard that the king is going to come this evening together with the National Assembly, to encourage the workers; that makes for joy, singing and dancing! No other country has seen such enthusiasm. Four hundred thousand people are going to enjoy the most wonderful spectacle on the 14th that the earth has ever offered up to heaven. Good day, dear friend, all I miss is your presence; but you may rest assured of your success.[16]

This letter was signed "Beaumarchais." But not long thereafter, when he dedicated a splendid copy of the text for the "Couronnement de Tarare" to the mayor of Paris, he signed himself "Caron, formerly Beaumarchais"—titles, one might observe, where titles are due.

The first performance of *Tarare* with its new ending was to take place on July 18, that is, immediately after the three-day celebration. However, the premiere was delayed until August 3. Beaumarchais described the performance to Salieri on August 15:

> Now, my dear Salieri, I must give you an accounting of your great success. *Tarare* has so far been seen three times. The opera was performed with the greatest care. The public reacted to it as a sublime piece of music. You now hold pride of place here. The opera, which has been making about 500–600 livres a year, took in 6,540 livres on the opening night of *Tarare*, and 5,400 livres on the second night. The performers kept strictly to my principle that the singing should be considered as a

bonus to the play, and for the first time they were considered the equals of the greatest talents in the theater; and the audience shouted: *Such music! Not a single superfluous note; everything is designed to have a great effect on the dramatic action!* What joy for me, my friend, to see that such justice is finally being done to you and that there is unanimous acclaim for you as the *worthy successor to Gluck.*[17]

Once again, as far as money was concerned, Beaumarchais had been successful. What he did not tell Salieri was how mixed the reaction of the public was to this "crowning." The aristocracy, sitting in their boxes, felt the opera went too far; others thought it was not decisive enough. Nor did Beaumarchais mention that he had been asked by the Comité de l'Opéra to explain his reasons for the epilogue to the newspapers, as the fuss was probably due to misconceptions. So Beaumarchais had abandoned his reserve, and had publicly and unmistakably declared his respect for the king. This was an author who had directed sharp words at the aristocracy in his play *La Folle journée,* and who had also openly attacked the church and the monarchy in *Tarare.* Hence his political declaration was not a formal disclaimer but an opportunistic rejection of the consequences of his own political influence. It was the attitude of a bourgeois who shortly thereafter was able to save his skin only by fleeing abroad.

The "Couronnement de Tarare" seems almost to predict the strictly limited success of the Revolution in the period between 1795 and the rise of Napoleon I. First there is a ceremonial event, at which an "autel de la patrie" and a statute book decorated with a golden crown are brought in; then Tarare is given the purple robe and scepter, and he and Astasie take their seats on the thrones. The first official acts consist of the abolition of monastic vows and celibacy (issues that were just being debated in the National Assembly), the divorce of Spinette and Calpigi, and the abolition of negro slavery in Zanzibar. The emancipated slaves thereupon perform an exuberant dance. But then a wild mob appears, shouting, "Everything has changed, we do not need to obey anyone anymore." The municipal council, the army, the peaceful citizens, farmers and their wives, and finally the priests of death confront the rabble in succession, while Tarare joins the citizens. This calms the populace. An allegorical representation of the throne, the altar and statute book, and above them the sun chariot and the genies of Nature and Fire from the prologue, end this epilogue.

Though Beaumarchais had invited Salieri to attend the premiere, he did not have time to go to Paris. As Hofkapell-meister he had official duties to perform at the various installation ceremonies for Leopold II, which commenced in the autumn of 1790. First there was his coronation as Emperor of the Holy Roman Empire on October 9, 1790, in Frankfurt-am-Main, which preceded the Habsburg-Bourbon double wedding.[18] Then came his inauguration as King of Hungary on November 15 in Pressburg; finally there was his enthronement in Prague as King of Bohemia on September 6, 1791. Salieri did not have to write any new operas for these important occasions, but he had composed a coronation *Te Deum* and was expected to be present with the court orchestra.

New rulers make changes among officeholders. Thus Count Rosenberg was replaced by Count Johann Wenzel Ugarte as the director of the court theater, and Salieri asked to be relieved of his duties as Hofkapellmeister. Everyone found it difficult to deal with the new emperor, as no one knew quite what to make of him. He was withdrawn, and his political plans were unclear. In any case, there was little opportunity to get to know him, as he was away a great deal just then; and in view of the tense political situation, he had no time for social life. Much of what was said about Leopold may have been prejudice, but the new emperor mistrusted those who had belonged to the intimate circle around Joseph II. He considered them responsible for the political mess he found, and surmised that they were insincere sycophants. As for music, he did not seem to have any particular interest in it, and his wife, Maria Ludovica, was expected to prefer the familiar melodious Neapolitan opera.

Salieri had as little access to the new emperor as Mozart did. If what Leopold II said about Salieri is true—that such an important composer should write operas instead of sitting at the Opera's pianoforte in the evenings—it reveals respect but no real conception of what Salieri had done for opera at the Nationaltheater. In fact, the emperor showed a general disregard for the Opera and its achievements when he appointed Weigl (Salieri's young student and assistant) to succeed his mentor without raising his meager salary of 600 gulden, and by delaying his certificate of appointment for a whole year. Salieri was thus permitted to relinquish his duties as Opernkapellmeister on condition that he write a new opera annually. It meant that he could give up the burdensome responsibility of administering the Opera, but was still committed to the Nationaltheater on a free-lance basis. However, he did retain his position of Hofkapellmeister, with all of its related duties.

Salieri had just turned forty. He had made his debut as an opera composer twenty years before, and had since written close to thirty operas, with varying success. Some of them, like *Les Danaïdes, Tarare*, and *Axur* belonged with the best and most spectacular works of his time; several of his works were performed all over Europe. He had been Kapellmeister of the Italian Opera for sixteen years, and held one of the most influential positions in Viennese musical life. But the high point of his career had been the operas he had written for Paris. Salieri was six years older than Mozart, and at the time of the latter's death he had already passed the peak of his career. Of the eleven works that followed, no more than two or three were of the caliber of his earlier ones.

In those days it was extremely rare to find great careers and unlimited creativity, combined with the skill acquired through lifelong experience, alertness, and concentration, continuing into old age. Of the older composers, only Gluck and Haydn, and of the younger ones only Cherubini, could be said to have been blessed in this fashion. Perhaps the failing of compositional ability at an age when today many are just beginning to see their star rise was the price paid for an unusually early start of artistic activity—which is not often found in the other arts. This early start and the pressure under which composers worked necessarily resulted in the relatively rapid exhaustion of their creative power.

Salieri was fortunate in that he had also been involved in other projects that kept him active into advanced old age. He taught composition and voice, was an important organizer of Viennese musical life, and, finally, composed music for use in church. Yet the end of his administration of the Opera was to have a deeper effect on his life than he realized, whatever relief he may have felt at first.

CHAPTER EIGHT

Setbacks During the Restoration
1791–1802

Ever since the reestablishment of the Italian opera in 1783, Lorenzo Da Ponte had been actively involved in the new productions of the Nationaltheater. He was not only a diligent dramatist willing to undertake any task, but his libretti contributed to some of the greatest successes of his time. His contemporaries linked his name with Mozart operas as well as with *Una cosa rara* and *L'arbore di Diana* by Vincente Martín y Soler; or with the text of *Axur*, and the adaptation of Stephen Storace's *Gli equivoci*, which was based on Shakespeare's *Comedy of Errors*. Even if one reproached Da Ponte for not creating his own libretti, there was no denying that his musical and dramatic instincts enabled him to be an excellent adapter of other people's texts. He worked not only with the most diverse composers, but dealt with many different genres and a great variety of settings.

Da Ponte's subjects ranged from mythological to contemporary themes. There were pastoral as well as conventional pieces dealing with mistaken identities, tales of gypsies, or oriental extravaganzas; and time and again he turned to rustic life (though without giving it a romantic transfiguration). But above all, Da Ponte was a poet who was willing to break with tradition and bring completely new forms to music theater. Mozart's *Le nozze di Figaro* and *Don Giovanni* and Salieri's *Axur* could not have been written without Da Ponte, because no other librettist could have adapted himself to their wishes and needs, and yet worked with such a sense of the theater. At any rate, there was no one in Vienna—not even Giambattista Casti—who could easily replace Da Ponte, and where could another poet of his caliber have been found to handle such varied tasks?

But whatever accolades posterity may bestow, the daily round at the Opera within which the temperamental Da Ponte had to work was quite another matter. He was evidently one of those people who were frequently the center of theatrical intrigues. His love affair with Adriana Del Bene may have been part of it. Whether this caused public disapproval because the singer was married and Da Ponte was an *abbate* is not easily ascertainable from the available documents; but one comes across it as an often-reiterated assertion that seems to reflect the prudish reaction of those who retail it. On the other hand, it is known that he wrote to the management of the theater to convince them to extend his friend's engagement.

Shortly thereafter Da Ponte received an inquiry from Martin y Soler in St. Petersburg as to whether he would like to become the court poet there. As he guessed that his lover's contract would not be prolonged, Da Ponte asked one of the subordinate Viennese officials whether he could resign his position early, and was told that he was under contract to Vienna until March 1792. During this period he became very angry over some slander. He demanded an interview with the emperor, which was refused, whereupon he wrote an impertinent letter to the monarch that increased the ill feeling toward him. He was finally informed that his services would no longer be required, that he would be compensated, but that he should leave Vienna promptly. This de-facto expulsion hurt Da Ponte so much that he did everything possible to be able to defend himself personally before the emperor and be reinstated. An unsuccessful audience with Leopold II did come about in Trieste, after which Da Ponte wrote several letters urging the emperor to arrive at a decision. Eventually, staking everything, he returned to Vienna again, but arrived on the very day when Emperor Leopold II unexpectedly died. The latter's son and heir, Franz II, saw to Da Ponte's ultimate dismissal, paying part of his travel expenses out of the police funds.

This inglorious departure put an end to Da Ponte's important work in the Viennese theater, and to his collaboration with Mozart and Salieri. No comments on him by Mozart have been passed on, whereas Da Ponte idolized Mozart in his memoirs. He lived to arrange for the first performance of *Don Giovanni* in New York in 1825. His relationship with Salieri, for whom he wrote or adapted five libretti, was businesslike and to the point. Da Ponte speaks of him with approbation and respect but without the warmth of friendship.

Under Leopold II, the new management at the Opera had no need of Da Ponte, and some of the decisions regarding the 1791 season showed other influences at work. Angelo Testori, a castrato, was engaged for the ensemble so that real *opera seria* could be produced again—which had not been seen during the entire Josephine era. And while Joseph II had eliminated ballet for reasons of economy, it was now reinstated. Finally, there were some innovations that indicated considerable indifference to and unfamiliarity with works of art. Single acts of operas were performed, and supplemented with ballets. The character of the Nationaltheater was so completely transformed that it is obvious why a composer like Mozart looked for other theaters for his works. He chose Emanuel Schikaneder's Freihaustheater auf der Wieden for *Die Zauberflöte*, where he was in the best of hands. Salieri, who was expected to create a new opera annually, kept a low profile. Not that he ceased to compose; by 1802 he had written eleven more operas. But the first of these was not performed until 1795, when the Nationaltheater was rented out to private interests.

Now that there was no more friction over theater business between them, Salieri and Mozart managed to have a completely relaxed relationship. There is no other way to interpret the letter Mozart wrote to his wife Konstanze about a performance of *Die Zauberflöte*, to which he had invited Salieri (whom he had formerly accused of "cabals") and the singer Catarina Cavalieri. Mozart also brought his son Karl Thomas (from his boarding school) and brother-in-law Franz Hofer to this production:

> Yesterday, Thursday the 13th, Hofer and I drove out to see Carl [sic]; we ate out there, then we all returned and at 6 o'clock I went by carriage to fetch Salieri and [deleted word] Cavalieri and took them to my box—then I quickly went to get Mama and Carl, whom I had left with Hofer meantime. You won't believe how well-behaved they [Salieri and Cavalieri] both were, and how much they not only liked my music but the text and everything else. Both of them said it was an *opera* worthy of being performed at the most important occasion for the greatest of kings, and that they would like to see it frequently as they had never seen a more beautiful and pleasing spectacle. He [Salieri] listened and watched with great attention, and from the *sinfonia* to the final chorus there was not a single item that did not elicit a "bravo" or "bello" from him; and they could not thank me enough for giving them this opportunity. They had intended to go to the opera yesterday in any case, but they would have had to go at 4 o'clock. This way they could see and hear everything in peace. After the performance I took them home and I had supper at Hofer's with Carl (October 14, 1791).[1]

These spontaneous comments of approval, perhaps even enthusiasm, were too real to be mistaken for suppressed envy or love-hate feelings. And Mozart was too sensitive not to discern hidden flattery or other hypocrisy, especially in Salieri, whom he had known for so long. The fact that Mozart invited Salieri to see *Die Zauberflöte* suggests friendly collegial intercourse between them. After all, Salieri was no longer the feared Kapellmeister with whom one had to ingratiate oneself, but where the new emperor was concerned, was now on an equal footing with Mozart. Besides, the composer of *Axur* had no reason to consider himself overshadowed by Mozart.

Mozart died suddenly, barely eight weeks later, after a short infectious illness, the cause of which has not been ascertained to this day. There is no evidence that Salieri managed to visit the sick man. He is said to have attended the benediction service in St. Stephen's cathedral, though no firm proof of that exists either.[2] What might he have been thinking as the prayers for the dead were sung? He was silent, and later had to contend with this silence being interpreted as evidence of his having

poisoned Mozart. Did he try to convince the Tonkünstler
Society to organize a memorial concert—as he had done for
Gluck—especially as Mozart's family was thought to have been
left without means? Mozart had contributed much of his talent
and time to the Society's concerts, but he had not been a
member, and evidently it was one of their strict principles not
to create a precedent. It is possible, therefore, either that Salieri
did not even try to arrange anything, or that his appeal was
turned down. In any case, no information exists on this subject,
and he should not be blamed for nothing being undertaken.
Salieri later gave free lessons to Mozart's youngest son, Franz
Xaver Wolfgang—as he did with almost all of his students.

Leopold II, who had so unwillingly succeeded his brother,
died suddenly not quite four months afterward. His twenty-
four-year-old son Franz thus had all too soon to take on the
heavy burden of the Habsburg empire. The emperor's death
was followed within six weeks by that of his wife. All the
funerals were conducted according to the pompous Habsburg
tradition, which involved a strict, impersonal, and complex
ritual whose symbolic significance was unlikely to mean much
any longer. Then, for the last time in the history of the Holy
Roman Empire, coronation ceremonies took place in Frankfurt-
am-Main, in Pressburg, and in Prague. Salieri performed his
duties as Hofkapellmeister on all of these occasions, but composed nothing new for them. The *Missa solemnis* by Vincenzo
Righini, which had been given two years earlier, was repeated
again in Frankfurt in 1792.

Casti had been back in Vienna since the summer of 1791,
and was still nursing hopes of becoming the royal court poet.
Although circumstances had changed completely, and *Cublai,
gran kan de Tartari* had not yet been performed, he promptly
wrote a new libretto for Salieri that was almost as problematic
as the previous one. But Salieri was not worried about having
his works performed; instead, as a free man, he composed
Catilina (an "opera tragicomica") for his own pleasure, a work
that could be consigned to his desk drawer if necessary.

The opera is based on the second Catiline Conspiracy,
which gave rise to Cicero's famous speech, "Quousque tandem"

(how much longer?) known to all students of Latin since time immemorial. As can be imagined, this material about a carefully planned conspiracy against the state did not contain anything humorous, and Casti did not add any comic characters. The comedy is created entirely by the fact that the portrayals are not in black and white, but have, so to speak, distinctive and colorful gradations.

Catilina is depicted as the archetypical sinister and uncontrolled libertine who is not afraid to plunge the state into ruin as he transfers his dissolute life to the political stage. He tries to secure his power by acquiring a dangerously large group of followers to whom he makes various promises. He is opposed by Cicero and Cato, who stand for moral and political virtue as well as the traditions of ancient Rome. The subject corresponds to that of the familiar pathetic Roman dramas, except that here it is parodied. This is achieved not by portraying Cicero as absurd, but by stressing his human weaknesses as well as his heroic qualities, even in an important scene. Thus, his fearfulness is shown openly in contrast to his pose as the eloquent speaker. For instance, the scene of the "Quousque tandem" is set in the Roman Forum rather than the Senate, and Cicero's delivery constantly falters as he faces the crowd, which is partially composed of Catilina's followers. Cicero thus gives the impression of a comic character without being entirely exposed to ridicule by Casti-Salieri. It is a moment of unsparing realism in a serious scene based on a historical subject; Cicero has to submit to such ambivalent experiences in order finally to emerge as victor over the conspirators. The treatment of Fulvia, Cicero's daughter, is similar. She is engaged to Curio, a vacillating follower of Catilina, and is initiated into the conspirators' group in a hilarious ritual. But once a member, she can then engage in the betrayal of Catilina that will lead to his elimination.

Salieri knew that with *Catilina* he was taking a bold step. The critical comments he added in his old age to some of his works recommend that this opera be read rather than performed, which means that Salieri was aware of its worth. Yet he kept pointing out that it required good actors who possessed a great deal of sensitivity.[3] The opera contains long recitative sections contrasted with large ensemble scenes. In the crowd scenes the chorus represents excited partisan groups, and thus plays an important role in the action.

There can be no doubt that with this work Casti and Salieri were swimming against the tide. No model existed for the portrayal of a subject weighted with so much pathos in such a reflective way that it revealed the comic aspects of serious and fateful events. But in view of the developments of the French Revolution—the constantly changing and confusing news of which was being followed in Vienna—and especially once the Jacobins seized power after the execution of King Louis XVI, the opera could not be staged. *Catilina* therefore remained in Salieri's desk drawer, and has not been performed to this day.

While Salieri was busy with his composition of *Catilina*, his student Franz Xaver Süssmayr was engaged in completing Mozart's *Requiem* at the request of Konstanze Mozart, so that it could be delivered to the person who had commissioned it. Süssmayr had become Mozart's student and assistant in 1791, but had probably studied with Salieri previously, and had gone back to him right after Mozart's death. One may assume that Salieri was informed of the special circumstances surrounding the *Requiem*, though it is unlikely that he offered Süssmayr any advice; after all, the latter had more precise knowledge of Mozart's wishes and idiosyncrasies. But Salieri attended the rehearsals for the premiere of this work (January 4, 1793), as Konstanze recalled decades later.

Salieri wrote another opera, *Il mondo alla rovescia*, based on a text by Caterino Mazzolà, fairly soon after *Catilina*. The subject had previously been dealt with by Carlo Goldoni (1750), when it was set to music by Baldassare Galuppi. But the material existed elsewhere as well; even Marivaux made use of it.

The story concerns an island where the social relationship of men and women is reversed. Women are in charge (in the private, the political, and even the military sphere), whereas men assume the traditional female role even to the extent of being passive in matters of love, and are portrayed as emasculated beings. However, the women find these reversed conditions difficult and have trouble resolving their conflicts. A ship arrives carrying Europeans (of course these are men), who gradually become influential and intervene in the existing controversies, restoring the "natural" order of things, which is celebrated by one and all at the end.

The concept of a "reversed world" is attractive, but it requires a philosophical mind to work it out. Mazzolà had not sufficiently distanced himself from Goldoni's burlesque, so that it turned into a shallow theatrical piece, to which Salieri raised no objection. Thus the character of an older lady general ("la generala di età avanzata") was written as a bass role, to be sung by a man dressed as a woman. It could of course have been transformed into political material, but Mazzolà was not Casti. The latter would not have missed the chance to turn the lady general into a satiric figure with the traits of the Empress Catherine II, who was still alive. Once again, Salieri fell victim to an inadequate libretto—or to his lack of critical perception.

Mosel criticized the work quite openly:

> The material may appear humorous at first, with men and women reversing their roles not merely in their occupations but also in their feelings and behavior; but the fact is that this opera cannot appeal to anyone unless they are bereft of all delicacy. For though it arouses laughter to see men doing women's jobs, or assuming the manners and shyness of girls, on the other hand it is quite offensive, even revolting, to see women and girls pursuing and pestering men with their declarations of love and caresses. This idea belongs with those that remain entertaining only as long they engage one's fantasy; but once they are actually portrayed they not only lose all that is entertaining but become unbearable. Moreover, the development of the piece can only be called deplorable.[4]

This opinion, delivered with all the prejudice of the Biedermeier period, reveals all too clearly how the concept of another world, seen as a logical counterpart to our own, was lost through lack of a decisive stance. Despite all the effort Salieri put into his composition, there is no satirical edge to the work. There are many sections for ensembles and rather lengthy finales in the opera, in the mode of the usual through-composed pieces that have little in common any longer with the traditional "numbers operas" of ten or twenty years earlier.

But even the best music cannot save an unsuccessful text, and a composer of opera has to accept the fact that he is considered responsible for his libretto as well.

Salieri now had time, and was not under any pressure in planning a program, engaging singers, distributing the parts, or having to fill last-minute vacancies in the cast. He had complete artistic freedom, and was not even committed to working with the official dramatist, although if he chose another librettist he had to bear the cost himself. As for Casti, he had at last achieved his goal of becoming court poet; in making the appointment, Franz II finally filled the position that had been held by Pietro Metastasio for more than fifty years.

Leopold II had originally engaged Giovanni Bertati, from Venice, to be the official dramatist, but he was replaced two years later by Giovanni De Gamerra. De Gamerra was an old acquaintance of Salieri's, and the latter had already twice sampled his dubious qualities as a librettist (*La finta scema* and *Delmita e Daliso*). De Gamerra had never held a firm position and had moved around a great deal, but he had written what Marcus Landau characterized as:

> . . . a satiric-comical epic of no less than 11,654 octaves, that is 93,000 stanzas, which he had printed little by little as of 1792 at his own expense. And who knows how much lengthier it might not have been had his wife's dowry been any larger; for, as he admitted himself, he only married her to be able to pay the printing costs of the epic which describes the infidelity of women. That explains the title of the questionable work (La Corneïde), in which he included things from his own life and some other tales, parts of which he took from the Decameron. What he lacked in humor he made up for in obscenity. And he had the audacity to preface the work—of which he himself was ashamed in his old age—with butchered verses by Dante.[5]

It was likely not to have been this work that finally led to his appointment, but his gifts as a smooth sycophant, which seemed to appeal to Emperor Franz.

Salieri soon collaborated with him on a comic piece set in ancient Greece, *Eraclito e Democrito*. Though these two philosophers, Heraclitus and Democritus, belonged to different periods, their disparate natures provided a suitable contrast for the purpose of this opera. In antiquity, Democritus was known as the laughing one and Heraclitus, because of his melancholy temperament, as the dark one. However, the opera respects historical fact in that the real Democritus is always being announced but never actually appears. Philosophy itself is not the subject of the piece but, as so often, the vain and unrealistic behavior of people who surround themselves with philosophers to reflect glory on themselves. And, of course, there are two lovers, who are permitted to come together only after certain minor obstacles. Thus Pulcheria loves Arcon, a student of Democritus, but she has not received any letters from him for some time. Heraclitus is currently visiting her father, who wants to arrange their marriage. For that reason she is to study with Heraclitus ("Lessons on how to cry? Oh, I like to laugh"). The servants think her father is a fool with an obsession about philosophers, which he certainly is.

Then Democritus is announced, and Pulcheria hopes to have a chance to inquire about Arcon. When Democritus appears, her father decides that as Heraclitus is little inclined to marry, for the sake of his reputation his daughter should marry Democritus. But she prefers to remain single, though she wants to escape secretly to look for her Arcon. She is now introduced to the supposed Democritus, whom she quickly recognizes as Arcon in disguise. Next, Democritus is announced once again, which makes the father suspicious until Arcon admits his real identity. The father is so angry that he wants to throw Arcon and his daughter, together with all the servants, out of the house, but Heraclitus advises him to let the couple get married: "Whoever wants to punish lovers needs only to unite them and, like unhappy slaves, they are then condemned to quarrel and complain eternally."[6]

This was not a very strong work; it was merely a fairly skillful piecing together of timeworn *buffa* characters and situations. Nor was it an especially intellectual or witty piece; at times it was even long-winded. Salieri had already tried, in his overture, "to give the audience an idea of the nature of the two philosophers, of the laughing Democritus and the melancholy Heraclitus," but they confront each other rather abruptly. Aside from that, he claims to have succeeded in expressing the text in music, and that some sections are "buonissimo." But in his later comments he admits that though the second finale contains "satisfying action and sections of good harmony," it is "on the whole perhaps much too circuitous for the theater and as a result a little too boring."[7] It was hard to tell that this was a work by the composer of *La grotta di Trofonio* and *La scuola de' gelosi* (not to mention *Axur*, which was a different genre altogether). Accordingly, the opera was soon forgotten; but one has to wonder why he wrote it in the first place. And why did he not work with Casti, who was a better and more successful librettist, and was apparently far more capable of inspiring him?

The reason may simply have been that while Casti had written two magnificent texts for Salieri (*Cublai, gran kan de Tartari* and *Catilina*), their political allusions made them unperformable. Casti, who had stayed with Count Rosenberg on his previous visits to Vienna, was now living in one of Prince Liechtenstein's palaces in the Herrengasse. He moved in high society, but also maintained close connections with people who were politically suspect, which the court regarded with distrust (see Chapter 5). He was now devoting his time to the preliminary work on his epic on the French Revolution, *Gli animali parlanti*, and made no effort to conceal his political views. Franz II, whose fear of the Jacobins was increasing, kept his police system working intensively. Casti speaks of a "place of the most suspicious and dangerous inquisition," and says:

> Anyone is considered a Jacobin who does not completely agree with the thousands and thousands of [dirty tricks] committed by the coalition since its beginnings. . . . Under these circumstances it would be inconceivable if at least nine-tenths of the population were not Jacobins, I mean those who still have a modicum of sense, of humaneness and honesty left.[8]

Not surprisingly, Casti could not remain in Vienna for long. Yet he did not develop a "diplomatic illness" until the summer of 1796, when he decided to go to Italy to cure a cough—but the political reasons for his departure were unmistakable. It is not known to what extent Salieri had kept in touch with the court poet up to that point, just as there is little information of any sort on the private life of the composer. In any case, there was no further chance for their collaboration.

Casti was not a wholehearted supporter of the Jacobins; he was far from condoning everything that went on during the French Revolution. But he supported the nation that took its destiny into its own hands for the first time when it faced the coalition of European powers. As a cosmopolitan, he was on the side of a beleaguered people. In contrast, Gamerra was one of those opportunists who always do what is most profitable; and as such people are generally not very farsighted, it meant playing up to the young emperor, for whom many a renegade was now willing to spy on and denounce others.

Salieri continued to work with Gamerra, whose political views were in stark contrast to those of Casti. Da Ponte notes in his memoirs that it was Gamerra who had denounced Casti as a Jacobin, whereupon the latter received a nocturnal visit from the secret police, who confiscated some papers and were then responsible for his expulsion. There is no documentary proof of this, but given Gamerra's character, it is not out of the question.

The new political culture in Vienna tended to produce a hasty distancing from the enlightened and liberal principles of the Josephine era. There were very few who did not reverse their previous, often vociferous political opinions in the period between 1792 and 1797. Not that most did so out of real conviction, or a sudden revelation concerning their former flawed views; the motive was usually opportunism and weakness of character.[9] There remained very few among Viennese writers, journalists, and pamphleteers of the Josephine period (like Johann Baptist von Alxinger and Aloys Blumauer, who more or less stopped writing) who did not openly switch to the side of Franzine reaction. The fear of being linked to the supposed Jacobin conspiracy, exposed in 1794 and ending in death sentences and imprisonments, was an additional deterrent to holding the wrong political views.

However, Salieri had nothing to do with any of these factions; he had no need to retract anything. He had never involved himself in questions of the day. In the Josephine period he had refrained from joining the Freemasons—even when it was fashionable to do so—and had never moved in suspect circles. The two operas based on Casti librettos, which might have been seen as controversial, had never been produced or even been considered for production. Only *Tarare* (including its "Couronnement") did not correspond to the conservative views held by Franz II, but in any case this version was unknown in Vienna. Salieri simply ignored the political changes that had taken place, and minded his own business. As Gamerra was the official dramatist, Salieri let him write the texts for his operas without regard to his other activities. Without realizing it, then, Salieri had gradually been developing into an enthusiastic Austrian patriot—not through active participation but through sheer passivity.

One libretto that Salieri had Gamerra adapt was an Italian version of *La Princesse de Babylone*. Again one wonders whether he chose this subject because no new texts were available, or because he was convinced that the subject was worthwhile. Perhaps it was due to his inclination not to give up on works he had begun but never completed. The French libretto, by Désiré Martin, had been rejected earlier because of its thin plot and because the staging was too elaborate for such a weak story. Perhaps what intrigued Salieri were its ornate, fairy-tale aspects that lent themselves to being set to music. He must also have been attracted by the chance to contrast with each other the three "protagonists" who represent the heroic-comic element of the libretto. At any rate, Salieri had almost completed the first act. But when he asked Gamerra for an Italian version, he quickly realized that what he had already composed was no longer suitable—as had been the case when *Tarare* was transformed into *Axur*.

La Princesse de Babylone takes place in "Tauris, the ancient Ecbatana," according to the libretto. It was actually Tabriz, which in those days was still considered identical with Ecbatana [Hamadan]. The location was important in order for *La Princesse de Babylone* now to become *Palmira, regina di Persia*. Palmira is the daughter of King Dario, whose country is constantly being devastated by a monster. It has been decreed that whoever kills the monster will receive the princess as his bride. Three princes compete for this honor: the fearful Alderano, who comes from Egypt; Oronte, a Scythian prince, who is overly confident; and Alcidoro, an Indian for whom Palmira feels concern and who ends up victorious. There are also a high priest and Rosmino, the general of the Persian army.

If one looks at the long list of extras, it is soon evident that they are required not because of an action-packed scenario, but for the lavish Asiatic court scenes and the numerous foreign retainers. The list includes "officers, satraps, grandees, priests, ladies, pages, Indian virgins, magicians, royal guards, Persian soldiers, Indian soldiers, Scythian soldiers, Egyptian soldiers, and grooms"; not itemized are the quantities of animals, such as horses, camels, and elephants. This was a windfall for the artists responsible for the décor. Any theater willing to produce it had to be prepared to spare no expense, and indeed the most important set designers were engaged; the work's long-lasting success was surely due to their skills. For instance, the enthusiastic references to the opera by Goethe were occasioned solely by the sets. In a letter to Schiller (August 14, 1797), he even maintains: "The sets of Palmira are examples from which one could abstract the theory of scene painting."[10]

Salieri's music contains several effective passages, such as a short vocal quartet without orchestral accompaniment that always elicited storms of applause. Then there are the strongly contrasting marches and arias of the three protagonists, and a contemptuous aria by the boastful Oronte, who is the only one to die in the battle (Alderano has already fled at the sound of the monster's roar). One other noteworthy item is a dramatic aria expressing doubts and changes in mood, sung by Palmira, a character who tends otherwise to be colorless. Though these are examples of a melodic *parlando* found elsewhere only in Salieri's French operas, they are isolated instances and do not make for a convincingly rounded-out work. Contemporary audiences were aware that the opera never measured up to *Axur*. It was obvious that the spectacular staging outweighed the content of the work—the trouble was that Gamerra was no Schikaneder.

This was Salieri's third opera to have its premiere in the

space of a year: *Il mondo alla rovescia* took place on January 13, *Eraclito e Democrito* on August 13, and *Palmira* on October 14, 1795. Even allowing that some work had been done on these operas at an earlier date—*Il mondo alla rovescia* was based on plans for an opera *L'isola capricciosa* commissioned by Venice in 1779—it suggests frenzied compositional activity undertaken in addition to various other tasks. Once before, when Salieri returned from Paris after *Tarare* was performed, he had produced four operas within two years, but at that time he was trying to overcome the stagnation at the Nationaltheater and revive its repertory. At present he was not responsible for the theater, which had been leased to Peter von Braun, nor was there any other outside pressure on him.[11] After the crises that had ended in his relinquishing his charge as Kapellmeister and his other administrative activities, Salieri had given himself a long break of over five years. Now it seemed as if he wanted to remind people of his existence—by providing quantity, but without being able to achieve the high quality of his previous efforts. Not even the great success of *Palmira* could disguise that fact.

Salieri had Gamerra write one more libretto for him, and began work on it right away. It was the opera *Il moro*, which, as Mosel tersely put it, "was not very successful." The story deals with a Moor who has amassed a great fortune as a pirate and who, now that he has more or less turned honest, wants to settle in Italy. He is determined to marry a white woman, but rather than advertising for one, he organizes a beauty contest, which proves a great attraction. The greedy Orgone smells money and wants to marry his daughter Stella to the Moor, but she is having a love affair with the Moor's secretary Ramiro, and elopes with him. The opera ends with the unexpected appearance of the Moor's wife, whom he had left in Africa with her eleven children—a sight that moves the penitent Moor to return to his family, and amazes the audience. Finally the secretary is allowed to marry his beloved Stella.

It is difficult to understand why Salieri undertook to compose music for a libretto that offered so little inspiration. Even Mosel, who was a great if not uncritical admirer of Salieri's talents, commented, "Indeed, this work offers little that is first-rate if one compares it to what one is accustomed to expect from *Salieri*."[12]

After this latest experience, Salieri took a break from writing operas for the next two and a half years, as if he himself had become aware of his artistic decline. But he was not inactive. The Tonkünstler Society celebrated its twenty-fifth anniversary in March 1796, and Salieri, who had been in charge of its concerts for years, contributed a cantata, *La riconoscenza (Gratitude)*. Its soprano solo was sung by his student Therese Gassmann, the daughter of his mentor, who had also been the society's founder. He prefaced the score with the following comment: "The author of this Cantata offers greetings and peace from the lap of eternity to the composer who will write the Cantata of Gratitude for the celebration of the half century, and to all those who will perform it." When that fiftieth anniversary celebration actually took place in 1821, Salieri was still very much alive, and arranged the program for it himself.

These years saw the first coalition war against France, whose real instigator was the Habsburg monarchy. Strangely enough, however, the actual declaration of war was made by France's King Louis XVI against his brother-in-law Franz, King of Hungary and Bohemia, who was crowned Emperor of the Holy Roman Empire on the very anniversary of the storming of the Bastille. Despite the complete isolation of France and its revolutionary upheaval, it carried on the war with a national fervor that gave it the strength to export the concept of a republic—especially to Italy.

The coalition, however, was a highly unstable and shifting alliance, marked by selfish special interests vying for territorial expansion. Even neutral countries such as Poland fell victim to the greed of the great powers. During the North Italian campaign of 1796–1797, a commander in chief (derided as the "little corporal") appeared who combined great military skill with far-reaching political plans. This was Napoleon, who captured the whole of Northern Italy, and most particularly Lombardy, in a lightning war. One incidental result was that the rule of the doges in Venice came to an end, and troops even advanced into Carinthia. Milan, Mantua, Modena, and parts of Parma now became the Cisalpine Republic, and Genoa became known as the Ligurian Republic.

On June 10, 1797, *Axur* was performed at the Scala in Milan "per celebrare la festa federativa della Repubblica Cisalpina." A more suitable work could not have been chosen, unless it were *Tarare*, including the "Couronnement de Tarare." And as an added fillip, the opera celebrated the creation of a republic—though it actually became a sort of French satellite state—in place of the Habsburg rule. Salieri made no comment on this adaptation.

Changing the locale of *Axur* had by no means depoliticized it; in Warsaw, where the opera was performed in 1792 and 1793, it had already been understood as a work celebrating liberation. But in Vienna, where people were more preoccupied with the constant problem of having to recruit fresh soldiers to fight the nimble French, the political reality of the work played a less important role. A new Viennese production, this time sung in German translation, was put on six months after the Milan performance. The opera had become so popular that it was performed on both sides of the front.

Once more the theater of war and the billeting of enemy troops had by-passed Vienna, but everyone had been prepared for it. Not only had all military and civil precautions been taken, but any inhabitants who could afford it had already fled the city and did not return until news of the peace negotiations (the Treaty of Campo Formio) was received. Still, an unexpected patriotism developed, as evidenced by the number of men who volunteered for the army and the donations made to the war effort. Artists also made their contribution. Not that the musicians formed an academic corps, as did those in the fine arts, but they provided propagandistic songs for the call to arms.

Even Beethoven did not consider himself above this, and Haydn composed his anthem "God save . . ." that soon became known everywhere. At the theater the audience actually had to practice it before the performance began so as to be able to sing it when Franz II arrived. Salieri held back at first; but when, following the peace treaty, Austria lost Belgium, and was instead awarded Venice with its "terra ferma" by Napoleon, he also wrote a patriotic song, *Il genio degli state veneti all'entrata delle truppe austriache in Venezia l'anne 1798*, based on a sonnet by Melchiorre Cesarotti. Naturally, this song on "the spirit of the Venetian state upon the entry of the Austrian troops" was promptly printed by Artaria—since propaganda always involves dissemination.

Peace did not last long, and war broke out again in 1799, especially in southern Germany. And this time Salieri wrote a long piece, *Der Tyroler Landsturm*, a cantata for four soloists, chorus, and orchestra, dedicated to "the brave nation of Tyrol and Vorarlberg." In May and November 1799, it was performed "for the benefit of inhabitants of Tyrol and Vorarlberg, who are victims of the devastation." It was not an important work, but a true expression of his feelings. The overture is almost a film of the events, which Salieri describes as follows:

> The sinfonia that opens the *Cantata* begins with the advance of the French into *Tyrol* aided by betrayal. They take over two mountain passes by sliding down the steep ice- and snow-covered sides of the rocks. The ringing of the *Tyrolean* bells to alert the reserves is heard, along with the sound of the French battle march. Helped by the royal army, the troops defending *Tyrol* advance to meet the enemy. The latter gains certain advantages in the first fray, expressed by the orchestra's repetition of the enemy's battle march. Meanwhile, the reserves are reinforced and the battle begins anew. Now the French are the losers. Curses come from their side as prayers are offered up by the *Tyrolean* reserves. In the heat of battle the enemies, angered by their losses, take their revenge in cruel destruction.[13]

Events continue in this manner until victory has come about, and the Austrian reserves sing "the Austrian national anthem: God save Emperor Franz!" (*The Marseillaise* is indicated as the French battle march.) This overture certainly provides a foretaste of Beethoven's battle symphony *Wellington's Victory*.

Shortly thereafter Salieri wrote a further cantata of gratitude for the heroic deeds of the people of Tyrol, *La riconoscenza dei Tirolesi*. Of course these are occasional pieces, "functional music" intended to inspire patriotic feelings; but they are also affirmations, stating that the composer of *Tarare* calls upon

Austrians to defend their country, that he considers Austria his nation and supports Franz II. Salieri witnessed the fall of the almost thousand-year-old Venetian republic of the doges, from which he himself had come, without remorse. And without hesitation he portrayed the French as cruel, malignant aggressors given to excesses, while the Tyroleans offer their prayers. We must note that these works were not written as commissions, nor were they compositions expected of the Hofkapellmeister, but personal contributions born of his own convictions. When the new coalition managed to gain a few military victories in the summer of 1799, Salieri wrote a mass and a Te Deum in the event of an imminent peace celebration. But they had to remain unperformed for the time being, as Napoleon, who had just returned from Egypt, was quickly able to reverse the military situation. The eventual negotiations at Lunéville merely confirmed the Treaty of Campo Formio, which subjected Austria to further deprivations.

The battlefronts during these coalition wars were distributed far and wide over Europe, and there were only two occasions on which Vienna feared for its own safety. Aside from that, life went on as usual in the metropolis of the Habsburg Empire, with hardly a sign of curtailment of its social activities. The city carried on in all its familiar splendor, and the aristocracy continued to enjoy the abundance of entertainment Vienna had always offered. Each evening there were operatic and theatrical performances, as though the war had not been going on since 1792. The lower classes, however, tended to become more irascible as rising prices made their economic situation worse.

Salieri now found some new material for an opera, and a young librettist to work with him. Aside from his name, Carlo Prospero Defranceschi, little is known about him or who was responsible for suggesting the text, which happened to be Shakespeare's *The Merry Wives of Windsor*. Several distorted versions of this play had already been shown in Vienna, with such titles as *Die lustigen Abentheuer an der Wien*, or *Hannibal von Donnersberg oder Der geitzige Soldat*. But it was not part of the repertory of serious works by Shakespeare produced by Friedrich Ludwig Schröder.[14]

However appealing the character of Falstaff for a composer, everything depended on the adaptation, for the play has too many characters and too many confusing subplots to be interpreted musically. The challenge was not merely to bring out the main theme of the plot in a suitable way—and this later applied to such composers as Otto Nicolai or Giuseppe Verdi as well—but also to maintain an extremely fast and witty dialogue that would distinguish the various characters without relying on burlesque action on stage. And it was precisely this that Defranceschi managed so well. In condensing the story into two acts, he dispensed with the entire subplot concerning Anna (the daughter of Mistress Page, known as Mistress Slender in the opera) and her three suitors, so that the story is limited to Falstaff and the two couples, Ford and Slender. The part of Ford is considerably enlarged, in that he not only appears as the jealous husband but has a wonderful love scene at the end when he is reconciled with his wife. Falstaff himself—true to Shakespeare—is not chiefly interested in erotic adventures; instead, he admits to his financial interests, which are directly related to his unlimited gluttony. The first scene already includes him as an uninvited sponger at a party where he flirts with Mistress Ford in her husband's absence.

The music of this opera belongs with Salieri's best. It is quite evident that librettist and composer worked closely together; the voluminous text has been pruned with the utmost skill by doing away with a schematic sequence of recitatives and musical numbers in favor of larger structures. For instance, Falstaff's big aria "Nell'impero di Cupido" is immediately followed by a solo scene in which Ford has a lengthy, dramatically heightened *accompagnato* and a big aria expressing anger. Or the smooth transition from a long, fast-paced discussion between Mistress Ford and Mistress Slender at the door, which gradually swells into a quartet with their husbands, who are standing to one side. A short recitative in the next scene is promptly succeeded by another big aria by Slender, in which he tries to imagine, and caricatures, a dialogue between his wife and Falstaff.

This concentration on larger musical passages naturally leads to the lengthening of the recitative segments. They in their turn are helped by the pace of the exchanges, their exceptionally light and deft humor, their lively and always surprising give and take. In this work, Salieri pays more attention to the harmonic changes of the harpsichord's *secco* interjections than he did in other operas. Of course, here too the librettist works in much comic material, as in the scene between Falstaff and Mistress Ford. Disguised as a "young lady," she talks with him in German, a language that he badly mangles. She tries to add to her credibility with a capricious aria, "Oh! I know all about men!" in which she does not lapse back into Italian again until the final section.

Salieri included several small bravura pieces in the opera, which were designed especially to impress the public. The instrumentation also contained surprising effects, such as eloquent solos, including a rare one for the cello, which was generally only an accompaniment to the singers. Most surprising of all is the facility of the music, maintained from beginning to end without ever becoming trivial; it interprets the text with an underlying serene wisdom and richness of nuance.[15]

This was one of Salieri's last operas, though he had not yet reached the age of fifty. The work shows no sign of failing powers or labored composition. It is a mature piece which sums up all his experience as a composer and practitioner of stagecraft, who often enjoyed rehearsing his own operas. But that type of composition needed peaceful and relaxed preparation, which had rarely been granted to him with his other works. Moreover, this was a libretto that could not depend on any schematic solutions, and demanded care. It could succeed only if he did not let himself be diverted by the numerous instances of lively and often coarse humor on stage. Each protagonist had to be considered as an independent individual with his own musical characteristics.

Salieri was proud of *Falstaff*, as his later comments on the opera indicate. He knew what he had achieved. Therefore, it was important to keep this librettist, and begin planning a new work with him. This time Defranceschi attempted to work out a subject without a literary model, one that would take the military and political situation into account. He intended it to be a light opera set in an alien, lawless, and wild region, with an obvious and entirely serious hero, yet one in which comic figures and amusing intrigues would not be out of place.

The librettist took as his point of departure a story transmitted by Plutarch about the twenty-five-year-old Caesar:

> . . . captured near the island of Farmacusa by pirates, who at that time already possessed a vast fleet of ships that were distributed all over the sea.
>
> At first he made fun of the pirates, who demanded only twenty talents as a ransom, and volunteered to pay them fifty. He then sent his companions to various cities to collect the money, and meanwhile he, a friend, and two servants remained among these murderous Cilicians. He paid them little heed and treated them so contemptuously that when he went to sleep he ordered them to be quiet. He lived among them this way for thirty-eight days; they were more like his personal guards than his captors, and he joked and toyed with them without the slightest fear. At times he wrote poems and speeches and read them aloud; he called those who did not admire them blockheads and barbarians and often jokingly threatened to have them hanged. The pirates enjoyed this very much, and looked on these courageous remarks as mere innocent, merry pranks.
>
> But as soon as the ransom money arrived from Miletus and he was set free, he manned some vessels in the Miletan harbor and sailed off against the pirates. He found them still at anchor along the island, and captured most of them.[16]

Defranceschi stayed close to every detail of Plutarch's tale, which also included humorous material. However, this was a story about men, so some female characters had to be invented. He therefore added a pirate bride and Gigi, a slave in Caesar's retinue, who is jealously loved by another slave named Tullus. Tullus behaves like a *buffo* character, and is the comic opposite of Caesar, the arrogant sovereign. He is the one who writes the poems and songs that Plutarch ascribes to Caesar. Naturally there is a violent fight over Gigi, who is desired by two of the pirates, a dispute that is promoted by the jealous pirate bride.

This makes up the bulk of the plot, while Caesar, in his customary victor's pose, waits for the ransom money to arrive. He spends his time reading, and lets nothing disturb him. The pirates are all foolish and simple representatives of their trade; at times they are even somewhat brutal. The ending is slightly different from Plutarch's in that Roman ships attack the island,

and Caesar saves himself by courageously jumping into the sea to reach the Romans. He leads the attack to capture the island, which is then set on fire.

As a "dramma eroicomico per musica," the opera *Cesare in Farmacusa* suited the tastes of the anti-Napoleonic period. In 1800–1801 there were altogether twenty performances of it; by 1808 a further ten productions had taken place, including one in Berlin in honor of the birthday of Friederike, the Queen Mother. *Falstaff*, on the other hand, was produced only four times. Yet its marvelous Shakespearean text makes the libretto of *Cesare in Farmacusa* seem banal. The latter's language is not very polished, and the obvious intrigues and jealousies surrounding Gigi are given too much emphasis. Nevertheless, Salieri gave a great deal of thought to the music; the piece is largely through-composed, and has attractive instrumentation with several solos for wind instruments. While it is evident that the work contains few big arias, it does have some clever parodic numbers.

A contemporary critic noted that "at times one is too obviously reminded of *Axur*," but made allowance for it by adding that it was "after all, a much too pleasant memory for it to be held against the composer, especially as the opera also has its own unique and masterful passages."[17] In connection with a performance in Leipzig, one reviewer referred to the opera as "somewhat cold and not without references to his earlier works."[18] As the text becomes increasingly superficial in the second act and is not very stimulating musically either, the work as a whole grows less and less interesting, though the staged battle at sea and subsequent fire may have been at least visually effective.

Once again Salieri had not sufficiently worked out the theatrical and musical-dramatic development with his librettist. If the general political mood of the times had not been in its favor, the opera would have been forgotten much sooner. As it was, audiences may have compared the wicked pirates to the French, whom one had to meet with Caesarean steadiness and decisiveness, and also with sufficient endurance for the fortunes of war.

Despite this, however, Salieri continued working restlessly and produced another opera four months after *Cesare in Farmacusa*. Defranceschi again wrote the text for it—"at least the greater part of it," as a flyleaf in the libretto ominously states. Apparently there was another, unnamed co-author. The work was entitled *L'Angiolina ossia il Matrimonio per sussurro* (*Angiolina or The Whispered Wedding*), clearly pointing to its model, Ben Jonson's *Epicoene or The Silent Woman*. It would appear that Defranceschi, though a budding lawyer, was well versed in Elizabethan literature. However, he had chosen a piece that consists almost entirely of slapstick, and that keeps elaborating on each blatantly humorous situation.

Jonson's play is about a rich old man who cannot stand the least noise, and who is at odds with the entire world. He wants to disinherit his nephew and decides to marry a quiet young person who, however, immediately after the wedding begins to make a lot of noise. She welcomes a growing number of guests who behave like a horde of monkeys. Finally, three particularly nasty villains promise to help the desperate old man if he will once more include the nephew in his will. After the old man has designated his nephew as his heir, the quiet wife's wig is torn off her head to reveal that she is a boy who has performed his role, including during the wedding, extremely well.

But the text of *Angiolina* is very different from Jonson's. In Defranceschi's version, Angiolina is herself the instigator of the intrigue because she loves the nephew of old Baron Valer, and is willing to marry the latter in exchange for his restoring the inheritance. To be sure, she needs the humor of Cicola, a barber who is to mediate between the baron and his nephew. Angiolina only becomes engaged to the old man, she does not marry him. Even so, there is great disturbance in the house. After a scene with the notary to arrange the marriage settlement, the conspirators remove their disguise so carelessly that the old baron discovers everything. He sees he has been betrayed, and is no longer willing to part with half of his estate. It is only when Angiolina threatens not to break off the engagement—so that the house would remain noisy—that the enervated old man gives in, and Angiolina is able to marry the nephew, who once more has his inheritance.

The German adaptations of this piece that soon appeared in various cities had subtitles like *Die durch Lärm gestiftete Ehe* (*The Marriage Created by Noise*), or *Die Heirat durch Getöse* (*Marriage Brought About by Continuous Noise*). With this work Salieri returned to his beginnings, so to speak; and it is characteristic that this is his only opera (aside from those written for Italy) that was produced at least three times in Italy. The other Italian operas he wrote for Vienna were hardly ever performed in Italy. All in all, it was a rather mindless comic piece, with clichéd characters and situations familiar from *buffa* operas dating back twenty or thirty years. The work was given only ten performances in Vienna.

Salieri himself concluded the second finale was flawed when he saw the reaction of the audience. He noted that the effect of many delicate passages was lost because of restlessness in the audience; they knew how everything would end and began to leave before the performance was over, which disrupted the ending.[19] But one should not simply criticize the audience; the composition deserves some blame for not holding their interest to the final chord. A reviewer who saw it in Prague calls the piece "a low farce with insignificant music by Salieri—surely the most trite he ever wrote."[20]

If, in this work, Salieri seemed to be retracing his steps, so to speak, it was only because the type of opera he had chosen resembled earlier dramatic *buffa* farces with recurring dramaturgical set pieces—undemanding entertainment to which no special attention is paid. But Salieri had clearly indicated right from the start which musical trend he would follow to emancipate himself. Even his early *buffa* operas contained many an allusion to what he had learned from and admired in Gluck. Yet although he had certainly gained great experience in the interim, and in *Angiolina* he was working on quite a different artistic level, there was nothing that could be described as trend-setting about it.

As refined as some of the details were, the music amounted to no more than an inferior evocation of earlier works. Not only had Salieri exhausted his ideas, he was apparently out of touch with what was happening in the development of opera. On the other hand, the unique status of *Falstaff* becomes clear if one studies Salieri's last works, such as *Angiolina*. *Falstaff* is not typical of any particular operatic category but is a *compositum mixtum*, in which musical concepts of the most varied origin and tradition are successfully blended. Salieri seemed to have a flair for these hybrid forms, as some of the earlier operas had shown. However, everything depended on a suitable text.

As Salieri's creative powers failed him, he appeared more readily willing to adapt himself to the limiting demands of the opera business, and to make compromises that were unsatisfactory in the long run. For example, he agreed to write *Annibale in Capua*, whose title role was to be performed by a castrato, to celebrate the opening of the theater in Trieste in May 1801. The singer chosen for the part was Luigi Marchesi, whom Nancy Storace had once imitated so perfectly in her role of the prima donna in *Prima la musica e poi le parole*. Commenting on *Annibale*, Mosel writes:

> One can tell from the work as a whole that the composer was tied to existing circumstances, and to the special needs of the available singers, which did not allow his talents free rein. Those musical passages in which he was able to use his principles and his discernment, contain what is a credit to him; but for the most part he was forced to write what was against his better and often-proved judgment, and then he is no longer his true self.[21]

One may well wonder at the famous composer's decision to accept offers that yielded so little, especially as in this instance he appeared to be a second choice. Domenico Cimarosa was to have written the inaugural opera, but he had died some months earlier. Furthermore, a work that had to be tailored to a specific cast stood little chance of being performed elsewhere, so that aside from the honorarium, of which Salieri had no urgent need, it brought him only local fame. Indeed, the opera received much acclaim in Trieste, which was not surprising, as the city had just recovered sufficiently from its secondary role to boast a new theater. Their engagement of the Viennese Hofkapellmeister was meant to express their close political ties with

Vienna. The librettist chosen was Antonio Simone Sografi, a Venetian lawyer, whose works had lately attracted attention for their republican orientation. This too cleverly symbolized the interplay of political forces in the free port city. But the result was that no other house chose this problematic opera. Furthermore, though Salieri had an invitation to go to Venice right after his engagement in Trieste, a longer stay in Italy was not feasible then, on account of the political situation, and so he returned to Vienna immediately.

However, this was not to be the final stage in Salieri's decline, for he let himself be talked into writing a *Singspiel*, *Die Neger*, for the Theater an der Wien. The author of the text was Georg Friedrich Treitschke, best known for his libretto for Beethoven's *Fidelio*. Treitschke was a famous butterfly collector who wrote a standard entomological work. He was the director of the Theater an der Wien and later of the Hofburgtheater, where he also served as administrator until his death. Furthermore, he was one of the most prolific of scribblers, and could turn out ten *Singspiel* adaptations in a year. A Viennese calumny describes him as the "gray-haired, well-nourished vinous manager of the Hofburgtheater, except when his own works are being performed."[22]

Die Neger was apparently one of Treitschke's first works, though not an example of innovative quality. It takes place on an English plantation in America. Anyone who expects the plot to pit Negroes against English plantation owners soon learns otherwise; in fact, it is all about Lord Falkland, who is missing and has been deprived of his holdings through the intrigues of his undaunted and evil opponent, Lord Bedford. The latter is now conspiring against the governor, whom he tries to poison. It is a grotesque tale of crime, at the end of which Jack, the Negro overseer of Bedford's slaves and the evil man's right hand, reveals himself as the missing and cleverly made-up Lord Falkland (not even mentioned in the list of characters). Aided by John, a Negro in the service of the governor, he uses his role to expose the criminal acts of Lord Bedford.

The reviewer of the *Allgemeine musikalische Zeitung* writes of it:

You can see how ordinary and inconsequential the plot of this opera is; . . . In portraying character it is not enough to have one person always speak virtuously and the other always speak viciously—for no one in the world ever displays his characteristics so blatantly all the time, least of all a dissolute person who tries to make his way by underhand means. Because the plot is of so little interest, and because the characters are contrasted by means of moral rather than psychological motivation, the entire work appears dull and drawn-out, which must have aroused special displeasure when it was performed.

Not only was the libretto considered to be poor; the composer also came in for his share of criticism for the complete failure of the *Singspiel*:

One could justly expect something excellent from the composer of Axur and La grotta di Trofonio, and so many other accomplished operas; but even this expectation was not satisfied. Though the first act, especially, has several very pleasing passages, and a march of the Negroes . . . which deserves an honorable mention, on the whole one missed the force and characteristics one has come to value more and more in the works of Mozart and Cherubini.[23]

Salieri had to endure being told that he had outlived himself; that his real and important contribution had essentially ended with *Axur*; that other, only negligibly younger, composers like Cherubini (also an Italian expatriate) had become the guiding stars of opera. But above all, he had to recognize that Mozart's triumph was only truly beginning now. The opera *Die Neger* was Salieri's last, a superfluous and sad epilogue to a stage career that had been uneven, yet crowned with brilliant highlights and extraordinary masterpieces.

CHAPTER NINE

Beyond Opera 1802–1825

Salieri wrote more than forty operas, and during those years of great productivity his family grew steadily; between 1777 and 1790 seven daughters and a son were born. Only the last of these children did not survive beyond the first year, unusual at a time of high infant mortality in which, on the average, only every third child reached its third year. However, Salieri's family was not entirely spared bereavement. One daughter, Elisabeth Josepha, died of scarlet fever at the age of seven in 1794; another, Francisca Antonia, died of pneumonia in 1796 when she was fourteen. Only four daughters survived their father.

The whole family lived in the house that Salieri's wife Theresa and two of her unmarried brothers had inherited from their father; it was in the Seilergasse next to the Gött-weiher Hof. Family life was very important to them, but unfortunately not a single letter exists that might shed some light on their domesticity. In the notes that Salieri wrote later and gave to Mosel, there is a description of a brief period in 1788 when Salieri was confined to bed with a leg injury. There he mistakenly refers to his "seven daughters," when two of them had not yet been born:

My wife generally sat by my bed with two of my daughters, working at a small table; my son did his studying at my desk; two of our younger daughters were in the next room knitting, keeping an eye on the three youngest girls who were playing with their dolls; I lay in bed and was happy to see that charming sight, in between my reading and reflecting. At seven o'clock my wife and children recited their evening prayers, and then continued their previous activities. Later my son sat down at the pianoforte, and if one of his sisters asked him to play a waltz the girls whirled around merrily. At nine o'clock my wife and a maid came to take care of my bad leg with fumigants and other medications prescribed by the doctor; afterwards one of my older daughters brought me my soup, and half an hour later my wife, my son and seven daughters— who kissed me, or kissed my hand—came to bid me goodnight. How pleasant those evenings were for me! What comfort and joy they brought to the heart of a loving husband and father![1]

Such recollections by the aging Salieri paint a family idyll without any indication that this was taking place in the house of a famous composer. When he refers to the waltz, which was hardly known in 1788, he probably meant one of the dances then in vogue. As for the pianoforte, it had become part of every comfortable bourgeois household, music being at the center of social life in the home.

Salieri must have read a great deal; all the memoirs of his contemporaries speak of a highly educated man. On the other hand, he was never one to bury himself in his study. He took every opportunity to go for walks in the Augarten, or make excursions farther afield, to the environs around Vienna, which he apparently liked to do in company. This sociability was inspired less by a desire to engage in conversation than to share his exuberance at being outdoors.

Such excursions yielded many simple canons, duets, terzettos, or quartets—depending on the occasion—meant for immediate performance. The texts for them were mostly amusing occasional verses he made up himself, or sayings, maxims, and quotations in verse, all of which he wrote down as compositions in a small book; some of them were published as "divertimenti vocali" or "scherzi armonici vocali." By and large, the texts are Italian, though there are some in German, Latin, or French as well. The assertion that during his lifetime Salieri spoke scarcely any German is untenable, though what he spoke was not free of errors; he had a habit of mixing bits and pieces of different languages in a fast-paced conversation, which was also said to be true of Gluck.

Perhaps this mixing of languages had something to do with his lively and bubbling temperament—a temperament that could also express itself in irascible outbursts. Yet Salieri was one of those who need harmonious and peaceful surroundings, and who prefer friendly and peaceful relationships to continuous feuding. He certainly tried to keep conflicts and dogmatism within bounds. The image conveyed of him in later legend—of a tortured conspirator, filled with enough hatred and jealousy to kill his rivals (especially Mozart)—is false. In his old age Salieri was occasionally plagued by fits of depression, which upset him greatly. Indeed, he was not always a very balanced person, being impulsive and spontaneous rather than controlled and impassive, but overall he was a happy, witty, and engaging individual, who blossomed in society. Apparently he had sufficient self-confidence to achieve his goals, though he remained self-critical and was not susceptible to flattery.

In fact, Salieri was an honest critic of his own work, especially from the vantage point of old age, and was fully aware of both his strengths and his weaknesses. However, his criticism all too frequently focuses on the crafting of a composition, without progressing to an evaluation of the work in its entirety. In this connection, it is significant that Salieri always examines the effect of individual numbers or of the formal unities of an opera, and also discusses their function within the musical and dramatic development. But he does not deal with the subject of the text, nor his own intentions. The later notes on his operas are thus primarily disparate observations, never treating a work as an artistic whole. One is sometimes tempted to wonder whether this is a characteristic of his critical commentary alone, or whether it is also true of his method of composition.

As of the 1790s, Salieri tended to compose small-scale pieces, such as canons and the various "scherzi armonici." Perhaps these not only express a change in his musical interests but also a growing inability to mobilize the concentration necessary for larger works. His last operas convey an impression of defiant efforts to overcome this weakness, but except for *Falstaff*, and despite individual interesting or well-crafted passages in the others, their overall compositional achievement becomes less and less convincing.

Evidently he now lacked the courage to embark on larger compositions in any category, and recognized his failing creative capacity. It is doubtful whether the stylistic changes that occurred in music around 1800 affected his waning output. He was, after all, considered one of the more innovative composers, at least up to the time he composed *Axur*. His best works had shown him to be independent of traditions, schools, or stylistic peculiarities. He tried everything, and adapted whatever he considered useful to his own musical and dramatic concepts. Thus the influence of Gluck is just as perceptible in Salieri's work as is his assimilation of the Neapolitan style; he incorporates his experience of French music as he does the Viennese *Singspiel*, and contrasts free *buffa* forms with elements of *opera seria* (as happened frequently in this transitional period). No doubt he listened closely to Mozart's operas as well. It was characteristic of him that the libretti he chose were also too varied to fit into any specific category. But some of the late operas show a regression in his musical language and dramaturgical ability to produce convincing solutions.

Salieri wrote most of his sacred music after 1800, and it is much more modest and conservative in its approach than his previous work. Within this category, he seemed to prefer graduals, offertories, and psalms. The music is not intended to be a dramatic paean in praise of God, but to inspire the listener to divine worship. Salieri saw church music as primarily liturgical, and felt it should serve that purpose as far as possible. An anecdote (unverifiable but typical of this attitude) has it that as Hofkapellmeister he never permitted Joseph Haydn's masses to be performed because he considered them too worldly, and ill-suited to religious service. Salieri's own sacred music is "utility music" in the best sense, never deviating from its religious task. It does not burden the listener with would-be originality, and is clearly organized; it possesses simple and pleasing melodies, few motifs, and plain harmonics. Salieri is not inclined to resort to sentimentality or high drama; his fugues are plain rather than lofty and drawn-out. The instrumentation has appeal, but avoids exaggerated effects.

As a composer of sacred music, Salieri did not have the slightest inclination to call attention to himself; he used conventional solutions and did not shy away from the frequent use of unison passages. Only in the masses and the *Requiem*, which he wrote for himself in 1804, are there quartets for soloists in addition to a chorus; these are written partly to contrast with the chorus, and partly to blend with it. The few solo numbers are very short, or else they alternate with the chorus. All this church music expresses personal faith and piety more than an independent artistic drive. Yet there is no expression of overwhelming religiosity; instead, one senses a tendency toward introspection in the last mass, and also in the *Requiem*, which has no fugue at all, and seems to possess some serene, almost popular elements as well.

Salieri's sacred music was intended almost exclusively for use at court, where he carried out his duties faithfully over many years and grew to be an increasingly staunch follower of the House of Habsburg. He did not indulge in the opportunism that led so many other convinced Josephinites to become overzealous apologists for the reaction. Salieri was too uninvolved in the politics of the day and too firm of character for such behavior. In his case, the change of heart was inspired by the universal patriotism that followed the French challenge to the European states.

This patriotic conviction saved Salieri from being a renegade, enabling him instead to become an objective member of the Franzine reaction. Unfortunately, the composer of *Tarare* was not perceptive enough to realize that this group was engaged in forging the "Holy Alliance," which sought to restore a viable form of the status quo ante; above all, they wanted to create an alliance between church and crown. Unlike his former librettist Beaumarchais, Salieri was too wrapped up in his work and had too little contact with critical individuals, so that he could sense no rupture with past policy. Perhaps this lack of sensitivity to ongoing social and historical developments was somehow linked to his failing creativity. In any case, from now on Salieri served both Habsburg dynasty and church. Indeed, most of his compositions of sacred music were written for royal occasions and to be enjoyed at specific performances. It remains to be seen whether Salieri initiated or was requested to produce such works. Retrospectively, at any rate, the seventy-two-year-old composer could justly comment to Friedrich Rochlitz: "These sacred pieces [were written] for God and my Emperor."

Included among Salieri's patriotic works was music for a nationalistic play, *Die Hussiten vor Naumburg*, by August von Kotzebue.[2] It was one of two hundred and eleven plays by this author, and while it was unbearably sentimental, it ably captured the widespread feelings of helplessness against Napoleon:

> According to historical evidence the Hussites, roused to the most cruel fanaticism, murder, and rapacity, laid waste the greater part of Bohemia, turned the loveliest cities and churches to ashes, and tortured to death all inhabitants who tried to resist them regardless of their age or sex. Under the command of their terrible leader, the infamous Procop, they invaded neighboring Saxony.[3]

The citizens of Naumburg are in the midst of harvesting, and enjoying a festival for the reapers when they receive this frightening news. Barricaded in their town, after various unsuccessful sorties they try to negotiate, but their representatives are brutally murdered. An old man suggests that defenceless children be sent to the enemy's camp to soften their hearts—and this finally succeeds. Now Procop is willing to bypass the town peacefully. The play ends with a hymn of praise to God by the liberated Naumburgers.

One or two well-known composers had agreed to write a choral piece for the play, and so make a communal political work out of it. Haydn had been among those asked, but had politely refused. Whatever music existed for the piece was not used when it was produced at the Hoftheater in Vienna, in March 1803. At that time, Salieri was commissioned to write the overture, choruses, and interludes. The work was performed seventeen times before Napoleon's entry into Vienna in 1805, which clearly demonstrates Salieri's ability to arouse patriotic feelings. Mosel writes:

> The overture belongs with his best compositions in this category; it expresses the cheerfulness of the country folk. The interlude between the first and second acts depicts the fear and confusion of the threatened Naumburgers, and is also one of the best instrumental pieces by our master. The introduction to the third act is no less excellent and, like the two foregoing compositions, it adds to the conviction that *Salieri* was quite capable of writing superb instrumental music when he was willing to make the effort. The interlude between the third and fourth acts, which represents the wild joy of the victorious Hussites, is forceful; and yet, like the introduction to the fifth act, which expresses the mothers' fear for their children, it is not up to the standard of the first interlude.[4]

The choruses were very simple and without embellishment; as Mosel points out, they were appropriate to the moving plot. The orchestral music for *Die Hussiten vor Naumburg* consisted of short mood pictures that were influenced by the changing emotions in the acts they introduced, though they did not describe the events.

It is a very different matter when it comes to the cantata *Gesù al limbo*, in which the overture attempts to portray the entire life story of Jesus in detail. Mosel comments:

> If this task appears to be beyond the confines of instrumental music, it was even less likely to be solved the way this work is organized, where the musical description of an event is limited to eight, or four, or even to two measures; and this is especially true if incidents such as Jesus among the scribes, the capture of Jesus, or his interrogation are included, which are impossible to express in sound. Hence the overture is a mosaic of short, quite varied and disconnected instrumental passages whose meaning no one would be likely to guess without having read the captions.[5]

This overly precise attention to individual details that never merge to become one large, cohesive whole has something amateurish and pedantic about it, especially as the life of Jesus does not need retelling and seems superfluous in connection with this cantata. For *Gesù al limbo* means Jesus in Purgatory, and treats a difficult theological problem that was not part of the Bible, and proposed only by the Church Fathers. Purgatory is the place where unbaptized infants and the virtuous who lived before Christ are supposed to go after death to await salvation by Christ. Thus Adam, Eve, and Abraham appear— even Jesus himself, of which Mosel did not approve, especially since there is a terzetto between Jesus, Faith, and Abraham, because "when the Savior speaks, all must remain silent and no voice is worthy of joining with His."[6] The musician-dramatist Salieri did not know what to do with such farfetched ideas; in fact, he deliberately mingled Jesus with others.

Salieri finally had a chance to have his big mass for double choir performed, as well as his *Te Deum*, which he had written five years earlier for an eventual peace celebration. Though there was as yet no peace in sight, there was an event to celebrate in Vienna that Salieri considered worthy of such music. Napoleon, who had been Consul, assumed the title of Emperor of the French in May 1804. This was a claim that the old Habsburg monarchy must have found quite intolerable. Franz II, who was to remain Emperor of the Holy Roman Empire until 1806, thereupon promulgated

> . . . a pragmatic law, in which the monarch called himself *Franz I, Hereditary Emperor of Austria*, so that as sovereign of the *House* and of the *Monarchy* he could preserve them, holding his title and hereditary rank in complete equality with the great powers—an equality that is guaranteed to Austria's rulers according to treaties and the law of nations, and that befits the age-old splendor of the House, and the populous realm that comprises large kingdoms and independent principalities.[7]

A large national thanksgiving ceremony took place in December (1804), at which Salieri conducted his mass and *Te Deum* for the first time. Joseph von Hormayr provides a description of the events as they occurred on December 8:

> . . . the ceremonial procession made its way from the Burg across the Michaelerplatz, through the Herrngasse, across the Freyung, the Hof and the Graben, past the Stock im Eisen to St. Stephen's cathedral, to hear the *Te Deum*. In the lead were the magnificent royal carriages carrying the royal chamberlains and the privy councillors all splendidly attired in court dress, each carriage drawn by six horses and accompanied by two runners and six lackeys in finery; these were followed by the carriages of the royal family—the Archduke Ferdinand with his sons, the Archdukes Franz, Ferdinand, and Maximilian, and the Archdukes Johann, Ludwig, Reiner, and Rudolph—accompanied by their private

tutors and chamberlains on horseback. After them came the sumptuous imperial carriage bearing *Franz I, Roman-German and Hereditary Emperor of Austria* and the Empress Maria Theresa, accompanied by the highest royal officials and captains of the guard, with the Lifeguards on either side, and the German and Hungarian Guards behind the carriage. They were followed by the resident governess and the dames de palais; a cavalry regiment and a battalion of grenadiers closed the procession. The army formed a guard of honor in the streets; the citizens paraded in the squares. Members of the Order of Teutonic Knights, the rest of the privy councillors, chamberlains, and seneschals, members of the government, of the upper classes, of the university and the city council were all waiting in St. Stephen's.[8]

Being so devoted to the House of Habsburg, Salieri's greatest concern was for peace for the Habsburg realm, and this festival must have seemed like its harbinger. He considered himself entirely Austrian, and now wished to convey a personal expression of gratitude to Emperor Franz. For though in most things Franz was the exact opposite of his uncle, Salieri respected him as the representative of a new régime with which he increasingly identified.

In his new patriotic zeal, he encountered a poem by an eccentric Hungarian nobleman, Ferdinand von Geramb, who created somewhat of a stir at this time. Though a marginal character of dubious reputation who had engaged in duels on several occasions, he had become a fervent patriot, and even put together his own volunteer corps to fight Napoleon. Later, while Geramb was in England to gather new volunteers, an attempt was made to arrest him for debts; over a period of twelve days he defended himself inside his apartment as if it were a fortress. He was expelled from the country and taken prisoner by the French, sharing a cell with the Bishop of Troyes, who converted him to the monastic life. Indeed, Geramb became a Trappist, and showed such enthusiasm for the strict rules of the order that he finally became the abbot general of the order.

Geramb's epic poem *Habsburg* appeared in an imperial folio de luxe edition, embellished with many engravings. In forty verses it praised the heroic deeds of the House of Habsburg as having been dedicated to peace from the very beginning. Here are two stanzas of this poem:

The mighty task is completed
world chaos and war have ended.
Franz rests with Austria undefeated,
and contemplates what he defended.
Leading your heroes, Franz,
inscribe into your will
That Habsburg's royal brilliance
ever its native land must fill.

Franz, second Rudolph of your clan,
you ordered feuds to cease,
and where the streams of blood ran,
to battlefield brought peace.
Once more the arts begin their dance
the plough takes up its work again,
with harvest crown peace does advance
to lead your coronation train.[9]

Even the most skilled and experienced composer was bound to find it utterly impossible to write music for forty such verses, and yet provide enough variety and inner suspense not to be terribly boring. Salieri sacrificed the very things that had previously characterized his work—a feeling for dramatic development and instrumental accompaniment that was more reflective than impressionistic—to a text that could not be improved by any amount of musical wit.

It was around this time (1805) that Salieri ceased to be an active composer. The *Requiem* of 1804, his major sacred composition, shows definite traits of being a terminal work. He thought he would be dying soon, and therefore wrote it for himself; perhaps this was the first sign of the old-age depression that so darkened his final years. And in this same period two deaths occurred in his family that troubled him profoundly. His only son, Alois Engelbert, died in September 1805 at the age of twenty-three; and his wife Theresa passed away eighteen months later, on May 30, 1807. Salieri now lived with two unmarried daughters who had to keep house for him. He insisted that it was their duty, which surely did not always make for a harmonious relationship. One can imagine how the family idyll gradually became transformed into a household run by a strict patriarch.

While Salieri gave up composing, he still participated in all sorts of musical activities, which seemed to increase as time went on. He continued to conduct the concerts of the Tonkünstler Society, on whose board he held a leading position, into his old age. As of 1807, the program alternated between Haydn's *The Creation* and *The Four Seasons*, which sold the most tickets. And ticket sales constituted the greater part of the benevolent fund for musicians' widows and orphans. Salieri took this task very seriously, not only for musical reasons, but because he had a decided social conscience. He could become very nasty if anyone organized a competing concert for the same evening, and perhaps lured some of the musicians away. Ludwig van Beethoven experienced this vividly when he planned his famous Akademie concert of 1808, at which the Symphonies nos. 5 and 6, the Piano Concerto no. 4, and the *Choral Fantasy* were first performed. The date he chose for the concert was December 22, the very date that had for years been reserved for the concerts of the Tonkünstler Society. Salieri's reaction caused Beethoven to speak indignantly of his "enemies" and of Salieri's "hatred," though the latter was not entirely in the wrong.[10]

But above all, Salieri devoted himself with great enthusiasm to his duties as Hofkapellmeister. This was not only a position as conductor, in which he was responsible for all the music connected with the court, but like a directorship, it also included all the administrative tasks. While it may originally have been customary for a Hofkapellmeister to contribute, rehearse, and perform primarily his own works, Salieri took the organizational aspects of his post especially seriously. Only on rare occasions did he present his own compositions of sacred music.

He was zealously concerned with establishing an exemplary functional orchestra. He tried to obtain the best possible players for the court orchestra, making the choice himself after auditioning musicians; and he also manifested an unusual solicitude for the orchestra. After all, he was in charge of arranging for leaves of absence and substitutes, and he tried to give permanent positions to any replacements who proved capable. As artistic director, he had no financial authority and had to defer in such matters as salaries and pensions to the nobleman, the *Hofmusikgraf*, responsible for court music. But he was a most effective spokesman for the needs of the orchestra, and almost always achieved results.

Since the orchestra had its own instruments, which had to be repaired or replaced regularly, Salieri took charge of supervising the instrument makers. He was equally dedicated when it came to maintaining the archives of the court orchestra, which housed a valuable collection of printed music. He laid down very strict rules so that these treasures could be carefully preserved.

Another of Salieri's duties involved the selection of the choirboys. He was renowned for his singing instruction, and the development and formation of their vocal and musical abilities was especially important to him. The pedagogical skills he had acquired early on were put to effective use here.

The rigor with which he carried out his official duties, and his unconditional support of all the needs of the musicians, made him a highly valued administrator. As he no longer did much composing himself and did not promote his own works, there was no occasion for envy. Moreover, he did not disdain the less important musical tasks. For instance, he played the pianoforte at the noteworthy premiere of Haydn's work *The Creation*. And at the big charity concert of December 8, 1813, at which Beethoven's battle symphony *Wellington's Victory* was first performed, Salieri directed the drums and cannon. He was a colleague who was approachable and willing to help at all times, a personality without whom Viennese musical life was inconceivable.

So it is not surprising that Salieri was promptly entrusted with important tasks when the *Gesellschaft der Musikfreunde* (Society of Friends of Music) was organized in 1814–1815. He was asked to be part of the governing board that had to devise the statutes and by-laws, and he was immediately put in charge of the institute for choir training, which had at least 272 members. Later, he also joined the concert and building committees. The latter committee was involved with the planning and construction of a conservatory. A first step in this direction was a school for voice in 1817, of which Salieri became the director (instrumental instruction was added in 1819).

Salieri's teaching career had begun right after the end of

his studies with Gassmann; it had been almost his sole source of income as a budding musician. At first he probably taught only pianoforte, but soon he added vocal instruction. One of his early students was Catarina Cavalieri, who made her debut at the age of fifteen. (Later she was the first to sing the role of Constanze in Mozart's *Die Entführung aus dem Serail*.) Salieri taught music for some fifty years, specializing in song and theory.

Music theory included the art of composition and the basics of counterpoint, as well as musical analysis, score reading, and an introduction to composition for voice. It was in the latter that Salieri was considered a leading authority. How else can one account for the fact that between 1793 and 1809, Beethoven frequently went to Salieri—whom he considered one of his teachers—to study questions of singing technique? It may not have been regular instruction, and later became more a sort of consultation, with its most intensive period lasting until 1802, but for Beethoven it was an important supplement to his contrapuntal studies with Johann Georg Albrechtsberger.[11]

Salieri taught most of his eighty students (and there may have been even more) free of charge, a responsibility he took upon himself throughout his life. He saw it as a way of expressing his gratitude to his teacher Gassmann, who had brought him to Vienna, taken care of him in his home for many years, and given him a thorough musical education. However, he did accept fees from those who came from noble or wealthy bourgeois families. His students of theory and composition, as well as of voice, included many illustrious names of the generations born between 1760 and 1810.

In addition to Beethoven, the composers who studied with Salieri included such names as Ignaz Umlauff, Peter von Winter, Anselm Hüttenbrenner, Joseph Eybler, Joseph Weigl, Franz Xaver Süssmayr, Giovanni Liverati, Simon Sechter, Ignaz Assmayer, and Carl Czerny. Other students included Meyerbeer, Franz Xaver Wolfgang Mozart, Ignaz Moscheles, Schubert, Karl Gottlieb Reissiger, Benedikt Randhartinger, and Liszt. Sometimes, as with Czerny or Meyerbeer, the instruction consisted of only a few lessons; in other instances the coaching went on over a period of years, as was the case with Schubert. Generally the focus was on composition for voice, together with the basic principles of counterpoint.

The memoirs of some of Schubert's circle of friends mention Salieri's classes, partly in connection with Schubert and partly with their personal experiences. For instance, Hüttenbrenner reports, "Schubert was very highly regarded by Salieri, with whom he studied *continuo* and composition."[12] Elsewhere he notes, "Our Salieri's favorite musicians were the *marksmen*, the *sight-readers*; he himself could play from the score like no one else; the treble and the baritone clef were as familiar to him as the rest of the well-known clefs."[13] Playing from the score, the "abc" of all aspiring Kapellmeister, seems to have been an important element in Salieri's teaching methods.

When teaching composition, Salieri most likely concentrated on pieces for voice. He assigned Italian texts, especially those by Metastasio, with whom he had himself studied declamation. Then he went over and corrected the assignments together with the students. Joseph von Spaun says of Schubert's lessons "that Salieri thoroughly disapproved of precisely the sort of composition to which his student was irresistibly drawn, namely the German Lied. The verses of Goethe, Schiller and others . . . were intolerable to the Italian . . . Salieri, along with Ernst von Schubert, desired that he [young Schubert] no longer spend time on compositions of that sort, and that he be more sparing with his own melodies . . ."[14] But that did not prevent Schubert from publishing five *Goethe Lieder* (Opus 5) in 1821, with a dedication to Salieri—perhaps by way of influencing the latter's taste.

Many of Salieri's voice students played important roles in concerts and opera. In addition to Cavalieri, they included such singers as Julius Cornet, Fortunata Franchetti-Walzel, Anton Haitzinger, Josephine Killitschgy, Katharina Kraus-Wranizky, Anna Milder-Hauptmann, Karoline Seidler, Katharina Wallbach-Canzi, and Karoline Unger. Salieri's lifelong involvement with the art of singing encouraged him to write a textbook for its instruction, which remains unpublished. Its special appeal lies in its having been written entirely in verse, each stanza designed for four voices; it was intended as a set of basic instructions for amateurs. Though this work was probably not used at the singing school of the conservatory, test questions from it were utilized.

The general esteem Salieri enjoyed also enabled him to exert some influence in practical matters concerning the performance of music. He was one of the first to acknowledge publicly the invention of the metronome by Johann Nepomuk Mälzel, and promoted its use.[15] He considered it important that posterity be made aware of the authentic conceptions of tempo, which are inadequately reproduced by verbal indications. Thus he not only metronomized the score of his work *Les Danaïdes*, but also passed on the metronome beat of Gluck's operas as he recalled them from performances, as well as the Haydn oratorios he had conducted in the composer's presence. The tempo is often surprisingly fast, as it is in the metronomic instructions given by Beethoven. Another essay[16] disputes the "maniera languida, smorfiosa" (overly sentimental manner) that had been adopted by string instrumentalists as well as singers; he considered this slurring of the intervals "a most tasteless style."

Salieri received many honors: he was made a member of the Swedish Academy, appointed a nonresident member of the French National Institute by Napoleon, and became an honorary member of the Milan Conservatory. When he was made a Knight of the Legion of Honor in 1815, and asked Emperor Franz if he might be permitted to wear the order, the latter first wanted to know what service had merited the award. For Franz II had had his problems with Napoleon; though he had even let him marry his own daughter, she had long since returned to live in Vienna as Marie Louise, Duchess of Parma. Salieri was able to assure the emperor that he had received his decoration from the Bourbons. On the occasion of the fiftieth anniversary of his service to the Habsburg court, Salieri received the golden Civilian Medallion of Honor on its golden chain; his students celebrated the event with a special gathering at which they performed their own vocal compositions for him.

Schubert noted in his journal on that day, June 16, 1816:

It must be delightful and uplifting for an artist to see all his students gathered around him, and to note how each one endeavors to contribute his best to the celebration. And it is almost entirely due to one of our greatest German artists that one hears in all these compositions only what is of a pure nature, and not any of that deliberate eccentricity which is now to be found in the work of most composers; the latter combines, confuses, and does not differentiate between the tragic and the comic, the pleasant and the unpleasant, the heroic and the pathetic, the holiest and the harlequinade; it drives man frantic instead of letting him feel love, and inspires his laughter instead of uplifting him. It is such eccentricity that this artist has banned from the circle of his students, and hence it must give him the greatest satisfaction to experience pure, holy Nature. For he was guided by Gluck, and came to understand Nature and preserve it despite the unnatural influences of our times.[17]

It is an odd declaration of loyalty. One important figure missing from the festivities was Beethoven. Though he was in Vienna at the time, he did not participate in this homage to Salieri by his students.

Not much is known of the external events of the aging Salieri's life. It appears to have been extremely regular, interrupted only by little excursions and two short journeys to Dresden and Bohemia. He did not overexert himself, and enjoyed being sociable. Mosel, who maintained close contact with him in this period, summarizes his routine as follows:

For several years *Salieri* devoted the morning hours from nine to one o'clock, three days a week, to the free instruction of talented young people of both sexes; the subjects of instruction included singing, *continuo*, and composition. On the other days his morning hours were taken up with his duties for the court orchestra and his transactions as Vice-President of the widows' pension institute of the Tonkünstler. He alternated his evenings at the homes of some of his artistically inclined friends, where he played or listened to music. The entertainment generally consisted of *Gluck's* immortal works, or the compositions of older Italian masters, and those of his own works which had either never been performed or else not heard in a long time. He rarely went to the theater, and to the extent that true dramatic music was ousted by trivial solfeggios and music resembling foolish circus pieces, he went ever less frequently. Whatever free time he had he spent reading and taking walks which, as a nature lover, he enjoyed above all else.[18]

At this time Salieri joined a social club called "Ludlams-Höhle,"[19] whose aims were to indulge in nonsense and drinking, in contrast to the satires that often formed part of political gatherings. In the club, Salieri was known as "Don Tarar di Palmira." It had over one hundred members, who were connected with the theater in one way or another, as actors, writers, musicians, or simply theatergoers. Carl Maria von Weber was also invited to join the society, but is said to have refused as long as Salieri was a member[20]—a result of the rumors of Salieri's complicity in Mozart's death, which had begun to crop up in his own lifetime. The most notable aspect of this totally apolitical association was its grotesquely ludicrous end; it was suspected of being a conspiratorial secret society, and was disbanded after a large-scale nighttime police raid. However, when this took place Salieri was no longer alive.

In December 1815 Salieri once more produced a work that showed that he was not merely an eighteenth-century composer, but an orchestrator skilled in the most recent post-classical trends in composition. This work, entitled *Vierundzwanzig Variationen für das Orchester über das Thema La folia di Spagnia*, was an original work of variations that could also be described as a method for teaching orchestration. Of special note are two substantial solos for harp and several solo passages for the violin. The treatment of the woodwinds was also highly effective, with its use of every conceivable shade of tone coloring, as was the somber brass instrumentation, without flourishes; in both, the variations keep very close to the theme. The work is a worthy forerunner of more recent works of this sort such as Benjamin Britten's *A Young Person's Guide to the Orchestra*. However, nothing is known about why it was written.

Unfortunately, this was the only new composition Salieri undertook; he now spent his time going over his older works again. How greatly his conceptions of music theater had regressed from his best period to a philistine harmlessness, a theater of shameless conciliation, is demonstrated by his reworking of *Les Danaïdes* into *Danaus*, an opera in four acts that was never performed in this version. The main idea was, as he himself says, "that brutal spectacles acquaint the people with brutal ideas, just as base ones plunge them ever more deeply into baseness."[21] On the one hand, the terrible slaughter of the fifty sons of Aegyptus by the Danaides was to be eliminated, though it is the center of the plot; on the other hand, Salieri wanted to save the moving music of the concluding choral scene in Hell because it belongs to the most forceful part of the whole opera. The librettist, Franz Xaver Huber, had no qualms about transforming this classical material into a sentimental play. In his version, Huber lets Hypermestra persuade Danaus to give up his murderous plan, and adds some other ideas of his own.

For instance, Danaus now experiences the famous scene in Hell as a dream—it is acted out onstage—whereas originally it concluded the opera. He is so terrified by his dream that he wants to prevent his daughters from committing the mass murder he has only just ordered. But at that very moment one hears the death cries backstage. Danaus grows desperate, especially once the Danaides return with their bloody daggers. But then Lynceus appears, and he and Hypermestra explain that it was all a ruse to make Danaus change his mind. Hypermestra's marriage to Lynceus can now proceed, as can the marriages of the Danaides to the sons of Aegyptus. As though he had been completely transformed, Danaus now declares, "Even if one of the gods were to demand that we commit a vicious crime, it would be our duty to refuse." The fearfully diabolical punishment he saw so vividly in his dream was in itself enough to change him. Nothing remained of the ancient Greek myth; instead, the opera propagates cheap theories of punishment as a deterrent.[22]

The exact date of this *Danaus* adaptation is unknown, but in 1818, Salieri began to rework *Tarare* as a three-act opera for a new production in Paris. And just as in *Les Danaïdes*, the real meaning of the work was completely reversed. While the main subject of the 1787 version was an alliance between a tyrannical monarchy and a corrupt clergy, and the subsequent betrayal of the latter, Salieri deleted all references to religion and clerical power in his revised work. Thus the essential intention of Beaumarchais' text was, so to speak, betrayed. A review by Georg Ludwig Peter Sievers in the *Allgemeine musikalische Zeitung* discusses the consequences of the changes:

> . . . each and every one of the reflections, whose daring, powerful, prosaic meaning previously made for the success of the piece, has been

eliminated, and Atar ends up as a penitent sinner who promises to reform, but who can still secretly nurse the desire to begin all over again and do even greater harm under more propitious circumstances. Thus Beaumarchais' boldest and most daring production has become a meaningless, weak parody of itself, and its author has had to let himself be transformed into an emasculated Calpigi! Indeed, the intention appears to have been to rob the piece of all its dramatic and moral interest, in order to turn it into a mere trellis for the unscented flowers of the art of the dance to climb. In its present form the piece really seems to exist solely for its ballets; they exceed anything that grand opera has produced until now.[23]

Salieri tried to keep as much of the existing music as he could in *Danaus* and *Tarare*, both by making numerous readjustments and by writing additional material as required by the altered libretto. However, the amount of newly composed music in each of them is relatively small. In *Tarare*, Salieri did not even shy away from having the much-admired aria normally sung by the sacrificial boy Elamir set to a new text for Spinette, Calpigi's "intriguing and flirtatious" wife. Thus music became material to be disposed of and moved around as needed, as in the old parodies; Salieri himself remodeled its emotional content, its "truth," so that "a beautiful passage" was reproduced and offered in a new guise.

Until 1822, the aged Salieri went over all his operas, "reading them one after the other," presumably making his handwritten comments in the scores at this time. He had before him a body of work that included the most varied forms; from the start, he had been open to different influences and had eagerly absorbed ideas from all sides, which he then blended into a specific and typical style of his own. Interpretation of the text was his starting point, and determined the nature of his musical decisions. This led to an altogether reflective, hence artificial, music by no means dependent on pretty melodies; in fact, it often lacked the typical Neapolitan melodic felicity and became somewhat choppy. Salieri never quite managed to write the sort of magnificent and haunting tunes that would become popular in the streets as well.

Free forms such as *cavatinas* and songlike pieces predominate in the formal arrangement of the vocal numbers; repetitions of text or even real *da capo* arias are rarely found. Even in the *buffa* operas there is a tendency toward through-composed sections, surely influenced by experience with the *tragédie lyrique*. There are many ensemble passages for which the scenic development is important. Often the finales are expanded but clearly arranged structures in which the frequent changes of tempo heighten the musical tension. Choruses are of great importance in Salieri's operas and musical comedies; in these he repeatedly achieved particularly lovely and impressive passages.

Salieri liked to use recitatives with orchestral accompaniment, even in the *buffa* operas. Such recitatives are very appealing harmonically in *Les Danaïdes*, and especially so in *Tarare*. Yet there are frequent instances in which his *secco* recitatives tend to be extremely simple and not especially varied harmonically. On the other hand, his musical comedies also contain *parlando*-like sections with nuances and transitions ranging all the way to *ariosos*, which he had tried out in *Tarare*.

The overtures are generally uncomplicated, often consisting of one movement whose sections are never developed. They mostly lack thematic relationship to the opera, and function purely as general introductions. That is surprising, given Salieri's specialty (though limited to certain works) of detailed and descriptive, almost pantomimic music that not only evokes an atmosphere—as in the popular "sea pieces"—but tries to tell a story. An early example of this is the *Armida* overture, but even in his old age Salieri used the technique again in the oratorio, *Gesù al limbo*, in which the orchestral idiom is very colorful and differentiated without in any way producing an exaggerated effect.

Salieri creates fine shadings rather than sharp contrasts. His treatment of the strings is especially varied, and he constantly provides solos for wind instruments. For instance, he added two English horns to *La Grotta di Trofonio* with great effect. And in conformity with Viennese custom, Salieri increased his orchestra by two clarinettists as of 1788. But his orchestral palette becomes fully developed only when it is used to describe extra-musical dramatic events and characterize people and situations. Salieri was a composer who needed the inspiration of action onstage and the challenge of transposing words into music. The fact that he wrote little instrumental music—with the exception of some early concertos and what presumably was his last great work, the *Orchestervariationen*—is due to his own recognition of where his true creative talent lay.

It is obvious, therefore, why Salieri adhered to the text unusually carefully. In his eyes, the natural word stress or prosody took precedence over melodic invention. Comprehensibility of the text was for him the key to dramatic music. He saw opera as musical theater; a combination of text, musical language, and stage action (including dance) was to provide a heightened scenic effect. This accounts for his tendency to write through-composed dramatic sections. In the vocal segments, his approach called for smaller musical forms that would fit together more easily. The large five-part *da capo* arias that predominated in *opera seria* were not suited to his dramaturgy. Such arias always contained a retarding, suspending factor and interrupted the development on stage, whereas Salieri was interested in the uninhibited flow of the action.

On the other hand, the *da capo* aria provided an opportunity to represent the reactions, the psychic states, and the excitement of the actors, and to stage events in a specially created musical form. Actors were able to express such emotions as passion or grief quite plainly while the action was halted; and such arias also served to display virtuoso singing. However, the newer dramatic technique had to portray the emotional changes of its characters in all their intensity as part of the ongoing theatrical action. This presented musical language with a completely new task of psychological insight and commentary. It is not by chance that at the same time as the typology of sentiments was done away with, the old *buffo*, woodcut-like figures developed into complex individual characters. As a result, the former distinction between *opera seria* and *opera buffa* became obsolete.

Salieri played a decisive role in the development of this type of music theater, which had to assert itself in the face of traditional Italian opera. Of course, he initially benefited from the support and guidance of Gluck, the first great opera reformer. Thus *Armida* and *Les Danaïdes* certainly reflect Gluck's influence, while each in its own way is quite independent and far from being epigonic. Salieri also learned much from Gluck for his comic operas, though here the dependence on suitable librettists is even more noticeable. All too often, he chose the resident librettist, making many compromises that could not be modified later. Hence there is a surprising imbalance in his career, with the production of great and important works alongside pieces of such insignificance that one would hardly suspect him of being their creator.

Encouraged by Gluck, Salieri was eager to experiment and take risks. And it is indicative of Gluck's farsightedness and Salieri's courage that the latter undertook *Tarare*, a work so radical in its text, as well as its musical and dramatic conception, that even French opera had no parallel. Salieri did not consider composing the music for this piece an onerous task; he became extraordinarily involved in it. Whatever he learned then concerning the treatment of text and declamation was also reflected in his later Italian operas. Moreover, the subject meant so much to him that he created an entirely new Italian version in *Axur*, which ensured the piece international success outside of France.

Notwithstanding all Salieri's success and the status he had acquired in his long career, by 1820 Mozart's star was increasingly in the ascendant; his posthumous acclaim was unlike that of any other composer. In contrast, once Salieri ceased writing any new operas, he had to face the fact that, as of 1810, his works were performed less frequently; this was especially true of his Italian operas. He had to acknowledge that his works— except for *Les Danaïdes* and *Tarare*—began to be perceived as outmoded; they were superseded by a new French trend in opera, whereas Mozart's creations survived independently of all subsequent musical developments. This was an entirely new, and irritating, experience for him. Added to it was the fact that he kept being questioned about Mozart, his relationship with him and his opinion of his work. Salieri is certain to have learned that there was occasional talk of Mozart having been poisoned, that his "Italian enemies" at the opera were the suspects, and that his own name had also been mentioned. But this was quite absurd, and no one really believed the poison story. However, the fact that the subject came up every once in a while was annoying, and resulted in immediate denials.

Those who knew Salieri were of course immune to such suspicions. Salieri kept silent and had little to say about Mozart, at any rate not in any public context that might have been recorded for posterity. It was probably the most sensible way to react, for anything he might have said would most likely have been interpreted unkindly. The only time he made an exception was in the company of his students, as shown by Hüttenbrenner in his recollections of Schubert:

> [Salieri] did not harbor a grudge against Mozart, who eclipsed him; but whenever he spotted a weak point in Mozart he drew his students' attention to it. Thus one day, when I was alone with Salieri, he divulged that Mozart had completely misinterpreted the final scene of the first act in "Titus." Rome is burning; the whole population is in revolt; the music ought to rage and be tumultuous; but Mozart chose a slow, solemn tempo and rather expressed dread and horror. I did not let Salieri confuse me, and still agree with Mozart's views. As far as I know, Salieri missed only one performance of "Don Juan." This work must have interested him particularly; but I have no idea whether he ever commented about it enthusiastically.

Hüttenbrenner then adds a most apocryphal comment:

> One day he said to me abruptly: *"He must grow, I must decline."* Out of reverence I did not dare ask him whether he was referring to Christ the Lord, to Mozart, or to Beethoven.[24]

That is the sort of thing that, if misunderstood, can feed rumors.

As Salieri grew older, he was not spared the effects of old age. In the autumn of 1820 he began to suffer from gout in his feet. This illness is generally accompanied by a great deal of pain that no amount of rest can alleviate, and by stiffening of the joints. The attacks appear to have been especially severe that winter. The following spring he was plagued by an eye infection. Still he continued with his normal activities and teaching, and even managed to go for walks. In June 1822 he met Friedrich Rochlitz, the important music critic of the Leipzig *Allgemeine musikalische Zeitung*. In an essay written years later, Rochlitz described this meeting, and especially the discussion about Mozart:

> Afterward we spoke . . . of Haydn and Mozart. He talked about their works with the respectful homage of an old man and the happy love of a youth. . . . Of Mozart's works he especially likes the quartets and of the operas, *Figaro*. "But the concerti—?" He admitted that they were to be considered the most superb of all of Mozart's instrumental pieces in terms of the wealth of exquisite and quite unique concepts, as well as the artistic and spiritual realization; but he thought that they too, particularly in their remarkable execution, went far beyond what their category required, but as concerti for the thin-toned pianoforte, they served the virtuoso poorly. "And the *Requiem*?" "Ah," he said solemnly, "that is beyond all description. That is imbued with an eternal spirit, a holy spirit, which took hold of Mozart after a very distracted life, and when facing death." —I am not replicating his own words, but their gist.

Rochlitz was also supposed to ask Salieri about available compositions for his publisher, Gottfried Christoph Härtel. In this connection, he writes:

> For your information, my dear H., I add the following: Salieri is such a friendly, cheerful man; and I am telling you this so that if he is unwilling to go along with your wishes, you do not misinterpret it and do him an injustice. He wants to have nothing further published. "Since retiring from the Opera," he said, "I haven't written anything except little songs to be sung in company, canons and the like, especially for singing outside; (even the verses are partly his own;) and church music. The world has such of my works as are intended for it. These smaller pieces are for friends; the sacred pieces are for God and my emperor." I think one has to respect that and not try to upset him.[25]

In addition to his teaching, Salieri continued to keep himself occupied with going over his former compositions. As Mosel reports, he tended to "study in the evenings until ten or eleven o'clock," as though he had "to compose everything all over again."[26] But in the spring of 1823 his old complaints set in again with the same severity. He tried Donau baths, and then sulfur baths in Baden in the summer, but there was little improvement. His entire constitution was so weakened now that he even fell at one point, severely injuring his head. From this time on Salieri was frequently confused, his physical condition grew steadily worse, and his legs became paralyzed. His decline was so rapid that it was no longer possible for his daughter to take care of him at home. In October 1823 he was admitted to a hospital, the Vienna Allgemeine Krankenhaus. When his student Ignaz Moscheles wanted to visit him there that same month, he needed to get permission from the authorities. Apparently Salieri's condition required official supervision.

There is no way of reconstructing what really happened, as there are no eyewitness reports. Only the rumor-like references by his contemporaries help one to imagine what happened to this feeble, obstinate, sometimes mentally confused old man, when he was admitted to a frightening hospital against his will. One such account comes from Anton Schindler, who apparently told Beethoven:

> He had to be taken to the hospital by force, because he would not bear the costs himself. On the 2nd day, while the attendants were having their midday lunch, he was caught trying to injure himself with a knife . . . He absolutely refused to take any *medicine* at home or to have it brought in . . . his daughters are already 30 years old but he refuses to allow them to marry, so as not to have to give them a dowry . . . his *Axur* still brings in good *royalties* each year.[27]

This was all part of Viennese gossip, as was the rumor that "*Salieri* cut his throat but is still alive," repeated by Beethoven's nephew Karl.[28] There is no factual evidence that Salieri attempted to commit suicide, though he did manage to inflict a knife wound on his neck in the hospital. It was known from Mosel's earlier comments that Salieri was subject to fits of depression in his final years. In his confused state of mind in the hospital, Salieri evidently recalled the slander that he had poisoned Mozart. But the day Moscheles visited him in the hospital, Salieri happened to be lucid and denied his guilt once more (see Introduction, p. 5).[29]

But Moscheles makes no mention of any injuries from a suicide attempt, which he would surely have noticed if Salieri had tried to "cut his throat" on his second day in the hospital. He may simply have been too tactful to refer to it; he merely states, "The very way he looked shocked me." Of course, that might have referred only to Salieri's general health. However, this much is certain: the rumor that Salieri accused himself of having been Mozart's murderer swept through Vienna. Even Schindler and Beethoven discussed it, as the *Konversationshefte* show. In the entry for January 25, 1824, Schindler notes, "*Salieri* is very poorly again. He is completely deranged. He keeps fantasizing that he is to blame for Mozart's death and poisoned him." Apparently Beethoven expressed his doubts, for Schindler continues, "It seems to be so as he wants to confess it, therefore it is true that everything receives its just reward."[30] Schindler thus corroborates this self-accusation, though neither he nor Beethoven believe it to be true.

Beethoven was much moved by Salieri's condition, for he keeps returning to the subject when talking to others. When the editor Josef Kilian Schickh suggested to Beethoven that he write a Requiem for himself, the latter immediately recalls Salieri's fate, and Schickh notes, "Children and fools tell the truth, and I wager a hundred to one that *Salieri's* statement of remorse is true!" Beethoven rejects this, and Schickh then adds, "The way in which Mozart died confirms the statement."[31]

Beethoven's next discussion with Schindler may have occurred on the same day, February 8, 1824. Schindler writes, "You are so somber again, illustrious master, what is wrong, what has happened to your happier mood lately?" Beethoven must have steered their conversation immediately back to Salieri again, for Schindler answers, "Don't take it so to heart, such is generally the fate of great men!" Apparently Beethoven described the accusation as slander, for Schindler tries to calm him as to the cause of Mozart's death: "There are many who can prove how he died and whether there were *symptoms*." Then it seems they came to speak of the relationship between Salieri and Mozart, whereupon Schindler replies, "But he must have damaged *Mozart* more with his criticism than *Mozart* affected him."[32]

There is no evidence of anyone having heard Salieri make the confession, nor of how the rumor was spread in Vienna. But apparently it became the talk of the day, and even the

Leipzig *Allgemeine musikalische Zeitung* referred to Salieri's disturbed state, though without repeating the rumor:

> Hr. Hofkapellmeister Salieri is seriously ill, and it is doubtful that he will recover. Old age leaves its destructive effects on the body as well as the mind. That is the universal destiny of mankind. Senectus ipsa est morbus! (November 19, 1823)[33]

After Salieri's supposed self-accusation, a number of his contemporaries certainly believed that he had poisoned Mozart. Beethoven's nephew also confirmed the rumors once more (January 27, 1825): "People are quite convinced now that Salieri is Mozart's murderer."[34] Statements of this sort would explain why various individuals kept referring to the topic and trying to clear Salieri of any culpability.[35]

Salieri was long past making any comments himself; his conversation with Moscheles was in fact his final legacy. But he lay tormented on his sick bed for another year and a half. He was pensioned with his full salary in 1824, but it is doubtful whether he was still able to understand the respectful and tactful letter from the *Hofmusikgraf*. After a detailed acknowledgment of his service, the letter states:

> Physical ailments then interfered with your activity and this sufficed to make you, who placed diligence above all else, take this step of entering your well-deserved retirement.
> Enjoy it to its fullest extent and fortify yourself, as always, with that magnanimity which belongs to a spirit such as yours; think of your noble, irreproachable, glorious career, and of your numerous friends and admirers, and make room among them to include him who leaves you with the most heartfelt compassion and expression of greatest respect.
> Moriz Graf v. Dietrichstein
> *Hofmusikgraf.*[36]

Salieri finally died almost a year later, on May 7, 1825, at eight o'clock in the evening. We will let Mosel, his first biographer, to whom we owe so much information about Salieri's life, report once again:

> His funeral procession included the entire personnel of the royal court orchestra, headed by Count *Moriz v. Dietrichstein*; all other Kapellmeister and composers present in Vienna,[37] numerous fine musicians and a large number of respected music lovers.

The memorial service, held some days later in the Italian Church, at which the great *Requiem* which the deceased had composed for himself was performed by his students and many other music lovers at his own request, was no less well-attended.

The mourning was just as universal as it was genuine, and was later replaced by an honorable, never to be forgotten memory.[38]

Those sentiments expressed Mosel's personal hopes. Unfortunately, though, Salieri was destined to enter a relatively lengthy obscurity. Now that interest in his work has been revived, there is every chance that he will at last occupy his rightful place in the history of opera and of music in general.

NOTES

Notes to Introduction

1. Otto Erich Deutsch, comp. and ed., *Wolfgang Amadeus Mozart. Die Dokumente seines Lebens*, Series 10, Supplement (Kassel, 1961), p. 380.
2. Franz Niemetschek, *W. A. Mozart's Leben nach Originalquellen beschrieben* (1798; facsimile of first ed., Prague, 1906), p. 34.
3. [Ignaz Ferdinand Arnold], *Mozart's Geist. Seine kurze Biografie und ästhetische Darstellung seiner Werke. Ein Bildungsbuch für junge Tonkünstler* (Erfurt, 1803), pp. 70–72.
4. Cited in John Warrack, *Carl Maria von Weber. Eine Biographie* (Hamburg-Düsseldorf, 1972).
5. Edmond Michotte, *La Visite de R. Wagner à Rossini*, reprinted in Rudolph Angermüller, *Antonio Salieri. Sein Leben und seine weltlichen Werke unter besonderer Berücksichtigung seiner "grossen" Opern*, Part 3, Appendix (Munich, 1971–74), pp. 35 ff. See also Edward Elmgren Swenson, *Antonio Salieri. A Documentary Biography* (Ann Arbor: Dissertation Abstracts, 1974), pp. 352 ff.
6. For a more detailed account, see chap. 9, "Beyond Opera."

7. Ignaz Moscheles, *Aus Moscheles Leben. Nach Briefen und Tage-büchern*, vol. 1 (Leipzig, 1872–73), pp. 84 ff.

8. Giuseppe Carpani, "Lettera del sig. G. Carpani in difesa del M° Salieri calunniato dell'avvelenamento del M° Moz-zard," *Biblioteca italiana o sia Giornale di letteratura, scienze ed arti*, 9 (Sept. 1824): 2262–76. This article contains the medical opinion by Vinzenz Eduard Guldener von Lobes, which is also given in Carl Bär, *Mozart. Krankheit—Tod—Begräbnis*, Schriftenreihe der Internationalen Stiftung Mo-zarteum, vol. 1, 2d. ed. (Salzburg, 1972). See also Otto Erich Deutsch, "Carpani's Verteidigung Salieris. Zur Leg-ende von Mozarts Vergiftung," *Schweizerische Musikzeitung* 97, no. 1 (1957): 8–16.

9. *Allgemeine musikalische Zeitung*, Leipzig, 19 Aug. 1824, col. 554; and 25 May 1825, col. 349 ff.

10. Friedrich Rochlitz, "Nekrolog," *Allgemeine musikalische Zei-tung*, 15 June 1825, cols. 408–14.

11. Cited in Ernst Stöckl, *Pushkin und die Musik. Mit einer an-notierenden Bibliographie der Pushkin-Vertonungen 1815–1965* (Leipzig, 1974), p. 125.

12. Cf. Volkmar Braunbehrens, "Mozart in den Orchesterkon-zerten des 19 Jahrhunderts," in *Freiburger Universitätsblätter*, 101 (Sept. 1988): 35–46.

13. Peter Shaffer, *Amadeus* (New York: Harper & Row, 1981), p. 94.

14. I. F. Edler von Mosel, *Üeber das Leben und die Werke des Anton Salieri, k.k. Hofkapellmeisters, Inhabers der goldenen Civil-Ehrenmedaille mit der Kette, Ritters der königl. französischen Eh-renlegion, Vice-Präses des Pensions-Institutes der Tonkünstler zu Wien für ihre Witwen und Waisen, Mitglied des französischen National Institutes und des musik. Conservatoriums zu Paris, dann der königl. schwedischen musikalischen Gesellschaft* (Vi-enna, 1827), pp. 199 ff.

15. Ibid., p. 5.

Notes to Chapter 1

1. The step-brother (from the father's first marriage) was called Francesco Antonio (born 1737), as was the eldest brother from the father's second marriage (born 1741). That was bound to cause some confusion. When Mosel refers to "the eldest brother," does he mean the one born in 1737 or the one born in 1741? Both were so much older than Antonio that they could already have completed their two-year course with Tartini when Antonio was starting his studies. One of them was a monk in Padua. Is it he whom Angermüller describes as having married Barbara Damichetti in 1764, in Legnago, and who then became the organist in that city's cathedral? Or was Swenson correct when he states that the older one, Francesco, was a monk in Padua, while the younger one became the organist in Legnago (he gives the wife's name as Barbara Danieletti, which may be a misprint; he cites different names and dates of birth for the children from this marriage from the ones indicated by Angermüller)? If Mosel is correct in saying that Antonio Salieri stayed with Francesco, the monk, in Padua, then the latter was not identical with the organist in Legnago. That is important, since a Francesco Salieri became known as a composer. Which one was it?
2. Mosel, p. 19.
3. Ibid., p. 20.
4. Ibid., p. 28 ff.
5. Ibid. p. 34.
6. Ibid., p. 41.
7. *Magazin der Musik*, ed. Carl Friedrich Cramer, 1, 1 (Hamburg, 1783): 17 ff.
8. Rudolph Angermüller, *Salieri*, Part 3, p. 27.
9. Ibid., p. 31.
10. Ibid., pp. 16–18.
11. Letter dated November 28, 1785, in Wilhelm Bauer and Otto Erich Deutsch, eds. and comps., *Wolfgang Amadeus Mozart. Briefe und Aufzeichnungen* (Kassel: Internationale Stiftung Mozarteum Salzburg, 1962–1975), vol. 3, p. 459.

12. Gustav Zechmeister, *Die Wiener Theater nächst der Burg und nächst dem Kärntnerthor von 1747 bis 1776*, Theatergeschichte Osterreichs, vol. 3, no. 2 (Vienna, 1971): 347 and 349.
13. Swenson, *Antonio Salieri*, p. 49.

Notes to Chapter 2

1. Mosel, p. 47.
2. Johan Henrik Kellgren, undoubtedly the most prestigious Swedish poet in the Gustavian period, was a confirmed disciple of Gluck. His close relationship with Gustav III, whose outlines for librettos he turned into finished texts, influenced the development of Gustavian opera.
3. *Wiener Theater Almanach für das Jahr 1795* (Vienna [1795]), pp. 48 ff; see also Gustav Donath (with addenda by Robert Haas), "Florian Leopold Gassmann als Opernkomponist," *Studien zur Musikwissenschaft. Beihefte der Denkmäler der Tonkunst in Osterreich*, 2 (1914), p. 46.
4. Meanwhile, Gassmann and Salieri lived on Heidenschuss 361 (now Strauchgasse 21).
5. Mosel, pp. 51–59.
6. In his biography (*Antonio Salieri*), Swenson incorrectly gives September 21, 1774 as the date of the death of Carl Jakob von Helferstorfer. Angermüller maintains in his volume (*Salieri* [1971–1974]) that despite the date of October 10, 1774, given on the marriage contract, the marriage actually took place a year later, citing Mosel (*Über das Leben*), who claimed that Salieri had already composed his opera *La secchia rapita*. I have greater faith in the Viennese chancery clerks' ability to list a correct date than in the aging Salieri's ability to recall the date of this opera and Mosel's subsequent account. The witnesses were Leopold Hofmann, the Kapellmeister at St. Stephen's (who had been Salieri's rival), as well as Leopold Auenbrugger, whose daughters Francisca and Marianne were Salieri's students. Auenbrugger

himself was a physician, who later became the librettist of Salieri's *Singspiel, Der Rauchfangkehrer.*

7. Angermüller, *Salieri*, Part 2:1, p. 41.
8. Mosel, pp. 59–61.
9. Bauer and Deutsch, *Mozart, Briefe*, vol. 3, p. 99.
10. Mosel, p. 62.

Notes to Chapter 3

1. *Maria Theresa und Joseph II. Ihre Correspondenz sammt Briefen Josephs an seinen Bruder Leopold,* ed. Alfred Ritter von Arneth, vol. 1 (Vienna, 1867–1868), pp. 359 ff.
2. Mosel, p. 63.
3. Ibid., pp. 62 ff.
4. Ibid., p. 66.
5. Ibid., p. 67.
6. Ibid., p. 68.
7. Ibid., pp. 69 ff.
8. Otto Michtner, *Das alte Burgtheater als Opernbühne. Von der Einführung des deutschen Singspiels (1778) bis zum Tod Kaiser Leopolds II. (1792),* Theatergeschichte Osterreichs, vol. 3, no. 1 (Vienna, 1970): 368, n. 25.
9. Mosel, p. 72.
10. Ibid., pp. 73 ff.
11. Bauer and Deutsch, *Mozart, Briefe*, vol. 3, p. 268.
12. Michtner, p. 84.
13. The aria "Se più felice ogetto" is sung by Publio in act 1, scene 5 of *Attilio Regolo*; "Basta, vincesti, eccoti il foglio," followed by an aria by Didone, comes from act 2, scene 4 of *Didone abbandonata.*
14. Bauer and Deutsch, *Mozart, Briefe*, vol. 3, p. 113.
15. Ibid., p. 296.
16. Ibid., pp. 179 ff.
17. Preparations for the reestablishment of the Italian Opera at the Nationaltheater had been under way since the autumn. Salieri was therefore able to take up his former position as *Vizekapellmeister* of the Italian Opera. The post

of pianoforte teacher for the Princess of Württemberg was filled by Georg Summer. Mozart writes about it most informatively on October 5, 1782:

> Well, the distinguished pianoforte teacher for the princess has now been appointed. I need only tell you what his salary is for you to form an idea of the skill of this master: 400 gulden. If it annoyed me, I would do everything in my power not to let it show, but as matters stand I don't need to pretend, thank God, because only the contrary would annoy me as I would naturally have had to give a negative answer, which is always unpleasant if one finds oneself in the unfortunate position of having to refuse a great lord. *Briefe*, vol. 3, pp. 236 ff.

Mozart found this salary so ridiculously small that had the emperor offered him the post he would have refused it. Yet in his position as *Konzertmeister* in Salzburg, he received 450 gulden, with surely more duties than a few pianoforte lessons. His father appears to have reproached him several times, as it involved a rather profitable additional job, even for a Mozart. Hence Mozart defends himself at some length on October 12, 1782:

> You write that 400 fl. as a guaranteed annual income is not to be looked down upon. If I were able to work my way up and could thus consider the 400 fl. as an extra, it would be guaranteed; but unfortunately this is not the case here; in this instance my main income would be 400 fl., and I would have to consider any additional earnings as a bonus, in fact a very uncertain and hence very minimal one. As you can easily imagine, one cannot deal with a princess as with any other lady; if a lesson is not convenient for her, then one has to wait. She is living with the Salesian nuns on the Wieden; if one does not want to go there on foot, one has to pay at least 20 pfennigs there and back, which means that only 304 fl. would remain of my salary. NB: If I only taught three times a week, and if I were made to wait, I would have to give up instructing my other students meantime, or any other business with which I might easily earn more than 400 fl. If I have to go there, I have to spend double my money on the trip because I have to go back again; if I were to stay out there, and it would surely be before midday, then at lunchtime I would have to eat at an inn where the food is bad and expensive. In forgoing other lessons I might even lose them entirely, as everyone considers their money to be just as good as that of the princess. And I would be losing time and the desire to earn more with my compositions. If one serves a great lord, in whatever capacity, it should be recompensed with the sort of salary that enables one *to serve him alone*, so that one does not have to seek

other duties to make up sufficient income. One must prevent poverty. Please do not think that I'm silly enough to mention to anyone else what I've written to you. But rest assured that the emperor *himself* is aware of his meanness and it is *only* for that reason that he did not consider me for this task. If I had applied, I would surely have been chosen, but not for 400 fl. And also not for a sum that would be considered cheap. I'm not looking for any other students, I can get enough of them; and without causing me the least inconvenience or trouble, two of them provide me with as much as the princess pays her master, who has nothing to look forward to save that he won't starve in his lifetime. You are well aware how poorly great lords reward the services one renders them. (Ibid., pp. 237 ff.)

Of course, this letter must be interpreted in its proper perspective. Mozart certainly needed students at this time, as he hardly had any other income, and two students did not provide him with 400 gulden annually, because "people of rank" generally spent some months of the year in the country. Moreover, it is unlikely that the emperor "*himself* [wa]s aware of his own meanness," because his attitude to services rendered and their just reward differed from that of Mozart. The latter was apparently very much disappointed at not having been given the position, and used this argument to build up a psychic defense for himself so as to protect his feelings of self-esteem. He was extraordinarily sensitive in such matters; however, his counterarguments were completely unrealistic.

Notes to Chapter 4

1. Swenson, *Antonio Salieri*, p. 88.
2. *Glucks Briefe an Franz Kruthoffer*, ed. and annotated by Georg Kinsky (Vienna, Prague, and Leipzig, 1927), pp. 49, 50, and 53.
3. *Magazin der Musik*, 1, 2 (Hamburg, 1783): pp. 1210 ff.
4. The Paris reviews of *Les Danaïdes* are given in their original French version in Angermüller, *Salieri*, 3, pp. 249–75. The most important and extensive discussion that appeared in the *Mercure de France* was also reproduced in German

translation in Cramer's *Magazin der Musik,* 2 (Hamburg, 1784), pp. 417–57.

5. Translation in Cramer's *Magazin der Musik,* ibid., pp. 432 ff., 448–53, and 456.
6. See Angermüller, *Salieri,* 2:1, p. 92.
7. Ibid., 3, p. 273.
8. Cf. the excursus on Da Ponte in Volkmar Braunbehrens, *Mozart in Vienna,* transl. Timothy Bell, New York: Grove Weidenfeld, 1990, pp. 203–9.
9. *Denkwürdigkeiten des Venezianers Lorenzo da Ponte,* ed. Gustav Gugitz, vol. 1 (Dresden, 1924), pp. 194 ff.
10. Ibid., pp. 198 ff.
11. Ibid., pp. 200–202.
12. Ibid., pp. 211–13.

Notes to Chapter 5

1. Michtner, p. 176. Casti's banishment from Vienna, or the payment of some sort of compensation to him, cannot be proved this way. After all, he complied with the emperor's wishes and temporarily delayed having the *Poema tartaro* printed. It was probably his own choice to accompany Count Joseph Fries on his trip to Italy in 1787. The 600 ducats referred to could be interpreted as a recompense for withholding publication. See also Herman van den Bergh, *Giambattista Casti (1724–1803). L'homme et l'oeuvre* (Amsterdam, 1951).
2. Deutsch, *Mozart. Die Dokumente,* 223. "No copy of this Cantata (KV appendix 11ᵃ) is known to exist. Nor has the text been preserved. The reference to Ophelia therefore hardly makes sense." However, in the context of the schedule of the Viennese Nationaltheater, the "reference to Ophelia" can easily be interpreted.
3. Michael Kelly, *Reminiscences,* ed. and intro. by Roger Fiske (London, New York, and Toronto, 1975), pp. 130–31.
4. Ibid., p. 125.
5. Bauer and Deutsch, *Mozart, Briefe,* vol. 3, p. 276.
6. Deutsch, *Mozart, Die Dokumente,* p. 193.

7. Bauer and Deutsch, *Mozart, Briefe*, vol. 3, pp. 276 ff.
8. Deutsch, *Mozart, Die Dokumente*, pp. 522 ff.
9. Nikolaus Harnoncourt has produced a record of this opera (Teldec) and combined it with Mozart's *Der Schauspieldirektor*. Unlike the care he usually gives to recordings and insists upon with the record companies, he decided not to make this a complete rendition of Salieri's work. The accompanying text refers to the fact that in Salieri's opera, "the *secco* recitatives as well as some of the arias [were] left out, so as to be able to get it onto one record." Apparently he was not that interested in Salieri's opera; just about half of *Prima la musica e poi le parole* has been cut, whereas the music of *Der Schauspieldirektor* is rendered in its entirety. The care given to the Salieri interpretation does not come anywhere near that given to the Mozart opera, and the recording therefore does not convey a really adequate impression of Salieri's opera. Though the apparent purpose of the recording was to reproduce both works performed on that noteworthy February 7, 1786, the real intention seems to be to show that Mozart was the greater composer. No one is likely to disagree with that, but it becomes a self-fulfilling prophecy if one does not reproduce Salieri's music in such a way that its qualities and special musical characteristics—whatever they are—can be experienced. The accompanying text does not even include a complete reprint of the libretto of Salieri's work, so that one is dependent on Harnoncourt's questionable retelling of the shortened sections in order to understand what it is about.
10. Kelly, p. 133.
11. Bauer and Deutsch, *Mozart, Briefe*, vol. 3, p. 536.
12. Niemetschek, pp. 25 and 22.
13. Mosel, p. 93.

Notes to Chapter 6

1. Mosel, p. 92.
2. Kelly, p. 101.

3. Salieri's presence in Paris is established for the first time in a letter from Beaumarchais (dated July 31), who wanted to see him before his departure for Versailles. This letter later became part of Goethe's collection of autographs. See Swenson, *Antonio Salieri*, p. 123.

4. Mosel, p. 93.

5. Ibid., p. 96.

6. Angermüller, *Salieri*, 3, p. 310.

7. Pierre Augustin Caron de Beaumarchais, *Théâtre complet. Lettres relatives à son théâtre*. Texte établi et annoté par Maurice Allem et Paul Courant (Paris, 1957), p. 368.

8. Angermüller, *Salieri*, 3, p. 397.

9. Ibid., p. 318.

10. Ibid., p. 325.

11. Kornmann, a Strasbourg banker, gained notoriety for having his wife imprisoned after she committed adultery with a family friend. Beaumarchais wrote various pamphlets in her defense, but used unorthodox means in his role of a "defender of justice." He accused Kornmann of turning his wife into a prostitute, and of being solely interested in her money. Beaumarchais even threatened to destroy Kornmann financially and tried to force him into bankruptcy. An attempt on Kornmann's life was never solved.

    Kornmann found a very articulate spokesman in Nicolas Bergasse, whose highly respected written statements accused Beaumarchais of corrupting public morality. Beaumarchais's reputation was severely damaged by this affair.

12. An attempt to produce this opera after more than 160 years (at the Schwetzinger Festspiele, 1988) met with complete failure. The reviews carried such headlines as: "Useless labor of love for Salieri" (*Mannheimer Morgen*), or "Salieri cannot be revived" (*Süddeutsche Zeitung*). The failure was not due to Salieri, but the fault of a production that could not begin to convey the daring of a work that was more a precursor to Richard Wagner's *Oper und Drama* than a throwback to the "baroque opera of Lully," as some critics maintained. The plot was rendered in such a way

that Monika Lanzendörfer could write of it (in the *Mann-heimer Morgen*, June 6, 1988): "The essential elements of the plot are comparable to Mozart's 'Entführung aus dem Serail' (of the year 1782, nota bene)." Others also made the same silly comparison. Thus Atar is described as being "almost identical to Mozart's Osmin." This performance, which was carried on many radio stations, will have contributed to the idea that Salieri is really nothing but an uninspired and unimportant rival of Mozart's, who deserves to be forgotten. The chance to reexamine *Tarare* was lost; the work still waits to be rediscovered.

13. Beaumarchais, pp. 369–79.
14. *Mémoires secrets*, June 14, 1787, cited in Angermüller, *Salieri*, 3, p. 339.
15. Ibid., p. 354.

Notes to Chapter 7

1. Mosel, p. 121.
2. Ibid., p. 129.
3. Beaumarchais sent the freshly printed score of *Tarare* to Salieri in Vienna as early as September 1787. Beaumarchais' accompanying letter is reprinted in Angermüller, *Salieri*, 3, p. 379.
4. Mosel, pp. 130 ff.
5. Da Ponte, vol. 1, p. 280.
6. Count Karl Zinzendorf, an essential source for comments on Viennese operas, noted only the lighting and sets. As for the piece itself, he states laconically, "La pièce fort platte." Cf. Michtner, pp. 412 ff., n. 56.
7. Casti's "argomento" is given in German translation in Rudolph Angermüller, "Die entpolisierte Oper am Wiener und am Fürstlich Esterhazyschen Hof," *Haydn Jahrbuch*, 10 (1978): 18–21.
8. Rudolph Payer von Thurn, ed., *Joseph II als Theaterdirektor. Ungedruckte Briefe und Aktenstücke aus den Kinderjahren des Burgtheaters*, (Vienna-Leipzig, 1920), p. 76.
9. Ibid., p. 82. Interestingly enough, Joseph II initially ex-

pressed the possibility—even if only hypothetically—of closing down the Opera as early as mid-May 1788, after learning of the failure of the premiere of *Don Giovanni*. Count Rosenberg-Orsini reported on the premiere on May 7, whereupon the emperor answered, "The opera's failure does not surprise me at all. Vienna only esteems what is new, and if one were to let them do without opera for a year, I believe it would be the only way to get them to enjoy a much more mediocre one" (ibid., p. 74).

This letter, frequently cited in Mozart literature, is here erroneously dated May 3, which must be a misprint, for it is supposed to have been written in answer to the report on the premiere, and must have been sent by return on May 13. The many misunderstandings regarding Joseph II's judgment of *Don Giovanni* are thus clarified. The emperor did not see this opera until after his return from the battlefront.

10. The opera was included in the program only three more times: on October 18 and 26, and November 1, 1789.
11. *Rapport von Wien*, Oct. 15, 1788, in Michtner, p. 272.
12. Bauer and Deutsch, *Mozart, Briefe*, vol. 4, 100.
13. As discussed in the commentary to this letter, ibid., vol. 6, p. 389.
14. Angermüller, *Salieri*, 3, p. 49.
15. Ibid., p. 51.
16. Ibid., p. 386.
17. Ibid., p. 396.
18. The opera *Axur* was performed in celebration of this wedding, when Archduke Franz (later Emperor Franz II), married his second wife, Maria Theresa. It had also been given at his first marriage in 1788 to the Princess of Württemberg (who died in February 1790). The occasion marked the first time Leopold II attended an opera.

Notes to Chapter 8

1. Bauer and Deutsch, *Mozart, Briefe*, vol. 4, pp. 161 ff.
2. According to new evidence discovered by Austrian histo-

rian Walther Brauneis, Salieri did indeed attend Mozart's funeral procession. See Christoph Wolff's article "A Requiem for Mozart: Some Myths Dispelled" in *The New York Times*, Dec. 1, 1991, Section 2, p. 32.

3. Angermüller, *Salieri*, 3, pp. 61–63.
4. Mosel, p. 145.
5. Marcus Landau, *Geschichte der italienischen Litteratur im achtzehnten Jahrhundert* (Berlin, 1899), pp. 668 ff.
6. The libretto for *Eraclito e Democrito* was issued in two printings in 1795. But the citations from it are from the handwritten manuscript of the score, which is in the Österreichische Nationalbibliothek, Vienna.
7. Angermüller, *Salieri*, 3, pp. 79–81.
8. Bergh, *Giambattista Casti*, p. 75.
9. Cf. Gustav Gugitz, "Johann Pezzl," in *Jahrbuch der Grillparzer-Gesellschaft*, ed. Karl Glossy, 16 (1906): 164–217; see also Gustav Gugitz, "Lorenz Leopold Haschka," *Jahrbuch der Grillparzer-Gesellschaft*, ed. Karl Glossy, 17 (1907): 32–127.
10. Friedrich von Schiller, *Briefwechsel zwischen Schiller und Goethe*, intro. by Franz Muncker (Stuttgart, 1892), vol. 2, pp. 140–41.
11. Peter von Braun (1758–1819) was a manufacturer, and banker to the court. He leased both court theaters from 1795 to 1806, and managed them at his own expense. In 1805 he produced Beethoven's opera *Fidelio*.
12. Mosel, p. 151.
13. Erich Schenk, "Salieris 'Landsturm' Kantate von 1799 in ihren Beziehungen zu Beethovens 'Fidelio,' " *Colloquium amicorum Joseph Schmidt-Görg zum 70. Geburtstag*, eds. Siegfried Kross and Hans Schmidt (Bonn, 1967), pp. 343 ff.
14. Friedrich Ludwig Schröder (1744–1819) was an actor and producer at the Burgtheater in Vienna, from 1781 to 1785, where he introduced Shakespeare to German audiences. As translations were not yet available, he made his own, not always faithful, adaptations. His star roles were those of Hamlet, Lear, and Henry IV.
15. The Hungarian record company Hungaroton produced

an excellent recording of the opera *Falstaff* in 1985 that does complete justice to the work in its facility, pace, and musical delicacy. The conductor is Tamás Pál.

16. *Des Plutarchus von Chäroneia vergleichende Lebensbeschreibungen.* Tr. from Greek and annotated by Johann Friedrich Salomon Kaltwasser, Part 7 (Magdeburg, 1803), pp. 3 ff. In a note, Kaltwasser writes: "In our currency twenty talents are equivalent to 25,625 thaler, but fifty amount to 64,062 thaler." Converted into gulden, that would be 38,400 and 96,000 gulden, respectively. Converted into 1992 rates, these sums amount to approximately 1 million and 2.5 million dollars.

17. The Dresden performance is reviewed in *Allgemeine musikalische Zeitung*, Feb. 24, 1802, col. 368.

18. Ibid., Jan. 8, 1806, col. 232.

19. Angermüller, *Salieri*, 3, p. 112.

20. *Allgemeine musikalische Zeitung*, Apr. 15, 1801, col. 497.

21. Mosel, p. 161.

22. C. von Wurzbach, *Biographisches Lexikon des Kaiserthums Oesterreich, enthaltend die Lebensskizzen der denkwürdigen Personen, welche seit 1750 in den österreichischen Kronländern geboren wurden oder darin gelebt und gewirkt haben*, Section 46 (Vienna, 1882), p. 105.

23. *Allgemeine musikalische Zeitung*, Dec. 12, 1804, col. 174 ff.

Notes to Chapter 9

1. Mosel, pp. 209 ff.

2. August von Kotzebue, *Die Hussiten vor Naumburg im Jahr 1432. Ein vaterländisches Schauspiel mit Chören in fünf Akten* (Leipzig, 1803).

3. Quoted from a handwritten libretto in the possession of Rudolph Angermüller. See Angermüller, *Salieri*, 2, 1, pp. 253 ff.

4. Mosel, p. 167.

5. Ibid., p. 168.

6. Ibid., p. 168 ff.

7. Baron Joseph von Hormayr, ed. and comp., *Wien, seine Geschichte und seine Denkwürdigkeiten*, vol. 5, 1 (Vienna, 1823–1825), pp. 146 ff.

8. Ibid., pp. 147–49.

9. Baron Ferdinand von Geramb, *Habsburg, ein Gedicht seiner k. k. Majestaet Franz II. bei Annahme der Oesterreichischen erblichen Kaiserwürde allerunterthänigst zugeeignet* (Vienna, 1805).

10. See Beethoven's letter to the publisher Breitkopf & Härtel, on January 7, 1809, in Emerich Kastner, ed., *Ludwig van Beethovens sämtliche Briefe*, new ed. (Leipzig, 1923), p. 126.

11. Johann Georg Albrechtsberger (1736–1809) was a composer of church music, and the Kapellmeister at the cathedral in Vienna. He was one of the most eminent teachers of composition of his time. His students included Beethoven, Czerny, and Hummel, and he was a good friend of Mozart, Haydn, and Dittersdorf.

12. Otto Erich Deutsch, ed. and comp., *Schubert. Die Erinnerungen seiner Freunde* (Leipzig, 1966), p. 26.

13. Otto Erich Deutsch, "Anselm Hüttenbrenners Erinnerungen an Schubert," *Jahrbuch der Grillparzer-Gesellschaft*, 16 (1906): 145.

14. Cited in Deutsch, *Schubert. Die Erinnerungen*, p. 76. Joseph von Spaun (1788–1865) was one of Schubert's closest friends.

15. A statement on the usefulness of Mälzel's metronome, signed by Salieri and Beethoven, appeared in the *Allgemeine musikalische Zeitung*, Vienna, Feb. 14, 1818, pp. 58 ff.

16. Angermüller, *Salieri*, 3, pp. 148 ff.

17. Otto Erich Deutsch, ed. and comp., *Schubert. Die Dokumente seines Lebens* (Kassel, 1964), p. 45.

18. Mosel, p. 180.

19. For a detailed account of "Ludlams-Höhle," see Ignaz Franz Castelli, *Memoiren meines Lebens. Gefundenes und Empfundenes. Erlebtes und Erstrebtes.* Ed. with introduction and notes by Josef Bindtner (Munich, 1914), vol. 2, pp. 1–60.

20. Warrack, *Carl Maria von Weber*, p. 177.

21. Mosel, p. 175.

22. It is astonishing to find concepts cropping up again here that belong to the time of the Inquisition; it goes to show how quickly the ideas of the Enlightenment were forgotten. Fifty years earlier, enlightened Europe had been debating Cesare Beccaria's work *On Crimes and Punishments*, which was translated into several languages, and in which, for the first time ever, the principle of retaliatory punishment was contrasted with the idea of rehabilitation.

23. *Allgemeine musikalische Zeitung*, March 24, 1819, col. 190 ff.

24. Deutsch, "Anselm Hüttenbrenners Erinnerungen," p. 142.

25. *Allgemeine musikelische Zeitung*, Jan. 2, 1828, cols. 8–10.

26. Mosel, p. 200.

27. Ludwig van Beethoven, *Konversationshefte*, vol. 5, eds. Karl-Heinz Köhler, Grita Herre, and Peter Pötschner (Leipzig, 1970), notebook 50, p. 40.

28. Ludwig van Beethoven, *Konversationshefte*, vol. 4, eds. Karl-Heinz Köhler, Grita Herre, and Ignaz Weinmann (Leipzig, 1968), notebook 46, p. 259.

29. Moscheles, vol. 1, pp. 84 ff.

30. Beethoven, *Konversationshefte*, vol. 5, notebook 54, p. 95.

31. Ibid., notebook 55, p. 136.

32. Ibid., p. 136 ff.

33. *Allgemeine musikalische Zeitung*, Nov. 19, 1823, col. 766.

34. Ludwig van Beethoven, *Konversationshefte*, eds. Karl-Heinz Köhler, Grita Herre, Renate Bormann, and Günter Brosche, vol. 7, notebook 83 (Leipzig, 1978), p. 114.

35. The following citation from the *Allgemeine musikalische Zeitung*, Aug. 19, 1842, col. 554 (about nine months prior to Salieri's death), serves as an example of this type of statement:

> *Société académique des enfans d'Apollon.* . . . In the talk given by Hr. Belle between the two events, he discussed the purpose of the society and the promotion of the arts in general terms. . . . Then the names of the most recent artist-members were announced, among them young Liszt; and finally there was reference to those members who had died, including Viotti and Salieri who received special attention. With the greatest fervor the speaker refuted a rumor of Salieri's hatred for Mozart that had recently made the rounds here.

36. Letter of June 15, 1824, in Mosel, p. 202.
37. Beethoven was not in Vienna, but in Baden near Vienna. It was probably important for Mosel to find a way of referring to Beethoven's absence without giving rise to any misunderstanding.
38. Mosel, p. 207.

BIBLIOGRAPHY

This bibliography lists all titles which were quoted from in the text, as well as the most important secondary literature on Salieri. Salieri's musical estate (scores of Salieri's operas, hand-written either by himself or copied by others, and prints) today is in the music collection of the Österreichische Nationalbibliothek, Vienna. This is supplemented by the archives of the *Gesellschaft der Musikfreunde* in Vienna. As part of the first volume of his three-volume Salieri monograph, Rudolph Angermüller put together a list of sources of Salieri's secular works, along with a list of the places where they were found. Salieri's church music is listed (this needs to be supplemented) in Rudolf Nützlader's dissertation.

Hermann **Abert,** *W. A. Mozart.* Revised and augmented edition of Otto Jahn's *Mozart,* 2 vols., 9th ed., Leipzig **1978.**

Rudolph **Angermüller,** "Salieri als Hofkapellmeister," in: *Österreichische Musikzeitung* XXV (**1970**), pp. 305–311.

Rudolph **Angermüller,** "Antonio Salieri und seine 'Scuola di Canto,'" in: *Beethoven-Studien,* ed. Erich Schenk, Vienna **1970.**

Rudolph **Angermüller,** "Aus der Frühgeschichte des Metronoms. Die Beziehungen zwischen Mälzel und Salieri," in: *Österreichische Musikzeitung* XXVI (**1971**), pp. 134–140.

Rudolph **Angermüller,** *Antonio Salieri. Sein Leben und seine weltlichen Werke unter besonderer Berücksichtigung seiner 'großen' Opern,* Munich **1971–74** (Dissertation Salburg 1970).
Teil I: Werk- und Quellenverzeichnis, München 1971 (Schriften zur Musik 16).

Teil II,1: Vita und weltliche Werke, Munich 1974 (Schriften zur Musik 17).

Teil III: Dokumente, Munich 1972 (Schriften zur Musik 19).

Rudolph **Angermüller,** "Zwei Selbstbiographien von Joseph Weigl (1766–1846)," in: *Deutsches Jahrbuch für Musikwissenschaft* 1971, vol. 16 (**1974**), pp. 46–85.

Rudolph **Angermüller,** "Aspekte Salierischer Kirchenmusik," in: *Mitteilungen der Internationalen Stiftung Mozarteum* XXI/1–2 (**1973**), pp. 19–21.

Rudolph **Angermüller,** "Salieris Gesellschaftsmusik," in: *Analecta musicologica* 17 (**1976**), pp. 146–193.

Rudolph **Angermüller,** "Reformideen von Du Roullet und Beaumarchais als Opernlibrettisten," in: *Acta Musicologica* 48 (**1976**), pp. 227–253.

Rudolph **Angermüller,** "Salieris Vorbemerkungen zu seinen Opern," in: *Mitteilungen der Internationalen Stiftung Mozarteum* XXV/3–4 (**1977**), pp. 15–33.

Rudolph **Angermüller,** "Bemerkungen zur Familie Salieri," in: *Wiener Figaro* XLIV (**1977**), 18. Oktober.

Rudolph **Angermüller,** "Die entpolitisierte Oper am Wiener und am Fürstlich Esterházyschen Hof," in: *Haydn Jahrbuch,* vol. 10, Eisenstadt/Vienna **1978**, pp. 5–22.

Rudolph **Angermüller,** "Salieris 'Tarare' und 'Axur, Rè d'Ormus' (1788). Vertonung eines Sujets für Paris und Wien," in: *Hamburger Jahrbuch für Musikwissenschaft* 5 (**1981**), pp. 211–217.

Theophil **Antoniček,** *Ignaz von Mosel. Biographie und Beziehungen zu den Zeitgenossen,* Dissertation Vienna **1962**.

Max **Arend,** *Gluck. Eine Biographie,* Berlin **1921**.

[Ignaz Ferdinand **Arnold**], *Mozarts Geist. Seine kurze Biografie und ästhetische Darstellung seiner Werke. Ein Bildungsbuch für junge Tonkünstler,* Erfurt **1803**.

Carl **Bär,** *Mozart. Krankheit—Tod—Begräbnis,* 2nd, augmented ed., Salzburg **1972** (Schriftenreihe der Internationalen Stiftung Mozarteum, vol. 1).

Pierre Augustin Caron de **Beaumarchais,** *Théâtre complet. Lettres relatives à son théâtre.* Texte établi et annoté par Maurice Allem et Paul Courant, Paris **1957**.

Cesare **Beccaria,** *On Crimes and Punishments,* New York **1963**.

Ludwig van **Beethoven**s *sämtliche Briefe,* ed. by Emerich Kastner, new ed., Leipzig **1923**.

Ludwig van **Beethoven.** *Konversationshefte,* ed. by Karl-Heinz Köhler, Grita Herre et al., vol. 7, Leipzig **1978**.

The English-language edition in print containing letters and conversations is Ludwig van **Beethoven,** *Letters, Journals and Conversations,* ed. by Michael Hamburger, Westport **1966**, repr. **1978**.

Herman van den **Bergh,** *Giambattista Casti (1724–1803). L'homme et l'œuvre,* Amsterdam **1951**.

Anton **Bettelheim,** *Beaumarchais. Eine Biographie,* Frankfurt a.M. **1886**.

Otto **Biba,** "Geselliges Musizieren rund um Wien. Beispiele aus dem Schaffen Antonio Salieris," in: *Wiener Figaro* XLIII (**1976**), pp. 8–18.

Werner **Bollert,** "Antonio Salieri und die italienische Oper," in: W. B., *Aufsätze zur Musikgeschichte,* Bottrop **1938,** pp. 43–128.

Volkmar **Braunbehrens,** *Mozart in Vienna,* New York **1990.**

Volkmar **Braunbehrens,** "Mozart in den Orchesterkonzerten des 19. Jahrhunderts," in: *Freiburger Universitätsblätter* 101 (September **1988**), pp. 35–46.

Maurice J. E. **Brown,** "Schubert and Salieri," in: *Monthly Musical Record* 88 (**1958**), pp. 211–19.

I. F. **Castelli,** *Memoiren meines Lebens. Gefundenes und Empfundenes, Erlebtes und Erstrebtes.* With an introduction and annotations newly ed. by Josef Bindtner, 2 vols., Munich **1914** (Denkwürdigkeiten aus Alt-Österreich, vols. 9/10).

Giovanni Battista **Casti,** *Opere,* Brussels **1838.**

Adelmo **Damerini/**Gino **Roncaglia,** "Volti musicali di Falstaff," in: *Chigiana* XVIII (Siena **1961**), pp. 23–31.

Denkwürdigkeiten des Venezianers Lorenzo **da Ponte.** Ed. by Gustav Gugitz. 3 vols., Dresden **1924.**

Andrea **Della Corte,** *Un italiano all'estero: Antonio Salieri.* Turin/Milan **1936.**

Otto Erich **Deutsch,** "Anselm Hüttenbrenners Erinnerungen an Schubert," in *Jahrbuch der Grillparzer-Gesellschaft.* Ed. by Karl Glossy, 16. Jahrgang, Vienna **1906,** pp. 99–163.

Otto Erich **Deutsch,** "Von der angeblichen Hinterlist Salieris gegen Schubert," in *National-Zeitung,* Basel, 29 July **1930.**

Otto Erich **Deutsch,** "Carpanis Verteidigung Salieris. Zur Legende von Mozarts Vergiftung," in *Schweizerische Musikzeitung,* 97. Jahrgang (**1957**), No. 1, pp. 8–16.

Max **Dietz,** *Geschichte des musikalischen Dramas in Frankreich während der Revolution bis zum Direktorium (1787–1795),* Vienna **1985.**

Gustav **Donath** (with additions by Robert Haas), "Florian Leopold Gassmann als Opernkomponist," in: *Studien zur Musikwissenschaft. Beihefte der Denkmäler der Tonkunst in Österreich* 2 (**1914**), pp. 34–211.

Alfred **Einstein,** *Gluck. Sein Leben, seine Werke,* Zurich/Stuttgart **1954.**

Franz **Farga,** *Salieri und Mozart. Musikgeschichtlicher Roman,* Stuttgart **1937.**

Ferdinand Freiherr von **Geramb,** *Habsburg, ein Gedicht seiner k.k. Majestaet Franz II. bei Annahme der Oesterreichischen erblichen Kaiserwürde allerunterthänigst zugeeignet* [Vienna **1805**].

Glucks Briefe an Franz Kruthoffer. Ed. and with commentary by Georg Kinsky, Vienna/Prague/Leipzig **1927.**

Glucks Briefe. Sel. and transl. by W. M. Treichlinger, Zurich **1951.**

Gustav **Gugitz,** "Johann Prezzl," in: *Jahrbuch der Grillparzer-Gesellschaft.* Ed. by Karl Glossy, 16. Jahrgang, Vienna **1906,** pp. 164–217.

Gustav **Gugitz,** "Lorenz Leopold Haschka," in: *Jahrbuch der Grillparzer-Gesellschaft.* Ed. by Karl Glossy, 17. Jahrgang, Vienna **1907,** pp. 32–127.

Gustav Gugitz → Da Ponte

Robert **Haas,** "Antonio Salieris vergessene Familie," in: *Festschrift Max Schneider zum 80. Geburtstag,* Leipzig **1955,** pp. 191–196.

Franz **Hadamowsky,** *Die Wiener Hoftheater 1776–1966. Verzeichnis der aufgeführten Stücke mit Bestandsnachweis und täglichem Spielplan.* Part 1: 1776–1810, Vienna **1966** (Musaion. Veröffentlichungen der Österreichischen Nationalbibliothek, Neue Folge, Reihe 1.4).

Eduard **Hanslick,** *Geschichte des Concert-Wesens in Wien,* Vienna **1869.**

Josef **Heinzelmann,** " 'Prima la musica, poi le parole.' Zu Salieris Wiener Opernparodie," in: *Österreichische Musikzeitung* XXVIII (**1973**), pp. 19–28.

Wien, seine Geschicke und seine Denkwürdigkeiten. Im Vereine mit mehreren Gelehrten und Kunstfreunden bearbeitet und herausgegeben durch Joseph Freyherrn von **Hormayr,** 9 vols., Vienna **1823–25.**

Walter **Hummel,** *W. A. Mozarts Söhne,* Kassel **1956.**

Adolphe **Jullien,** *L'Opéra en 1788. Documents inédits extraits des Archives de l'Etat,* Paris **1873.**

Adolphe **Jullien,** "Salieri. Sa carrière en France," in: *Revue et gazette musicale* XXXXII (**1875**), Februar–Juli.

Adolphe **Jullien,** *La Cour et l'Opéra sous Louis XVI. Marie-Antoinette et Sacchini, Salieri, Favart et Gluck,* Paris **1878.**

Michael **Kelly,** *Reminiscences,* ed. and intro. by Roger Fiske, London/New York/Toronto **1975.**

"Michael **Kelly**'s Lebenserinnerungen." Transl. by Cäcilie Chrysander, in: *Allgemeine Musikalische Zeitung,* 15. Jahrgang, Leipzig **1880,** No. 12–33.

Georg **Kinsky,** "Glucks Reisen nach Paris," in: *Zeitschrift für Musikwissenschaft* VIII (**1925/26**), pp. 551–66.

Ludwig Ritter von **Köchel,** *Die kaiserliche Hofmusikkapelle in Wien von 1543–1867. Nach urkundlichen Forschungen,* Vienna **1869.**

August von **Kotzebue,** *Die Hussiten vor Naumburg im Jahr 1432. Ein vaterländisches Schauspiel mit Chören in fünf Akten,* Leipzig **1803.**

Marcus **Landau,** *Geschichte der italienischen Litteratur im achtzehnten Jahrhundert,* Berlin **1899.**

Giuseppe **Magnani,** *Antonio Salieri: musicista legnaghese,* Legnago **1934.**

Maria Theresia und Joseph II. Ihre Correspondenz sammt Briefen Josephs an seinen Bruder Leopold. Ed. by Alfred Ritter von Arneth, 3 vols., Vienna **1867/68.**

Otto **Michtner,** *Das alte Burgtheater als Opernbühne. Von der Einführung des deutschen Singspiels (1778) bis zum Tod Kaiser Leopolds II. (1792),* Vienna **1970** (Theatergeschichte Österreichs Bd. III: Wien, Heft 1).

Otto **Michtner,** "Der Fall Abbé Da Ponte," in: *Mitteilungen des österreichischen Staatsarchivs* 19 (**1966**), pp. 170–209.

*Aus **Moschele**s Leben.* Nach Briefen und Tagebüchern herausgegeben von seiner Frau, 2 vols., Leipzig **1872/73.**

I. F. Edler von **Mosel,** *Ueber das Leben und die Werke des Anton Salieri, k.k. Hofkapellmeisters, Inhabers der goldenen Civil-Ehrenmedaille mit der Kette, Ritters der königl. französischen Ehrenlegion, Vice-Präses des Pensions-Institutes der Tonkünstler zu Wien für ihre Witwen und Waisen, Mitglied des französischen National-Institutes und des musik. Conservatoriums zu Paris, dann der königl. schwedischen musikalischen Gesellschaft,* Vienna **1827.**

Wolfgang Amadeus **Mozart,** *Briefe und Aufzeichnungen.* Complete edition, ed. by the Internationale Stiftung Mozarteum Salzburg, collected and with commentary by Wilhelm A. Bauer and Otto Erich Deutsch, vols. I–IV (text), vols. V–VI (commentary, edited by Joseph Heinz Eibl), vol. VII (index, created by Joseph Heinz Eibl), Kassel etc., **1962–75.** An English-language edition of Mozart's letters is *Letters of Wolfgang Amadeus Mozart,* ed. Hans Mersmann, Dover **1972.**

Mozart. *Die Dokumente seines Lebens.* Collected and with commentary by Otto Erich Deutsch, Kassel etc., **1961** (Neue Ausgabe sämtlicher Werke, series X: Supplement).

Franz **Niemetschek,** *W. A. Mozarts Leben nach Originalquellen beschrieben.* Facsimile of the 1st edition 1798, Prague **1906.**

Georg Nikolaus von **Nissen,** *Biographie W. A. Mozarts.* Nach Originalbriefen, Sammlungen alles über ihn Geschriebenen, mit vielen neuen Beylagen, Steindrucken, Musikblättern und einem Facsimile. Ed. by Constanze, Wittwe von Nissen, fruher Witwe Mozart, Leipzig **1828.**

Walter **Nohl,** "Ist Mozart von Salieri vergiftet worden? Neues Material zu einer alten Frage," in: *Die Musik* XXXI (**1938/39**), pp. 389–392.

Gustav **Nottebohm,** *Beethovens Unterricht bei J. Haydn, Albrechtsberger und Salieri,* Leipzig/Winterthur **1873** (Beethoven-Studien, vol. 1).

Rudolf **Nützlader,** *Salieri als Kirchenmusiker,* Dissertation Vienna **1924.**

Rudolf **Nützlader,** "Salieri als Kirchenmusiker," in: *Studien zur Musikwissenschaft* XIV (**1927**), pp. 160–178.

Alfred **Orel,** *Der junge Schubert. Mit ungedruckten Kompositionen Schuberts nach Texten Pietro Metastasios,* Vienna/Leipzig **1941.**

Joseph II. als Theaterdirektor. Ungedruckte Briefe und Aktenstücke aus den Kinderjahren des Burgtheaters. Collected and with commentary by Rudolf **Payer,** Vienna/Leipzig **1920.**

Richard **Perger,** *Geschichte der k.k. Gesellschaft der Musikfreunde in Wien.* 1 Abteilung: 1812–1870, Vienna **1912.**

*Des **Plutarch**us von Chäroneia vergleichende Lebensbeschreibungen.* Transl. from the Greek and with annotations by Joh. Friedr. Sal. Kaltwasser. 7. Teil, Magdeburg **1803.** The most comprehensive English-language edition is *Parallel Lives,* 11 vols, Loeb's Classical Library, Cambridge: Harvard University Press, n. d.

Carl Ferdinand **Pohl,** *Die Gesellschaft der Musikfreunde des österreichischen Kaiserstaates und ihr Conservatorium,* Vienna **1871.**

Josef **Richter,** *Die Eipeldauer Briefe 1785–1797.* A selection, ed., with an introduction and annotations by Eugen von Pannel, 2 vols., Munich **1917** (Denkwürdigkeiten aus Alt-Österreich, vols. 17/18).

"Die Tagebücher von Joseph Carl **Rosenbaum** 1770–1829." Ed. by Else Radant, in: *Haydn Jahrbuch*, vol. V, Eisenstadt/Vienna **1960**.

Julian **Rushton,** "Salieri's 'Les Horaces.' A Study of an Operatic Failure," in: *Music Review* XXXVII (**1976**), p. 266.

Albert **Schatz,** "Giovanni Bertati," in: *Veröffentlichungen für Musikwissenschaft* 5 (**1889**), pp. 231–271.

Erich **Schenk,** "Salieri's 'Landsturm'-Kantate von 1799 in ihren Beziehungen zu Beethovens 'Fidelio,' " in: *Colloquium amicorum. Joseph Schmidt-Görg zum 70. Geburtstag.* Ed. by Siegfried Kross and Hans Schmidt, Bonn **1967**, pp. 338–354.

Friedrich von **Schiller,** *Briefwechsel zwischen Schiller und Goethe*, intro. by Franz Muncker, 4 vols., Stuttgart **1892**. The English-language edition was published as *Schiller's Correspondence with Goethe*, transl. by L. Dora Schmitz, in: Kuno Francke, *The German Classics of the Nineteenth and Twentieth Centuries*, vol. 3, New York **1969**.

Fritz **Schröder,** "Antonio Salieri: ein Lehrer Beethovens," in: *Das Musikleben* V (**1952**), pp. 78–80.

Schubert. Die Dokumente seines Lebens. Collected and with commentary by Otto Erich Deutsch, Kassel etc. **1964**.

Schubert. Die Erinnerungen seiner Freunde. Collected and ed. by Otto Erich Deutsch, Leipzig **1966**.

Carlo **Serini,** "Antonio Salieri," in: *Rivista Musicale Italiana* XXX (**1925**), pp. 412–433.

Peter **Shaffer,** *Amadeus*. New York **1981**.

Jane **Shatkin Hettrick,** "A Thematic Catalogue of Sacred Works by Antonio Salieri. An Uncatalogued Holograph of the Composer in the Archive of the Vienna Hofkapelle," in: *Fontes Artis Musicae* III (**1986**), pp. 226–235.

Robert **Sondheimer,** "Gluck in Paris," in: *Zeitschrift für Musikwissenschaft* 5 (**1922/23**), pp. 165–175.

Ernst **Stöckl,** "Zur sowjetischen Diskussion über Mozarts Tod," in: *Die Musikforschung* 17 (**1964**), pp. 275–283.

Ernst **Stöckl,** *Puškin und die Musik. Mit einer annotierenden Bibliographie der Puškin-Vertonungen 1815–1965*, Leipzig **1974**.

Edward Elmgren **Swenson,** " 'Prima la musica e poi le parole.' An Eighteenth Century Satire," in: *Analecta musicologica* (**1970**), pp. 112–129.

Edward Elmgren **Swenson,** *Antonio Salieri. A Documentary Biography*, Ann Arbor, MI **1974** (Dissertation Cornell University).

Ernst **Tittel,** *Die Wiener Musikhochschule. Vom Konservatorium der Gesellschaft der Musikfreunde zur staatlichen Akademie für Musik und darstellende Kunst*, Vienna **1967**.

Edith Hays **Walton-Myers,** *Antonio Salieri's "La cifra." The Creation of a Late Eighteenth-Century Opera*, Ann Arbor, MI **1978** (Dissertation Northwestern University 1977).

John **Warrack,** *Carl Maria von Weber. Eine Biographie*, Hamburg/Düsseldorf **1972**.

Egon **Wellesz,** "Giuseppe Bonno (1710–1788). Sein Leben und seine dramatischen Werke," in: *Sammelbände der Internationalen Musikgesellschaft* XI (**1909/10**), pp. 395–442.

Const. v. **Wurzbach,** *Biographisches Lexikon des Kaiserthums Oesterreich, enthaltend die Lebensskizzen der denkwürdigen Personen, welche seit 1750 in den österreichischen Kronländern geboren wurden oder darin gelebt und gewirkt haben,* 60 parts, Vienna **1856–91**.

Gustav **Zechmeister,** *Die Wiener Theater nächst der Burg und nächst dem Kärntnerthor von 1747 bis 1776,* Vienna **1971** (Theatergeschichte Österreichs vol. III: Vienna, no. 2).

Agnes **Ziffer,** *Kleinmeister zur Zeit der Wiener Klassik,* Tutzing **1984** (Publikationen des Instituts für österreichische Musikdokumentation vol. 10).

LIST OF ILLUSTRATIONS

INDEX